CW00688684

Lives of Scottish Women

Women and Scottish Society, 1800–1980

William W. J. Knox

Edinburgh University Press

Again, for Patty

© William W. J. Knox, 2006

Edinburgh University Press Ltd
22 George Square, Edinburgh

Typeset in 10.5/13 Sabon
by Servis Filmsetting Ltd, Manchester, and
printed and bound in Great Britain by
Antony Rowe Ltd, Chippenham, Wilts

A CIP record for this book is available from the British Library

ISBN-10 0 7486 2409 0 (hardback)
ISBN-13 978 0 7486 2409 6 (hardback)
ISBN-10 0 7486 1788 4 (paperback)
ISBN-13 978 0 7486 1788 3 (paperback)

Contents

Acknowledgements

Many people have contributed to the writing of this volume. There are, in the frontline of assistance, the archivists and librarians on whom we depend so much. I would particularly like to thank the staff of the Special Collections department of the University of St Andrews, the School of Scottish Studies, University of Edinburgh, the National Archives of Scotland and the National Library, Edinburgh, the Royal Free Hospital Archive and the Women's Library, London, who helped in so many ways that it would be impossible to list them all. All I can say is that collectively you made researching my subjects an enjoyable and rewarding experience. I would also like to thank the Research Committee of the School of History at St Andrews for providing me with the necessary funding to undertake research in London. My daughter, Kimberley, also deserves a mention in this instance for acting as my unpaid research assistant while there. Lorna Harris did a splendid job transcribing rather low quality tapes into a readable typescript.

I have also benefited from discussions with students past and present, of the Department of Scottish History, concerning the intellectual issues the book attempts to grapple with. Their sharp intellects and quick wittedness forced me to rethink my assumptions about women's history in general, and my subjects, in particular, on a number of occasions.

Finally, my thanks go to the commissioning editor of Edinburgh University Press, John Davey, whose recent retirement has meant that not only has Scottish history lost a champion, Scottish historians have lost the most encouraging and supportive editor anyone could wish for. John taught me more than I can mention regarding the economics of publishing, and the art of writing. His going will be a great loss to us all.

To end on a personal note I want to express my thanks to my wife, Patty, and my children, David, Kimberley, Liam and Natasha for their unflagging support, their occasional criticism, and most of all for their love. Also to David and Clem for producing the most beautiful grandson, James, that anyone could wish for. Finally, to my good friends Ian and Nan Gourlay for the interest and enthusiasm they have shown in the project. They all make the whole endeavour worthwhile.

Plates

Abbreviations

AASS	American Anti-Slavery Society
AFASS	American and Foreign Anti-Slavery Society
BFASS	British and Foreign Anti-Slavery Society
CPCW	Committee for the Protection of Coloured Women
CPGB	Communist Party of Great Britain
CSCMEWE	Committee for Securing the Complete Medical Education of Women in Edinburgh
DWWG	Dundee Working Women's Guild
EIC	East India Company
ELES	Edinburgh Ladies Emancipation Society
ESMW	Edinburgh School of Medicine for Women
GES	Glasgow Emancipation Society
GFASS	Glasgow Female Anti-Slavery Society
GLES	Glasgow Ladies Emancipation Society
LEA	Ladies' Educational Associations
LSMW	London School of Medicine for Women
NCW	National Council for Women
NJCSR	National Joint Committee for Spanish Relief
NUWM	National Unemployed Workers Movement
NUWSS	National Union of Women's Suffrage Societies
ODC	Open Door Council
PCF	Communist Party of France
RAMC	Royal Army Medical Corps
RCM	Royal College of Music
SAMED	Scottish Association for the Medical Education of Women
SFWSS	Scottish Federation of Women's Suffrage Societies
SWH	Scottish Women's Hospitals
TAS	Total Abstinence Societies
TAS	Traveller's Aid Society
WFL	Women's Freedom League
WLUA	Women's Liberal Unionist Association
WSPU	Women's Social and Political Union
WWS	Women's Working Society
YWCA	Young Women's Christian Association

Introduction

Writing biographies presents special challenges and creates both moral and methodological problems for the historian. These might be fairly easy to define theoretically, but in practice much more difficult to resolve. Fundamentally, the biographer must ask: what is the appropriate approach to adopt in trying to understand the actions and motivations of an individual? Do we try and recreate the mindset of an individual by absorbing ourselves in their writings, both public and private, or should we reject this as impossible as other people are unknowable? The celebrated biographer Philip Ziegler[1] has argued that 'biographers must aim to embrace the totality of the subject's life', and urged them to never lose 'their hunger for the minutiae of their subject's everyday life'. Following Ziegler, one would want to know about minor details such as his taste in ties, or her perfume, whether they took a bath or a shower, whether they preferred claret to burgundy, and so on.[2] By absorbing ourselves in such trivial and seemingly inconsequential information the subject might somehow reveal their true self, or at least provide insights into themselves and their actions that are unattainable from documentary texts. But if we can add to our knowledge of the subject and become more sensitive to the nuances of their character through interrogating the mundane, how far should we go in empathising with them? The earliest biographies were adventures in hagiography in the sense that they sought to emphasise the specialness of a king or a saint vis-à-vis the rest of society.[3] However, in spite of the greater objectivity of biographical writing, the temptation to write hagiography remains as the more one comes to know an individual the greater the tendency towards empathy and that leads, if overdone, to inevitable distortions and unreasonable justifications of conduct. If the subject is still alive then the possibility of collusion between subject and biographer is, of course, all the greater, even if the latter attempts to hold an objective position. An example of this might be Robert Skidelsky's much criticised biography of Oswald Mosley.[4] Written in 1975, the book powerfully demonstrated the dangers of charisma in overriding a talented historian's judgment and training. As a result, Skidelsky's biography failed the most basic historical tests of objectivity and record. Skidelsky's shortcomings raised another important issue for biographers. Where is the line to be drawn between fact and fiction? When does the historian's imagination come into play, especially when documentation produces silences rather than answers? Myths become reality, and conversely reality can assume mythical status. Robert the Bruce and the Spider, Isaac Newton and the Apple, might be a couple of the best known examples of this kind of thing, but there are obviously many, many more. Even in this volume we encounter the juxtaposition of myth and reality. Every biographer has told the same story of Mary Slessor's conversion to Christ when as a child an old lady threatened her with the burning fires of hell. A nice story and one that Slessor colluded in. But in the annals of Presbyterian history her experience could be reproduced ad nauseam since it was part of the conversion/repentance basis of Presbyterianism: St Paul on the Road to Damascus. The reality was that on her mother's side she was from a devoutly religious family.

These are just some of the major issues that all historians face when writing biography. I have deliberately eschewed an internal approach in favour of an external one as I do not know any of my subjects. I have never seen them lose their tempers, shed tears, laugh, flirt; I have never observed the inflections and nuances of their speech, the smiles and smirks and other non-textual signs that alert us to the hidden self. They only exist for me in their writings, letters and diaries, their works and other peoples' observations and interpretations of them. This echoes Bernard Crick, in his critically acclaimed study of George Orwell, who argued that all the biographer can do with their subjects is to 'observe their behaviour in a variety of different situations and through different perspectives'.[5] Thus, my approach is one that is empathetic, but critical; one that seeks to understand actions and motivations but does not claim privileged or special knowledge. Essentially, these are essays in interpretation, and bearing in mind the limits of space and time, could be nothing else since the main objective was to explore the dynamic relationship between individual women and the patriarchal society they inhabited in nineteenth- and twentieth-century Scotland.

The subjects in this volume were not chosen at random, indeed, inclusion was the result of a fairly long process of reflection and debate on the nature of female subordination over the last 200 years or so. A major influence in determining my approach was Theodore Zeldin's work on nineteenth-century France in which he uses the experiences of specific individuals to personalise the historical experience of the French people at important moments in their history.[6] Another influence was Lytton Strachey's *Eminent Victorians* (1918). Although a much flawed analysis of nineteenth-century British history, Strachey's book remains one of the most influential and pioneering works into exploring the possibilities of group biography as a way of summing up an age or epoch. Under these influences, the intention was to choose a woman whose story or experience, although interesting and provoking in its own right, also provided insights into wider issues facing women in Scotland in the course of the last 200 years or so. For example, the Duchess of Atholl, Scotland's first female MP, and the first woman to hold Cabinet rank in a Conservative government, was selected because her political experiences, interesting and irritating in equal measure, opened the way to a discussion of women and representative participatory politics. Elsie Inglis, the Edinburgh doctor and war hero, was chosen not only because her story was little short of amazing in terms of courage, but because it allowed for some exploration of the theme of women and militarism. The personal is therefore hugely important in this set of studies, but only insofar as it establishes a basis for a wider discourse on the nature of women's private and public lives in this period.

Of course, such an approach is open to criticism regarding the exclusivity of the selection process. Were these women not exceptional and therefore as such unrepresentative of the broad mass of Scottish women and their lives? Why these ten, and not others, is another obvious and pertinent question. Firstly, the intention was to move away from what might be termed the 'usual suspects' of female biography in Scotland. Thus a conscious decision was made not to include Mary Queen of Scots, Flora MacDonald, Saint/Queen Margaret, indeed, any woman who had lived before 1800. This is not to say that their stories are not important or relevant, but it was felt that a new set of female actors, whose activities, dilemmas and problems were more immediately recognisable to women in contemporary Scotland, was needed. And although many of the chosen subjects will be known in academic circles, to the general public they are obscure figures, but a number of them, such as Sophia Jex-Blake, campaigner for medical education for women, are deserving of more popular recognition; indeed, why do we know more about Florence Nightingale than Jex-Blake? Simple: Florence did not question existing constructions of femininity, while Sophia posed a fundamental challenge to what was and was not possible for women in the second half of the nineteenth century. Her activities opened the doors of Scottish and British universities to succeeding generations of women. Secondly, all these women in some way shaped the development of modern Scotland in both direct and indirect ways, and in doing so affected the lives of other women. Whether it was Jex-Blake and university education, or Lady Frances Balfour, daughter of the Duke and Duchess of Argyll, and the campaign to win the vote for all women, or Eliza Wigham's championship of women's rights and anti-slavery in the first half of the nineteenth century, Scottish and indeed British society was irrevocably changed through their activities.

However, not all the women were political activists; some changed perceptions through their writings and others through notoriety. Jane Welsh Carlyle sat at home most of the time writing letters that articulated the simmering discontent of middle-class women with domesticity and the growing desire for a life less ordinary and more socially meaningful. Jane's death in 1866 marked the transitional point in which private emotions became the stimulus for public protest by middle-class women over a whole range of issues, from education to the franchise. Similarly, the writer Willa Muir analysed the contemporary position of women in Scotland and the history of subordination in a series of influential novels and shorter polemical pieces of writing. Madeleine Smith, on the other hand, by being charged and tried for the murder of her French lover, whom she had sex with outside of marriage, redefined the feminine in bourgeois society. Her trial and eventual acquittal posed serious questions for traditional views concerning female sexuality and the innate nurturing quality of women. Generally, then, inclusion was based on importance, or the way an individual's life, although less celebrated, highlighted an important aspect of women's lives. Mary Brooksbank, Dundee weaver and poet, is an obscure figure outside of her native city, but the fact that she was one of the first women to join the British Communist Party made her an interesting subject as it opened up the wider issue of women's relationship to the Left in Britain.

Of course, other women could have been chosen in their place, for example, Isabella Bird,[7] the renowned Victorian traveller, who had interesting things to say on the British Empire and women's rights in Victorian Scotland, might have been included, as might Jane Smeal, anti-slavery and women's rights campaigner. There is also no inclusion of women scientists, but then there were very few before 1950. The most important – Mary Somerville – has been comprehensively covered in a number of impressive biographies.[8]

The issue of inclusion was partially resolved by another important consideration: the existence of sources, that is, diaries, letters, autobiographies, and so on, which by reading provided a basis to challenge existing historiography of such iconic figures as Jane Welsh Carlyle, Mary

Slessor and Sophia Jex-Blake. Although it was not possible to read all the sources relating to a subject, and in the case of Jane Welsh Carlyle impossible, since there are 3,000 letters, most of the existing material was researched. The only exception was Eliza Wigham, of whom there exists only the flimsiest of sources on which to construct her story, but given the size of her contribution to the development of the women's movement in Scotland it was felt appropriate to include her in the volume. The sources themselves are rather problematic and as such have to be carefully handled. In a number of cases a great deal of the primary material has been destroyed on the instructions of the subject. Margaret Todd, the biographer of Sophia Jex-Blake, was permitted access to her private papers on the condition that she would burn them once the biography had been written. All biographies since of Jex-Blake have relied on the carefully selected fragments of correspondence and diary extracts reproduced in Todd's volume. Mary Slessor also ordered all her personal papers to be destroyed on her death as she was afraid that they subsequently might have been invested with some magical or mystical properties. What exists today of Slessor's voluminous correspondence are the letters written mainly in the early 1900s to her friend and confidante District Commissioner Charles Partridge. The importance of the destruction of texts is that it leaves us with a view of the subject that has been conditioned by them. In some ways, and in spite of our adherence to objectivity, we end up colluding with the dead or their agents in conveying a set of images of them that they have actively influenced and one which they even may have approved of. However, even where the primary sources are abundant we may still fall into the trap of collusion. We know Jane Welsh Carlyle mainly through her letters and journals, although other witnesses' observations also provide clues to her character and to her relationship with her husband, Thomas. The purpose of her correspondence was to construct or organise her life, to make it not only intelligible, but bearable. In doing so Jane entertains, informs and impresses the reader and draws them, and ultimately us, into a collusive interpretation with her of her life.[9] The ways in which she defined herself and her marriage succeeded in convincing Thomas, and later biographers, of his guilt, of his wasting of her talent in the service of his career. Jane leaves us an overwhelming image of self-sacrifice and, as a result, we are compelled to share her sense of frustration at being recognised as only the helpmate of genius rather than a talent in her own right.

The other important source for the biographer is a subject's autobiography. These are normally written as a form of self-justification for one's past deeds and decisions, but those written in the confessional mode can

represent an individual's quest for self-knowledge, even if this goal is ultimately unattainable. Until recently this form of literature was dismissed
by literary critics as a simplistic narrative device mainly associated with
women's literature, which, as Valerie Baisnee points out, had been considered in some quarters as a 'giant autobiographical act', implying that
women could only write about their own lives and little else.[10] The last
twenty years or so has witnessed a seismic shift in literary criticism and
autobiography has become fashionable as a genre, indeed, an individual
writing their story at a given time is now considered to have been writing
'about the whole of humanity of that period'.[11] Only four of the women
in this volume – Frances Balfour, Katherine Atholl, Willa Muir and Mary
Brooksbank – penned an autobiography with varying degrees of success.
Balfour's and Atholl's stories straddle the nineteenth and twentieth centuries, while Brooksbank and Muir write mainly about the twentieth
century. Only Muir's autobiography can be considered introspective, the
others fail to address the dramas and emotional crises of their private
lives and concentrate instead on their public persona, the one that was
concerned with political struggle and important causes. Thus, Balfour
fails to mention her husband's descent into alcoholism, Atholl ignores
her husband's serial adultery, and Brooksbank also tells us little about
her married life except that she was happy. Pain is excised in these stories,
and the desire not to offend the living or the memory of the dead is very
evident. Muir stands out in this respect as she confronts the difficulties
in her relationship with her husband, Edwin, and addresses her frustrations with living with genius. But as honest and soul-bearing as she is in
this respect, her account of her relationship with her son is a dishonest
and somewhat weak attempt at self-justification. Thus, it is doubtful if
autobiography, the telling of an individual's story, can somehow speak
for the experience of humanity at a particular period as there exists
within the pages too many inconsistencies, too many excisions and unreliable memories. But what autobiography does provide is a basis for
examining the intersections between public and private experience, particularly if the individual is less well-known. In these cases we acquire
fragments of and glimpses into 'ordinary life, private drama, personal
success and failure, sometimes heroism, sometimes the underside of
fame'.[12]

It is clear that all primary sources that shape the way we view a subject
and his or her life contain unwary traps for the naive as well as the experienced writer. The modern trend towards psychoanalytical approaches
to biography has created even more unwitting snares for the contemporary biographer. It also demonstrates the quite impossible task of finding

the true self in one's subject: something that reinforces Bernard Crick's point regarding observation and perspective, and underscores Lytton Strachey's interpretative approach, of filtering out the mass of indigestible minutiae concerning a subject's life. As he says, in the preface to *Eminent Victorians*, by moving away from what might be termed worthy standard biographical approaches to a life, it becomes possible to attack the subject 'in unexpected places', shooting 'a sudden and revealing searchlight into obscure recesses, hitherto un-divined'.

However, most of what has been written from a theoretical perspective on the art and nature of biography concerns individual subjects, while this volume strays into less well-explored literary/historical territory – group biography. The subjects, as explained above, were chosen to illustrate some aspect of women's experiences over the last two centuries. The first chapter examines the life of Jane Welsh Carlyle and the domestic lives of middle-class women in the early to mid Victorian period, as well as detailing what it was like to play second fiddle to genius. The second chapter explores, through Eliza Wigham's life, the public lives of women in this period and chronicles the origins and development of the women's movement in Scotland. Chapter 3 deals with Victorian ideas on female sexuality and the challenge to these strongly held beliefs posed by the revelations concerning unmarried sex during the trial of the Glasgow femme fatale, Madeleine Smith, for murder in 1857. While Smith and Welsh Carlyle challenged gender stereotypes in highly personal ways, other women after 1860 confronted them more openly. One of the main arenas of conflict was education and Chapter 4 details the heroic struggle of Sophia Jex-Blake to gain acceptance to the medical faculty of the University of Edinburgh and open the doors of the institutions of higher learning to all women. Education, of course, was only one part of the strategy of equality, the other was the franchise. Chapter 5 focuses on the role of Lady Frances Balfour in the general agitation of women in Britain for the franchise, while Chapter 8 looks at the life of Katherine Ramsay, Duchess of Atholl, a lifelong opponent of votes for women, who ironically became Scotland's first female MP. Both chapters include reflections on women and politics in Scotland in the post-1918 era. Chapter 7 explores a complex set of moral issues concerning the relationship between women and warfare. Elsie Inglis' decision to establish field hospitals at the front in France and Serbia during the First World War posed important questions as to what constituted the feminine and paved the way for the use of women as combatants in warfare. While these women were pursuing equality in the world of politics, Mary Slessor, the subject of Chapter 6, had already achieved fame and real power in Africa. Her rise from humble weaver to become the first female vice-consul in the British Empire not only raises issues regarding the part played by women in the imperial project, but also shows how women could exploit loopholes in the ideology of patriarchy to empower themselves. Indeed, like the women political activists, Slessor's experience explodes the theory of separate spheres, in which women inhabit the private while men the public. The penultimate chapter deals with the inconsistencies between feminism as an ideology and its practitioners, feminists. Willa Muir wrote some interesting studies on the place of women in Scottish society and more generally on the history of female subordination,[13] and attacked existing institutions such as marriage and the church for the role they played in the subordination of women, but in her own life she willingly accepted a part that reduced her to one of service to genius. The final chapter looks at the life of Mary Brooksbank and of working-class women living and working within a hard and unforgiving environment. These experiences radicalised Mary, who joined the Communist Party, but she was part of a very small band, on the whole, and in spite of the progressive nature of its policies, the Left has failed to mobilise women in Britain in large numbers.

Mary's experiences highlight some of the dissimilarities between the women chosen for inclusion in this volume. One of the problems in writing about women is that we, as K. D. Reynolds points out, see them only in terms of their gender, while men are free 'to construct themselves in line with (or to acquire their identity) from class, religion, race or any other ongoing concept of their choice'.[14] Outside of the obvious fact that they are both female, there is very little that connects the Duchess of Atholl with Mary Brooksbank. One lived a life of luxury and privilege, the other one of poverty and hardship. Moreover, the Duchess exercised a degree of power that involved the subordination of men of inferior social classes, something which was denied to Mary. But however wide the disparities of wealth and power, they both experienced subordination in socio-economic and political structures that were predicated on male dominance, albeit in different forms. Emotionally, the importance of the father-figure in these women's lives cannot be overstressed. Welsh Carlyle wore black for seven years after her father's death; Brooksbank's, Inglis' and Wigham's social views were heavily influenced by their respective fathers; Smith went as far as murder to cover up her liaison with her French lover so as not to offend her father; and Willa Muir was drawn to Edwin as he represented a father-figure she never knew. The impact was, however, not always positive. Mary Slessor's father was drunken and abusive and his behaviour indelibly influenced her views of men and alcohol. Only those of the upper classes were more influenced by their mothers than their fathers: a phenomenon that was perhaps the result of the distant, shadowy role men in this social class played in their children's lives. Frances Balfour's mother influenced her from an early age into taking an interest in social questions and this she carried with her into adulthood.

Individually, these subjects all represent some aspect of women's lives in Scotland over the last two centuries. The disparities between them make it difficult to argue that they collectively make up the totality of the female experience, or that together they form the basis for the construction of a theoretical model of subordination. What they do is offer a window and hopefully some light into the history of women's struggle in this country for equal rights with men, and the different routes taken to achieve this. The pursuit of equality and the outstanding women who undertook it thus becomes the main theme of this volume. If these women find the recognition they undoubtedly deserve then the effort will be repaid many times over.

NOTES

1. Ziegler has written biographies on Harold Wilson, Lord Mountbatten and Edward VIII.
2. P. Ziegler, 'Biography: the Narrative', in I. Donaldson et al. (eds), *Shaping Lives: Reflections on Biography* (Canberra, 1992), pp. 225–6.
3. J. L. Clifford, 'Introduction', in J. L. Clifford (ed.), *Biography as an Art: Selected Criticism 1560–1960* (Oxford, 1962), p. x.
4. R. Skidelsky, *Oswald Mosley* (1975).
5. B. Crick, *George Orwell: a Life* (London, 1980).
6. T. Zeldin, *France 1848–1945: Politics and Anger* (Oxford, 1979); *France 1848–1945: Intellect and Pride* (Oxford, 1980).
7. O. Checkland, *Isabella Bird and 'Woman's Right'* (Edinburgh, 1996).
8. C. E. Patterson, *Mary Somerville and the Cultivation of Science 1815–40* (1983); K. A. Neeley, *Mary Somerville: Science, Illumination and the Female Mind* (Cambridge, 2001).
9. A. Christianson, 'Rewriting herself: Jane Welsh Carlyle's letters', *Scotlands*, 2 (1994), p. 52.
10. V. Baisnee, *Gendered Resistance: the Autobiographies of Simone de Beauvoir, Maya Angelou, Janet Frame and Marguerite Duras* (Amsterdam, 1997), p. 4.
11. Baisnee, *Gendered Resistance*, p. 5.
12. J. Strouse, 'Semiprivate lives', in D. Aaron (ed.), *Studies in Biography* (Cambridge, MA, 1978), p. 124.
13. W. Muir, *Women: an Inquiry* (London, 1925).
14. K. D. Reynolds, *Aristocratic Women and Political Society in Victorian Britain* (Oxford, 1998), p. 4.

1

Jane Welsh Carlyle: Living with Genius (1)

ᴥ

Of the women discussed in this volume, Jane Welsh Carlyle, is perhaps the most private and the least public. Her world revolved round the home, husband, and the minutiae of everyday life, rather than the dramatic arenas of political struggle and women's rights. Yet, in spite of this, more publications have been devoted to discussing her life than any of the others. Indeed, without fear of exaggeration, it can be said that rarely has a woman and her marriage come under such close scrutiny as hers. But, then, Jane was married to a genius – Thomas Carlyle. He was a historian and philosopher, one of the intellectual colossuses of nineteenth-century Britain. At first glance, compared with Thomas, Jane appears inconsequential: the woman behind the great man. Like other women who have stood in her shoes, she was seen as sacrificing her life and talent to further the career of her husband. While he wrote the weighty tomes on history and society, she cleaned and cooked, sewed and swept, ran the house and made his life as comfortable as she could. Jane it seems was there simply to service genius. The truth, however, is much more than this. Jane was not simply a footnote in the history of a great man; in fact, she was one of the great letter-writers of the nineteenth century and even a fleeting glance at her correspondence with family and friends shows not only her literary merit, but establishes her as an exceptionally witty and insightful commentator on both domestic and public matters. Indeed, her letters, of which over 3,000 have survived, provide an insight into the life of middle-class women at this time that is far removed from the Victorian stereotype of the 'angel in the house'. They allow us a unique insight into bourgeois marriage in the early to middle decades of the nineteenth century and convey, among other things, the frustration of gifted women with no outlet for their talents outside of home, church and philanthropy, as well as the emotional and psychological problems of living with such a troubled and tortured figure as Thomas undoubtedly was. While the domestic side of her life has generally been of less interest to biographers, from the highly controversial original by Anthony Froude through to the most recent award-winning publication by Rosemary Ashton,[1] this exceptional chronicle of nineteenth-century domesticity has rightly fascinated social historians. Jane's letters provide the basis for a historical interrogation of the intimate, inner details of bourgeois society as represented in gender relationships in the home and in marriage. Using this approach, the major questions concerning the Carlyles' marriage which have long been the basis of biography – for example, was the marriage consummated; who was to blame for Jane's unhappiness, herself or Thomas; would Jane have realised her talent as a writer if he had not overshadowed her – can be placed within the broader context of gender relationships rather than simply as a means to understand the psychodrama of two ill-suited, but ultimately dependent, lovers. The other advantage of adopting a gendered approach is that it allows for a more detached analysis of the Carlyles, one that avoids the kind of partisanship that has led to the construction of a two-dimensional Thomas, who is either depicted as an insensitive and overbearing monster or, alternatively, as a devoted husband, who had the misfortune to be married to Jane, an attention-seeking hypochondriac.

Regardless of what view one takes of the Carlyles and their marital difficulties, it seems rather unlikely given her upbringing that Jane would have found herself later married to the socially awkward and gloom-prone Carlyle, although there is much to suggest that her childhood would have a profound affect on her relationships with the men in her life. She was born in Haddington in 1801, the only child of John, physician, and Grace Welsh. Her childhood was an extremely happy one, and Jane, or 'Jeannie' as she was called, enjoyed and revelled in the attention her doting father paid her. Writing some years after her death, Carlyle remarked: 'Of her father she always spoke with reverence: he was the only person who had any real influence over her.'[2] John Welsh was in many ways determined that his daughter should be the son he never had, and because of this he gave in to practically all her demands. From an early age she showed a talent for Latin and was reading Virgil when only nine.[3] When she asked to be allowed to study Latin more academically, a very unusual step for a girl to take in early nineteenth-century Scotland as it was a subject reserved for male pupils who intended to go on to university, Jane was allowed to attend school in Haddington. She proved to be a very precocious girl who had a love of learning and life, indeed, so great was her thirst for study that she used to tie a weight at bedtime to her ankle so that she would not oversleep. It was not unknown for Jane to be in school at the earliest hour. She recalled herself being found in class by her teacher, James Brown, asleep at seven in the morning 'after two hours of hard study'.[4] By the age of fourteen Jane had completed a tragedy and had written some verse. Although far too flirtatious, talented and sharp for a provincial town, she proved very popular with the young men and was referred to as 'the flower of Haddington'[5], but privately she thought the place 'the dimmest, deadest spot . . . in the Creator's universe'.[6] Of her flirtatious nature, Carlyle wrote: 'If flirting were a capital crime, she would have been in danger of being hanged many times over.'[7]

When she was ten years old Jane made the acquaintance of Edward Irving, a mathematics teacher at Haddington, who was hired at the age of eighteen by John Welsh as a tutor for her. The hours were between 6 a.m. and 8 a.m. Irving was handsome and flamboyant and Jane developed an infatuation for him that later blossomed into love. She sent him a lock of hair, something that she did not privilege any other admirer, including Carlyle, with.[8] However, Irving moved to Kirkcaldy in the summer of 1812 for a better-paid teaching position; one that also allowed him to devote time to his theological studies in Edinburgh. While working in Kirkcaldy he became engaged to the daughter of the local minister, Isabella Martin, in 1816, but, in spite of this, he continued to pay calls on Jane, who by this time was attending Miss Hall's finishing school in Edinburgh and residing with her cousin. Jane saw a future for herself as Irving's wife and there is little doubt that he encouraged her feelings. But this ambition was thwarted by the fact that Isabella's parents felt the engagement, although only verbally contracted, was both legally and morally binding. As a result Irving, who by now had decided on a career in the church, was left with the choice of work or love. He chose his career and in 1820 he married Isabella.

This was a double blow to Jane as a year before John Welsh had died of typhoid contracted from a patient he had been treating. Jane found it extremely hard to come to terms with the loss of her father as he had meant so much more to her than anyone else, including her mother. As a mark of respect she wore black until the day of her wedding in 1826. Carlyle said that so affected was Jane by the death of her father that 'to the end of her life, his title even to me was "He" and "Him" [and] not above twice or thrice, quite late in years, did she ever mention (and then in what sweet slow tone!) "my Father"'.[9] By referring to her father almost continuously in the third person, Jane constructed an emotional barrier between herself and the event, which may have in the short term softened the blow of the tragedy, but in the long term it prevented her from coming to terms with the reality of his death. She vowed two purposes for the life ahead: 'to be a comfort to my poor mother, & to make myself worthy of being reunited to my adored father'.[10] However, her construction of masculinity, based on an adoring and loving father, would make it very difficult for any man, far less the self-absorbed and increasingly trying Carlyle, to live up to her expectations.

In spite of the end of Jane's relationship with Irving, he continued to call on her and her mother, and it was he who introduced her to Carlyle during a visit to Haddington in late 1821. Coincidentally, Carlyle had also suffered the pain of emotional rejection and a broken engagement. While working as teacher in Kirkcaldy he had become engaged to Margaret Gordon, later by marriage Lady Bannerman. Margaret's aunt, with whom she stayed, disapproved of Carlyle and that was enough to put an end to the relationship. Thus, when they met both were on the rebound from failed emotional entanglements and somewhat vulnerable. Carlyle was immediately smitten by Jane's vivacious personality and her looks and agreed to act as her tutor in German. He wrote to his brother that in spite of his dyspepsia, he returned from Haddington 'so full of joy that I have done nothing but dream of it'.[11] Some ten years later in a short story he said of Jane that 'never was there such another beautiful, cruel, affectionate, wicked, adorable, capricious little gipsy sent into this world for the delight and vexation of mortal man'.[12]

Entranced, Carlyle used every trick in the book of flattery and manipulation to win Jane's hand. He flattered her literary skills and intellectual ability, encouraging her to believe that 'she had great future as an author, that she was the best German student imaginable'.[13] Thus, she was to write a sonnet every day, begin a tragedy and an essay on some striking change in the nation's history. On top of this, as part of her education, Carlyle mapped out a programme of study that included the main historical works from ancient times, a reading list of major works in literature, as well as continuing with her French and German classes. Jane initially responded enthusiastically to Carlyle's suggestions and when he recommended four hours of study, she decided on eight. But unfortunately the zeal very quickly began to temper itself and the study regime became less intensive. As Jane herself admitted: 'I am a shuttlecock of a creature: I have no stamina.'[14] Although she continued with her languages, she spent much of her time going to tea parties, playing chess and shuttlecock with one of her admirers, Dr Fyffe, and as Drew says, 'flirting with any other young man who happens to be available'.[15] She was also being seriously courted by a local Haddington man, George Rennie, the nephew of the architect of London's Waterloo Bridge, and at one time 'she considered herself practically engaged to him'.[16] However, Rennie's decision to go to Italy saw her wash her hands of him, saying, 'Oh, the devil take him! He has wasted all the affections of my poor heart.'[17]

When Jane proved to be somewhat lacking in the discipline necessary to become a serious writer, Carlyle, now without competition, changed his strategy. He began to idealise domesticity and portrayed the notion of being the mistress of a home as 'the highest destination of even the noblest woman'.[18] However, in spite of the flattery and manipulation, Jane found herself unable to reciprocate Carlyle's obvious feelings of affection and love. For a start her mother disliked him. She saw in Thomas a poor financial prospect (a view shared by Jane) and forbade any contact. Jane had to keep a secret correspondence going until her mother's attitude to Carlyle softened. But more important than her mother's disapproval was the fact that at this point she had no desire to marry Carlyle or any other suitor. In a letter to Thomas at the end of 1821, Jane says: 'Falling in love and marrying like other misses is quite out of the question. I have too little romance in my disposition to marry you or any other man; and too much ever to marry without love.'[19] She also made certain that if someone married her it would not be for her money as in 1823 Jane executed a deed transferring the whole of her father's property worth £200–300 per annum, which he had left to her, to her mother.

The relationship carried on in a platonic manner and mainly through written correspondence. This suited Carlyle since in many ways he was more impressive on paper than in the flesh. But even as late as 1825, a year before marriage, Jane still rebuffed all Carlyle's entreaties and declarations of love. She wrote to him saying:

> I love you . . . but I am not in love with you; that is to say, my love for you is not a passion which overclouds my judgement and absorbs all my regard for myself and others. It is a simple, honest, serene affection made up of admiration and sympathy.[20]

One year later they were married, an event that raises a number of questions that have lingered since Froude's first biography of Carlyle. According to Froude, Jane had married beneath herself; she was still in love with Irving; Carlyle was distinctly 'second best'; she only married him out of sympathy; and Carlyle loved his mother above Jane. However, while it is fair to say that Jane prior to marriage did not feel the kind of physical passion for Thomas that one might expect of lovers, she was not indifferent. Indeed, if one examines her letters at the time she was in many ways besotted with his intellect and honesty. Writing to Eliza Stoddart in February 1822 she dismissed critics of Carlyle, saying that they would claim:

> he is poor . . . and in the next place . . . [they would] set him down as unpolished and ill-looking. But . . . they would not tell you he is among the clever-

est of men of his day . . . [who] possesses all the qualities I deem essential in a husband – a warm true heart to love me, a towering intellect to command me, and a spirit of fire to be the guiding star – light of my life.[21]

Jane wanted a genius for a husband and she succeeded in finding one, but she had to wrestle emotionally with the idea and work hard to convince herself that she was making the right decision and that is why the letters at this time are so contradictory in terms of her emotions. They reflect the doubts and insecurities she had in making such a match with a man with no certainty that his genius would be recognised by society. Perhaps, it had also taken this long to excise the passion she had felt for Irving, as it was not until July 1825 that Jane was prepared to reveal to Thomas that she had '*once*, passionately loved' him.[22]

However, after five years of dithering, the marriage finally took place at Jane's grandfather's farm, Templand (in Nithsdale, near Penfillan), in the presence of her immediate family and Carlyle's brother, John.[23] From the outset Thomas made it clear that the marriage was to be based upon a traditional patriarchal model, stating: 'The man should bear rule in the house not the woman . . . I must not and I cannot live in a house of which I am not the head.'[24] Jane it would appear colluded with her subordination from the beginning and, as Kaplan notes, her marriage was premised 'not only on her recognition of her husband's genius but also on her total identification of his mission and his values'.[25] Thus, Jane's life became one of service to genius and only Carlyle and his work gave meaning to hers. As Aileen Christianson says, 'she centred herself in this periphery making a triumphant virtue of her situation as a genius' helpmate'.[26] Only very occasionally, as we will see, did she ever challenge her subordination within marriage; however, that does not mean to say that she was not conscious of it. In a letter to a friend, Jane criticised the patriarchal attitudes of Carlyle saying that 'he thinks us an inferior order of beings – that is, an order of beings born to obey'.[27]

As a newly married woman Jane played the dutiful wife to perfection. Their first home was in Comely Bank, Edinburgh – 'a perfect model of a house', according to Carlyle.[28] With little in the way of income and a lifestyle by necessity frugal, the Carlyles did not accept dinner invitations, as they had no means of reciprocating them. In spite of this, many visitors called to talk, among them Francis Jeffrey, founder of the *Edinburgh Review*, Christopher North, of *Blackwood's Magazine*, and John Wilson, Professor of Moral Philosophy at the University of Edinburgh, among others.[29] Although they had a maid, Jane was forced for the first time to turn to domestic matters. As Carlyle recalled, 'until she married, she had never minded household things', but within a short space of time 'she could do everything and anything, from mending Venetian blinds to making picture-frames or trimming a dress'.[30] When the Carlyles moved from Comely Bank, where Jane was happy, to Craigenputtock (a high moorland farm standing on Dunscore Moors, sixteen miles from Dumfries), where she was not, there was an appreciable increase in her repertoire of domestic skills.

The years at Craigenputtock, that 'savage place', were among the unhappiest for Jane. The social isolation, the grinding poverty, Carlyle's irritability, his mean-hearted brother Alexander and his fiery sister Jean, all combined to make her life wretched. In an extremely candid letter to a young female friend in Carlisle, Jane detailed the misery of rural life and her sense of domestic inadequacy:

> Craigenputtock a whit less of a peat bog, and [a] most dreary, untoward place to live at! In fact, it was sixteen miles distant on every side from all the conveniences of life – shops and even post office! Further, we were very poor; and further and worst, being an only child, and brought up to 'great prospects', I was sublimely ignorant of every branch of useful knowledge, though a capital Latin scholar and a very fair mathematician!! It behoved me in these circumstances to *sew*! . . . Also it behoved me to learn to *cook*! No *capable* servant choosing to live at 'such an out of the way place', and my husband having 'bad digestion', which complicated my difficulties dreadfully . . . it was plainly my duty as a Christian wife to bake at home! So I sent for Cobbett's 'Cottage Economy', and fell to work at a loaf of bread . . . it came to pass that my loaf got put into the oven . . . I remained the only person not asleep . . . One o'clock struck . . . and then three; and still I was sitting there in an intense solitude, my whole body aching with weariness, my heart aching with a sense of forlornness and degradation. That I who had been so petted at home . . . who had never been required to do anything but *cultivate my mind*, should have to pass all those hours of the night in watching *a loaf of bread*! Which mightn't turn out bread after all! Such thoughts maddened me till I laid my head down on the table, and sobbed aloud.[31]

Jane's loneliness was made worse by Carlyle's working routine that, because of its intensity, led to a general disregard for those around him. As Jane explained in a series of letters written between 1828 and 1834 to Ellen Twistleton,

> it wasn't as if I saw anything of Carlyle – he went to his own room after breakfast and worked till an hour before dinner, & always rode alone . . . then he came to dinner all worked up, as bilious people always are by a rule . . . he was dangerous, there was no freedom of communication during dinner; then he went for a walk for an hour.[32]

A question asserts itself regarding Thomas' routine: was it to avoid intimacy with his wife? This leads to a further, and more debated, question: was the marriage consummated? The source of this speculation was Froude when he remarked – in *My Relations with Carlyle* (1903) – that rumour had it that the Carlyles' marriage was 'not a real marriage, and was only companionship'.[33] The notoriously unreliable novelist Frank Harris, in an article in *The English Review* (1911), embroidered on this remark by claiming that Carlyle had confessed to him in 1878 that 'he had never consummated his marriage'. In his autobiography – *My Life and Times* (1925) – Harris went even further, claiming that Jane's physician in later life, Sir Richard Quain, had declared her to be *virgo intacta*. These suggestions, mainly anecdotal, unleashed a frenzy of counter claims as to the virility of Carlyle and a fierce assault on the reliability of Froude and Harris by those close to Thomas, in particular his nephew, Alexander Carlyle, and the distinguished physician, Sir James Crichton-Browne.[34] Alexander Carlyle went as far as to claim that Jane was pregnant but had a miscarriage during the journey from Craigenputtock to London.[35] Historians have dismissed the nephew's claim as highly unlikely,[36] and, at the same time, shown little sympathy for allegations of the anti-Carlyle camp. Even a cursory reading of the letters that passed between Jane and Thomas in the early years of marriage shows two people completely in love and devoted to each other. Examples of their passion for each other can be seen in the following extracts, which could be multiplied many times over. Thomas wrote to her from his mother's home at Scotsbrig during their first separation:

> I promised that I would think of you *sometimes*; which truly I have done many times, or rather all times . . . as if till now I had never known how precious my own dearest little Goody was to me, and what a real Angel of a creature she was! I could bet a sovereign that you *love* me twice as well as you ever did; for experience in this matter has given me insight. Would I were back to you! I would have ten thousand kisses, and my own Jane's heart would beat against her Husband's![37]

When on a visit to her mother at Templand, Jane pining for her husband writes:

> Goody, Goody, dear Goody, – you said you would weary, and I do hope in my heart that you are wearying. It will be so sweet to make it all up to you in kisses when I return. You will *take me* and hear all my bits of experience, and your heart will beat when you find how I have longed to return to you . . . Darling, dearest, loveliest . . . I think of you every hour and every moment. I love you and admire you like – like anything . . . Oh, if I was there I could put

my arms so close about your neck and hush you into the softest sleep. Good night. Dream of me.[38]

The passion is obvious and reciprocated and there is little to suggest that they were incompatible sexually at this point in their marriage. It would appear, however, that the physical side of their relationship diminished over time, particularly as Thomas became increasingly devoted to his writing and Jane became worn down with medical problems, real or imagined. At the end of the day, as Rosemary Ashton recognises, 'No amount of speculation, or reviewing the speculation of others, can take us further into the mystery at the heart of this, or any other, marriage.'[39]

The long rural sojourn came to an end when in 1834 the Carlyles moved to Cheyne Row, in unfashionable Chelsea, London – 'our little household', as Jane described it. This was the kind of environment in which Jane thrived, and she confessed to Carlyle's sister, Jean, that in 'most respects my situation is out of sight more suitable than it was at Craigenputtock'.[40] There were interesting people to meet and converse with, there was the general hustle and bustle of city life, and there were the social occasions, such as balls and the theatre, to attend if one cared to. In the city, the mundane and the petty events of everyday life could be the stuff of high drama in the hands of a skilful and imaginative story-teller and writer, as Jane undoubtedly was. Her audience included some of the most important cultural and political figures of the nineteenth century. Charles Dickens, Giuseppe Mazzini, John Stuart Mill and John Ruskin, among others, all made their way through the front door of 5 Cheyne Row. While there Jane would regale them with witty cameos of domestic life that created a sort of drama documentary of domesticity replete with accurate impersonations of servants and friends and neighbours and told with a venomous wit. One of her favourite subjects was the extravagance of middle-class Englishwomen. She wrote to her mother:

> Englishwomen turn up the whites of their eyes, and call on the 'good heavens' at the bare idea of enterprises which seem to me in the most ordinary course of human affairs. I told Mrs Hunt, one day, I had been very busy *painting*. 'What', she asked, 'is it a portrait?' 'Oh! No', I told her, 'something of more importance – a large wardrobe'. She could not imagine, she said 'how I could have the patience for such things.' And so, having no particular for them herself, what is the result? She is every other day reduced to borrow my tumblers, my tea cups; even a cupful of porridge, a few spoonfuls of tea, are begged of me, because 'Missus' has got company, and happens to be out of the article; in plain unadorned English, because 'missus' is the most wretched of managers, and is often at the point of having not a copper in her purse. To

see how they live and waste down here, it is a wonder the whole city does not 'bankrape', and go out o'sicht; – flinging plateful of crusts . . . into the ashpits! . . . I never cease to be glad that I was born on the other side of the Tweed, and that those who nearest and dearest to me are Scotch.[41]

Frugality was forced on the Carlyles in spite of the success of Thomas' history of the French Revolution and other pieces of work. In this the Carlyles were no different to other members of the middle class in Britain. Kathryn Gleadle points out that 40 per cent of middle-class households in mid-nineteenth-century Britain lived on between £100 and £300 per annum and, in spite of an increase in household duties and large families, there was only limited domestic help in the shape of a maid, or skivvy.[42] These women's lives were far from the Victorian ideal of the 'angel in the house', that pampered creature whose raison d'être was to create within the home a haven of peace and order for her husband and children, while adding the necessary gloss of decoration and refinement expected of educated women, such as embroidery and piano playing. Cleaning, for instance, became a major task as the interior of the middle-class home became cluttered with all sorts of material artefacts, from tables to chairs, ornaments to carpets, kitchen utensils to bed linen, and so much more. The complexities of running a middle-class household had become so involved that Victorian women adopted a more scientific approach to household management. The key to this was order and thus a range of devices, including weights and measures, gongs and clocks, regulated the use of materials and defined daily routines for the family. Account books and budgets also allowed for the planning of expenditure. Thus, by these means a rationalisation of housework took place over the course of the first half of the nineteenth century.[43]

Jane's letters provide a unique chronicle of domestic life and the expectations placed on middle-class wives, as well as detailing the duties they performed in the home in the period 1830–60. Apart from the assistance of a maid and, occasionally, her mother, Jane had to perform all the tasks of household management, and, at the same time, deal with workmen and play hostess to a steady stream of callers, although being childless she was spared the duty of the religious and moral instruction of children. Some indication of her daily routine and the division of labour in her home is provided in a letter to Carlyle in 1835:

Mother and I have fallen naturally into a fair division of labour, and we keep a very tidy house. Sereetha [maid] has attained the unhoped-for perfection of getting up at half after six of her own accord, lighting the parlour-fire, and actually placing the breakfast things . . . I get up at half after seven, and prepare the coffee and bacon-ham (which is the life of me, making me hungrier the more I eat of it). Mother, in the interim, makes her bed, and sorts her room. After breakfast, mother descends into the inferno, where she jingles and scours, and from time to time scolds Sereetha till all is right and tight there. I, above the stairs, sweep the parlour, blacken the grate – make the room look cleaner than it has been since the days of Grace MacDonald [her former servant]; then mount aloft to make my own bed . . . then clean myself . . . and sit down to the Italian lesson. A bit of meat roasted in the oven suffices two days cold, and does not plague us with cookery. Sereetha can fetch up tea-things, and porridge is easily made on the parlour-fire; the kitchen one being allowed to go out (for economy), when the Peesweep retires to bed at eight o'clock.[44]

Servant keeping and their management was, of course, not only the primary social division between the working class and the middle class, it was also one of the arenas in the distribution of power within home that women controlled. In a small household such as Cheyne Row the relationship between mistress and servant was much more intimate and the control greater than in a large household. The long hours of work and the constant drudgery, as well as the restrictions on men friends and the patronising attitude of the employer, made it a disagreeable occupation for young women, and this led to tensions and fallings out. Jane in her thirty-two years at Cheyne Row went through thirty-four maids. Thea Holmes put this down to the fact that she 'expected too much of them, and alternatively spoilt them and lost her temper with them, so that in almost every case a violent scene terminated the engagement'.[45]

However, in spite of her continuing problems with servants, Jane's mood at this point, having made the transition from the social isolation of Craigenputtock to the dizzying social milieu of the metropolis, is quietly triumphant. But as Carlyle's reputation grew there were increasing strains placed on the marriage, through his need for solitude, and her need for recognition and fear of social invisibility. Any kind of noise seemed to irritate Carlyle. Jane, in a letter to her mother, spoke of the inability of either of them to get any sleep due to a cockerel crowing in the middle of the night, saying:

We are gone to the devil in the sleeping department . . . last night they had him [Thomas] up at three. He went to bed again and got some sleep . . . but I, listening every minute for a new screech that would send him down a second time and prepare such wretchedness for the day could sleep no more . . . If this goes on, he will be in Bedlam; and I too.[46]

Perhaps, because of city noise Carlyle spent more and more time away from London, indeed, it would interesting to calculate the actual time they spent away from each other. Letters continually pass between them from Scotsbrig, Carlyle's mother's home in Scotland, to Chelsea, and from across other parts of Britain. Jane was clearly finding life with Carlyle extremely trying as she vainly tried to cope with his irritability and inconsideration for anyone other than himself. For example, when Jane was clearly unwell in July 1843, he left for Wales, while she struggled to supervise the refurbishment of Cheyne Row and deal with all the upheaval. She wrote to Carlyle, 'I am in a complete mess and . . . I shall be for a time, times and half,' and pointedly reminded him that she had faced the first night alone, thankfully 'neither robbed or murdered'.[47]

The responsibility and the loneliness were beginning to take their toll on Jane's physical health. Kaplan notes that by 1841 she was 'constantly ill and dissatisfied. She felt her husband considered his work more important than her welfare',[48] and the feeling that she had only status as the wife of this literary lion, and not as a talented individual in her own right, led to the plaintive cry 'I too am here'. In a letter to her friend and confidante, John Sterling, she confessed that her mental state had suffered:

> Three weeks of solitude have passed very strangely with me. I have been worn out by what the cockneys call 'mental worry' . . . as soon as I had the house all to myself, I flung myself on the sofa, with the feeling, 'I would not, if I might, be blest, I want no Paradise – but rest' . . . Day after day has found me stretched out my sofa with a . . . book, which I have read . . . 'one eye shut, and the other not open'. Evening after evening, I have dreamt away in looking into the fire, and wondering to see myself here, in this great absurdity of a world! In short my existence since I was left alone has been an apathy, tempered by emanations from the 'Minerva Press' . . . One has to die at one's post, has one not? The wonderful thing for me is always the prodigiously long while one takes to die.[49]

The ennui and the insecurities Jane suffered from were compounded by the death of her mother in early 1842 from an apoplectic stroke following a long illness. On hearing of her mother's imminent death Jane caught the first available train from London to Liverpool and from there she was to travel to Scotland. Events overtook her and Grace Welsh was already dead by the time she had reached Liverpool. Like the loss of her father, Jane was grief stricken over her mother's death. She refused to travel to Templand and collapsed in Liverpool remaining in a darkened room until she felt well enough to return to Chelsea. Such was the intensity of her sorrow she could not bear the company of others and for some time no one was admitted entry to the house. Her only source of comfort was her cousin Jeannie: 'the dearest little soul I ever tried living beside . . . she sleeps with me, and comforts my nights as well as my days.'[50]

Grace Welsh's death had removed the last remaining source of undemanding love; a love craved by Jane and something that a husband, no
matter how attentive and loving, could not replace. She remarked: 'What
are friends for – what is a husband even, compared with one's Mother?
Of her love one is always so sure! It is the only love that nothing – not
even misconduct on our part – can take away from us.'[51]

Perhaps as a reaction to the loss of her mother Jane's physical condition began to deteriorate further, as did her relationship with Carlyle.
Harriet Martineau used to say that Jane had eight influenzas annually,[52]
and indeed, she rarely wrote a letter that did not at some point refer to
a past or present illness. As Drew says, 'There never seems to be a time
when she is not tugging with influenza like a fly among treacle, or pros-
trated with sick headache, convulsed with colic, wild with face-ache,
demolished by sleepless nights, bedevilled with neuralgia . . . weak as a
dish cloth.'[53]

As to the cause of her suffering Jane herself traced it to her childhood
and her entry to puberty. Apparently from an early age she suffered from
migraines and later from heavy menstrual bleeding; thus her illnesses
were part of a continuum of medical problems.[54] It was one's unfortu-
nate lot in life, something to be borne stoically, or in Jane's letters, hero-
ically. Another view, and one expressed by Carlyle's brother Jack, a
doctor, was that her illnesses were psychosomatic, the result of too much
brooding over life and her condition. He recommended that Jane find
some kind of occupation or involvement in some activity outside the
home; although apart from engaging in philanthropic activity, which
Jane was not interested in, it was impossible for a middle-class woman
to find work other than writing, which had the advantage of being performed in the home. Jack Carlyle was in many ways correct in his diag-
nosis of Jane, although his prescription was unrealistic and his lack of
sympathy obvious. As Kathy Chamberlain points out, her illness was a
form of speech: a way of manifesting a deep sense of failure and dissatisfaction with her life and her need for love. Thus, her 'fifteen years' long
illness' was a form of attention seeking from a man increasingly devoid
of the means to address the needs of his wife. To make matters worse
there was little emotional compensation for Jane. Her father and mother
were both dead, there were no siblings, and she was childless. Religion
may have helped but Mrs Carlyle had on occasion made 'sweeping dec-
lamations against the Christianity and the Church'.[55] Another possibility was a romantic attachment. Jane was known to be flirtatious and even
when married had a host of male admirers, or 'lovers' as she referred to
them, including Erasmus Darwin, Godefroi Cavaignac, Leigh Hunt, and

Mazzini, among others. But none carried admiration into admissions of desire. A lesbian relationship was possible. Geraldine Jewsbury declared her love for Jane in romantic terms, writing: 'I love you my darling . . . I feel towards you much more like a lover than a female friend.'[56] But her protestations of love came to nothing. Jane's feelings towards Geraldine were more of annoyance rather than of longing. Thus, it is hardly surprising that with no consolations, either spiritual or romantic, 'a consistent cry of the heart was "I am miserable – pay attention", this coming from the daughter of a doting father who had died when she was only eighteen'.[57]

That the root cause of the illnesses was psychological rather than physical is demonstrated by her continued capacity to respond to love and her liking for exciting and pleasurable experiences. Motherly love could restore her to health incredibly quickly. When visiting her mother in August 1841 she spent the first two days in bed quite ill and was the centre of Grace's love and attention. Jane remarked that the 'comfort of these two days was indescribable', and 'what a rehabilitation of the flesh all this was for me'. In no time she was 'up again – running about looking at every thing, and extacizing over every thing as if I just been imported from the backwoods'.[58] The stimulation of good company could also have restorative effects. As Drew puts it:

> Mingled . . . with her accounts of . . . her perpetual bad health . . . are accounts of perpetual recoveries. As she says, one day she is ill in bed, the next in full puff at an entertainment; in the morning she has 'cholera' and in the afternoon she is dining out. In spite of her influenzas, she never misses one of Carlyle's lectures. On one occasion . . . she describes how one day in 1855 she is lying, a physical wreck, on the sofa, unable to make any effort, when the door opens and George Rennie, after an absence of many years abroad, walks in unexpectedly to see her. She jumps up and kisses him 'a great many times', and the result is a miracle of healing.[59]

However, although Jane's illnesses were in essence psychological, both she and Thomas contributed to their poor health by eating food and drink that could only have inflamed digestive problems, such as bread, meat, potatoes, coffee and tea. They ate little or no vegetables and regarded fruit as 'of no use but to give people a colic'.[60] They also took remedies and, in the case of Jane, substances that adversely affected her physical being. Sleeplessness and pain saw her turn to morphine for relief, which she formed an addiction to. A warning from her doctor as to the harmful consequences of too much exposure to the drug saw her at various times turn to whisky, wine and gin for relief, but in extremes she would always return to morphine.[61] Another remedy was to stay indoors during winter months, although this only served to make her headaches worse and caused her to brood even more negatively about her lot in life.

Her relationship with Carlyle turned sour during this time. This can be seen in the way she addressed him in her letters. As one might expect in the first years of marriage they are addressed to 'my dearest husband of me', 'darling', then to 'my dear husband', and end 'yours faithfully Jane W. C.', and, finally, 'Mr T. Carlyle' or 'Mr C.'. The celebrated painting by Robert Tait of *A Chelsea Interior* shows just how cold and distant the relationship had become by the 1850s. In the painting Thomas lights his pipe by the fireplace and Jane sits in a chair in the corner of the room, both staring into an empty space. The cause of this emotional detachment was undoubtedly Thomas' relationship with Harriet Baring, later Lady Ashburton, a woman so unlike Jane in every possible way. While Jane was delicate and small, Harriet was a large woman, but as Carlyle put it, 'one of the cleverest creatures I have met with, full of mirth and spirit; not very beautiful to look upon . . . [but] the most like a dame of quality of all that I have yet seen'.[62] She became his 'daughter of the Sun'; his 'daughter of Adam most beautiful'; his 'own Queen'.[63] Jane's description of Lady Baring is more acute: 'She is immensely *large* – might easily have been one of the *ugliest* women living – but *is* almost *beautiful* – simply thro' the intelligence and cordiality of her expression.'[64]

Baring was the first real competitor for Jane for the attention of Carlyle. She undoubtedly entranced him from the first moment he met her at a dinner in February 1839 at Bath House in London. From that moment, until her sudden death in Paris in May 1857 from a disease of the uterus, he was besotted with Baring; however, Jane was little aware of the relationship until 1843. Their friendship greatly distressed and humiliated Jane, by making her the subject of gossip and innuendo, and its persistence brought clashes of personality and social class. As her friend, the novelist Geraldine Jewsbury, explained in a letter to Froude, what distressed Jane was that while Carlyle was quite happy to place his work before her, when it came to Baring he lingered in the 'primrose path of dalliance for the sake of a great lady who liked to have her philosopher in chains'.[65] Jane's notes in her journal hardly disguise her contempt and jealousy in equal measure for Carlyle's studied neglect of her and her feelings. In October 1855 she writes: 'That eternal Bath House. I wonder how many thousand miles Mr C. has walked between there and here'; and the following month she notes: 'Alone this evening. Lady A. in town again; and Mr C. of course at Bath House.'[66] In this mood, all Carlyle's protestations of innocence and love were treated with sarcasm. When he goes, without her, on holiday with Baring and her husband to their shooting-lodge in Scotland in late summer 1856, Jane writes in an angry and wounded manner, complaining that his 'letters' are simply a few disingenuous lines mouthing platitudes about missing her and their home, saying:

> When you go to any house, one knows it because you choose to go; and when you stay, it is because you choose to stay. You don't, as weakly amiable people do, sacrifice yourself for the pleasure of 'others'. So pray do not think it necessary to be wishing yourself at home, and 'all that sort of thing' on paper. 'I don't believe thee'![67]

Added to the neglect were the petty social humiliations and insults Jane suffered at the hands of Baring. As Jewsbury noted, 'Lady A. was excessively capricious towards her, and made her feel they cared more about *him* than about *her*.'[68] For example, at Christmas in 1855, Baring gave Jane a made-up silk dress, the kind of gift that would only be given to a housekeeper or a woman of a similar social status. Given the precise understandings of the nuances of class at this time, as Surtees points out, 'Harriet must have thought this perfectly fitting for Jane', although she was livid and refused the gift.[69] The incident tells us much regarding the social confidence and the lack of deference of the middle class towards the aristocracy in mid-nineteenth-century Britain. The enfranchisement of the former in 1832 and the introduction of free trade after the abolition of the Corn Laws in 1846 were expressed it seems in social as well as in political terms. Jane refused to be the object of Baring's obvious patronising and superior manner, declaring some years before that 'the Lady has a genius for *ruling* – whilst I have a genius for – not being *ruled*'.[70]

Feelings of humiliation and jealousy led Jane to consider leaving Thomas as early as 1846. Her marriage she felt was a 'stupidity rather than a heroism . . . my life is crushed out in it'.[71] She wrote to Mazzini detailing the emptiness and meaningless of her life with Carlyle, and that she was leaving Cheyne Row and had no point of return in mind. Consolingly, he wrote, saying:

> None can help you but yourself. It is only you who can, by a calm, dispassionate, fair re-examination of the past, send back to nothingness the ghosts and phantoms you have been conjuring up. It is only you who can teach yourself that, whatever the *present* may be, you must front it with dignity, with a clear perception of all your duties . . . Your life proves an empty thing, you say! Empty! Do not blaspheme. Have you never done any good? Have you never loved? Think of your mother and do good.[72]

These sentiments, however, were flights of fantasy, and when Jane again contemplated the same scenario in1862, she pointedly commented that 'I sometimes feel that I should like to run away. But the question always arises, where to?'[73] Such was the almost total level of dependency of married women on their husbands it was almost impossible for a woman to exit an unhappy marriage. Before the introduction of the Married Women's Property Act in 1870 married women had no right to their earnings and personal property. What was hers was his. When Jane's mother bequeathed Craigenputtock, with a yearly rental value of £200–300, to her in 1842, Carlyle quite legally appropriated the rent and property. Moreover, until the passing of the Matrimonial Causes Act of 1857, which introduced secular divorce in England, dissolving a marriage was an expensive legal process that involved an Act of Parliament; in fact, the expense was so great that only four women had achieved divorce by this route.

The degree of Jane's, and by inference other women's, reliance on her/their husband[s] was made clear in an amusing, but cutting, letter – *Budget of a Femme Incomprise* – written to Carlyle in 1855. In its paragraphs the ongoing confrontations over household expenditure in the middle-class home, which at a deeper level can be interpreted as conflicts over the desire of women for more freedom and independence, are laid bare:

> I don't choose to speak on the *Money question* . . . When you tell me 'I pester your life out about money' – that 'your soul is sick with hearing about', that 'I had better make the money I *have* serve, at all rates – hang it! Let *you* alone of it'; all that I call perfectly unfair . . . If I were greedy, or extravagant, or a bad manager; you would be in 'staving me off' with loud words: but you cannot say *that* of me . . . At least I am sure that I never 'asked for more' to myself from you or anyone – not even from my own Mother in all my life; and that thro' six and twenty years, I have kept house for you, at more or less cost according to given circumstances, but always on *less* than it costs the generality of People, living in the same style . . . You asked me at the last money-row, with 'withering sarcasm', had I the *slightest* idea of what amount of money would *satisfy me* . . . Was there any conceivable sum of money that could put an end to my eternal botheration? I will answer the question as if it had been asked practically and kindly. Yes! I have the strongest idea of what amount of money would 'satisfy' me . . . £29, divided into quarterly payments would *satisfy* me.[74]

If Jane left Carlyle her prospects would have almost certainly have been bleak. Penniless, she would have either been forced into accepting the charity of relatives, and the petty indignities that went with it, or into finding a position as a governess, which at her age would have been unlikely. Like most women in Victorian Britain finding themselves in an unhappy marriage there was little or no alternative than to stoically put up with one's lot, while hoping that her partner might experience a speedy and terminal demise. Harriet Baring's sudden death in 1857 solved the problem and Jane's feelings of affection for Carlyle were quickly restored. Letters once again begin endearingly and are addressed to 'darling' and 'dearest'.

Of course, some women, such as the anti-slavery campaigner Eliza Wigham, argued in the 1840s and 50s for women's rights, for equality with men, and even Jane's friend Geraldine Jewsbury in her novel – *The Half Sisters* (1848) – publicly contested traditional assumptions regarding marriage, but Jane was not among them. She dismissed overt challenges to female subordination, saying: 'I am so weary of hearing about these *rights* of ours – and always to the tune "don't you wish you may get them".'[75] She questioned her subordination in the domestic sphere and through this came to doubt whether marriage was the ultimate state of fulfilment for women. In an intemperate letter, very bitter in tone, Jane emotionally implodes when conveying her frustration and resentment over her own experience of marriage to her young friend, Miss Barnes, who had just become engaged, stating:

> And you are actually going to get married! you! already! And you expect me to congratulate you! or 'perhaps not' . . . Frankly, my dear I wish all the happiness in the new life that is opening to you . . . But congratulations on such occasions seems to me a tempting of Providence . . . Will you think me mad if I tell you that when I read your words, 'I am going to be married', I all but screamed? Positively it took away my breath, as if I saw you in the act of taking a flying leap into infinite space . . . After you had walked out of our house together that night, and I sat down there in the dark, and took a 'good cry'. You had reminded me so vividly of my own youth, when I, also an only daughter – an only child – had a father as fond of me, as proud of me. I wondered if you knew your own happiness. Well! knowing it or not, it has been enough for you, it would seem . . . But of you father? Who is to cheer his toilsome life, and make a home bright for him? His companion through half a lifetime gone! . . . Oh, little girl! little girl! do you know the blank you will make to him?[76]

Privately, Jane – interestingly writing in French – also questioned the marriage laws that set double standards for men and women. She felt it grossly unfair that women could lose their families because of some misconduct on their part, while the men who through their studied neglect or actual cruelty drove them to it went unpunished. With a direct reference to her marriage to Thomas, Jane argued that a harsh and difficult man could drive a woman, perhaps not to misconduct, but to 'something, and something not to his advantage, any more than hers'.[77]

It was, therefore, in the domestic sphere where the issues of subordination were to be confronted and ultimately resolved. But this was a sphere that Jane was losing control of as her illnesses became increasingly debilitating. She had been in generally poor health for some years and this already had taken its toll on her appearance. Nowhere is this more visibly demonstrated than in Robert Tait's celebrated photograph of Jane. In it she looks drawn and very old, rather than a woman of fifty-four years. However, in the last years of her life she experienced more severe mental and physical problems. Neuralgia in her left arm after a fall in September 1863, clinical depression during the period December 1863 and September 1864, feelings of insanity, suicide, loss of appetite and weight, and other problems, all took their toll on her. Carlyle was moved to describe Jane as a 'suffering aged woman, accepting her age and feebleness'. Although she rallied and recovered her spirits after her depression, Jane's death came quite soon and in unexpected circumstances. While out with her dog, Tiny, on 21 April 1866, it was knocked down by a carriage and she suffered a fatal shock: as the *Dictionary of National Biography* put it, 'she was found sitting with folded hands in . . . [her] carriage dead'.[78] Fittingly, she was buried in her father's grave in Haddington. Carlyle died fifteen years later.

We know Jane Welsh Carlyle mainly through her letters and journals, although other witnesses' observations also provide clues to her character and to her relationship with Thomas. The purpose of these letters, as Aileen Christianson recognises, was to construct or organise her life, to make it not only intelligible, but to make it bearable. In doing so she entertains, informs and impresses the reader and draws him or her, and ultimately us, into 'a collusive interpretation with her of her life'.[79] The ways in which she defined herself and her marriage succeeded in convincing even Carlyle, as *Reminiscences* makes clear, and later Froude, of his guilt, of his wasting of her talent in the service of his career. Jane leaves us an overwhelming image of self-sacrifice and, as a result, we are compelled to share her sense of frustration at being recognised as only the helpmate of genius rather than a talent in her own right. In a letter to Carlyle she speaks sarcastically of her role, saying:

> the greatest testimony to your fame seems to me to be the fact of my photograph . . . stuck up in Macmichael's shop-window. Did you ever hear anything so preposterous in your life . . . it proves the interest or curiosity you excite; for being neither a 'distinguished authoress', nor a 'celebrated murderess' . . . it can only be as Mrs Carlyle that they offer me for sale.[80]

However, the heroic presentation of self in her correspondence, witty and lively as it was, should not be accepted unreservedly. Thomas was undoubtedly self-centred and obsessive and increasingly irritable, particularly during the years writing his biography of Frederick the Great. Jane described her life with him at this time 'as like keeping a madhouse'.[81] But in spite of his obvious faults and idiosyncrasies, Jane was in some ways the architect of her own unhappiness. The standard of masculinity used to measure a man was her father and no man could scale these preposterously dizzying heights. Love in the real world was conditional, not undemanding, and her grudging acceptance of this reflected the immaturity of women who seek a father-figure as a partner, or men who seek in a wife a substitute for their mother. Jane strove to recreate Thomas in the mould of her father, but without much success. She nurtured his talent, freed him from all forms of responsibility, even to the point of dealing with the Commissioners of Inland Revenue in 1855, and located herself on the periphery of his career. The reward for her devotion was Thomas' long fixation with Harriet Baring and his neglect of her sexuality. The jealousy and resentment this generated in her made Jane only too aware of her subordination within marriage, but what to do? The short answer was nothing. She retreated more and more into the private sphere and sought attention and solace in illness and its relief, usually morphine, and, when that did not work, alcohol. She even took up smoking at one point.

The answer may have been a life less domestically orientated, but women in her position had, with highly restricted occupational opportunities, very few outlets for their frustrations other than arguing with their partners, complaining to other women, or immersing themselves in religion and/or philanthropy. Jane was adept in the areas of argument and complaint, but her tone is always either self-pitying or self-parodying. There is, as Anne Skabarnicki points out, no attempt 'to grapple with an issue, pursue an idea, or dissect an argument that did not have a purely narrow and personal relevance'.[82] Moreover, at no time did she express any regrets concerning failed ambition or the lack of creative fulfilment. Her frustration was fixed on her husband, not on the lack of a career.[83] Jane's letters, which are the only indication we have of her literary talent, chiefly consist of gossip, tittle-tattle, advice on home improvements, scolding workmen and servants, and serve to underscore the view that she had 'no vision beyond the domestic, no focus beyond self'.[84] Writing needs discipline, structure and thought: qualities that seem to be missing in her letters. This suggests that, perhaps, writing serious literature was beyond her ability. Failing to carve out a niche in the public sphere as a writer, Jane, like most women at this time, had little alternative but to collude in her subordination. But in this instance collusion did not equate with satisfaction. Somewhat contradictorily we also glimpse in Jane the simmering discontent of middle-class women with domesticity and the growing desire for a life less mundane and more socially meaningful. Jane's death in 1866 marked the transitional point in which private emotions became the stimulus for public protest by middle-class women over a whole range of issues, from education to the franchise.

NOTES

1. J. A. Froude, *Thomas Carlyle: a History of his Life in London, 1834–1881* (London, 1890) and *Letters and Memorials of Jane Welsh Carlyle*, 2 vols (London, 1883); R. Ashton, *Thomas and Jane Carlyle: Portrait of a Marriage* (London, 2003).
2. T. Carlyle, *Reminiscences* (London, 1881), p. 207.
3. Carlyle, *Reminiscences*, p. 206.
4. Quoted in A. Christianson, 'Jane Welsh Carlyle's private writing career', in D. Gifford and D. MacMillan (eds), *A History of Scottish Women's Writing* (Edinburgh, 1997), p. 235.
5. *Dictionary of National Biography* (London, 1908).
6. E. Drew, *Jane Welsh and Jane Carlyle* (London, 1928), p. 22.
7. Carlyle, *Reminiscences*, p. 208.
8. V. Surtees, *Jane Welsh Carlyle* (Salisbury, 1986), p. 14.
9. Carlyle, *Reminiscences*, pp. 71–2.
10. Quoted in I. Campbell, 'Grace Welsh and Jane Carlyle', *Carlyle Newsletter*, 1 (1979), p. 17.
11. Quoted in Drew, *Jane Carlyle*, p. 31.
12. T. Carlyle, 'Cruthers and Jonson', *Fraser's Magazine* (1831), quoted in Drew, *Jane Carlyle*, p. 32.
13. F. Kaplan, *Thomas Carlyle: a Biography* (Cambridge, 1983), p. 109.
14. Drew, *Jane Carlyle*, p. 40.
15. Drew, *Jane Carlyle*, p. 41.
16. L. and M. Hanson, *Necessary Evil: the Life of Jane Welsh Carlyle* (London, 1952), p. 39.
17. Quoted in Drew, *Jane Carlyle*, pp. 33–4.
18. Kaplan, *Carlyle*, p. 109.
19. Quoted in Drew, *Jane Carlyle*, p. 34.
20. Quoted in Drew, *Jane Carlyle*, p. 50.
21. Letter to Eliza Stoddart, 8 February 1822 in A. and M. McQueen Simpson, *I Too Am Here: Selections from the Letters of Jane Welsh Carlyle* (Cambridge, 1977), p. 8.
22. Letter to Thomas Carlyle, 7 July 1825 quoted in Ashton, *Thomas and Jane*, p. 17.

23. Ashton, *Thomas and Jane*, p. 71.
24. Quoted in Kaplan, *Carlyle*, p. 116.
25. Kaplan, *Carlyle*, p. 178.
26. A. Christianson, 'Rewriting herself: Jane Welsh Carlyle's letters' *Scotlands*, 2 (1994), p. 52.
27. Quoted in K. Chamberlain, 'Illness as speech in the life of Jane Welsh Carlyle', *Carlyle Studies Annual*, 19 (1999–2000), p. 64.
28. Ashton, *Thomas and Jane*, p. 75.
29. N. Brysson Morrison, *True Minds: the Marriage of Thomas and Jane Carlyle* (London, 1974), pp. 81–2.
30. Carlyle, *Reminiscences*, p. 210.
31. Letter to Mary Smith, 11 January 1857, quoted in M. Smith, *The Autobiography of Mary Smith* (1892), pp. 309–11.
32. Quoted in K. J. Fielding, 'The cry from Craigenputtock', *Times Literary Supplement*, 13 August 1999.
33. J. A. Froude, *My Relations with Carlyle* (London, 1903), p. 4.
34. Sir J. Crichton-Browne and A. Carlyle, *The Nemesis of Froude* (1903).
35. Drew, *Jane Carlyle*, pp. 132–9.
36. Hanson, *Necessary Evil*, p. 139.
37. Letter to J. Carlyle, 14 April 1927, in T. Bliss, *Thomas Carlyle: Letters to his Wife* (London, 1953), p. 23.
38. Quoted in Drew, *Jane Carlyle*, p. 83.
39. Ashton, *Thomas and Jane*, p. 76.
40. Letter to Jean Aitken, August 1835, in Froude, *Letters and Memorials*, p. 19.
41. Letter to Grace Welsh, 1 September 1834, in Froude, *Letters and Memorials*, pp. 3–4.
42. K. Gleadle, *British Women in the Nineteenth Century* (Baskingstoke, 2001), p. 52.
43. P. Branca, *Silent Sisterhood: Middle-class Women in the Victorian Home* (London, 1975), pp. 22–47; L. Davidoff, *Worlds Between: Historical Perspectives on Gender and Class* (Cambridge, 1995), pp. 73–102; C. Hall, *White, Male and Middle-Class: Explorations in Feminism and History* (Cambridge, 1992), pp. 75–93.
44. Letter to T. Carlyle, 12 October 1835, in Froude, *Letters and Memorials*, vol. 1, p. 26.
45. Thea Holmes, *The Carlyles at Home* (Oxford, 1965), pp. 14–15.
46. Quoted in Hanson, *Necessary Evil*, p. 267.
47. Letter to T. Carlyle, 4 July 1843, in Froude, *Letters and Memorials*, vol. 1, p. 145.
48. Kaplan, *Carlyle*, p. 282.
49. Letter to J. Sterling, 29 April 1841, in Froude, *Letters and Memorials*, vol. 1, p. 99.
50. Quoted in Hanson, *Necessary Evil*, p. 269.

51. Quoted in Hanson, *Necessary Evil*, p. 270.
52. Chamberlain, 'Illness as speech', p. 65.
53. Drew, *Jane Carlyle*, p. 160.
54. Kaplan, *Carlyle*, p. 237.
55. Quoted in Surtees, *Jane Welsh Carlyle*, p. 204.
56. Quoted in Holmes, *The Carlyles*, p. 300.
57. Chamberlain, 'Illness as speech', p. 67.
58. Chamberlain, 'Illness as speech', p. 68.
59. Drew, *Jane Carlyle*, p. 164.
60. Drew, *Jane Carlyle*, p. 161.
61. T. Holmes, *The Carlyles*, p. 52.
62. Quoted in Hanson, *Necessary Evil*, p. 241.
63. Quoted in Hanson, *Necessary Evil*, pp. 316, 338, 364.
64. Quoted in Hanson, *Necessary Evil*, p. 297.
65. Froude, *Letters and Memorials*, vol. 2, p. 49.
66. Quoted in Drew, *Jane Carlyle*, p. 154.
67. Letter to T. Carlyle, 18 September 1856, in Froude, *Letters and Memorials*, vol. 2, pp. 68–9.
68. Froude, *Letters and Memorials*, vol. 2, p. 49.
69. Surtees, *Jane Welsh Carlyle*, p. 227.
70. Quoted in Hanson, *Necessary Evil*, p. 329.
71. Quoted in Holmes, *The Carlyles*, p. 304.
72. Quoted in Hanson, *Necessary Evil*, p. 336.
73. Letter to Mrs Austin, 23 October 1862, in Froude, *Letters and Memorials*, vol. 2, p. 241.
74. Letter to T. Carlyle, 12 February 1855, quoted in Ashton, *Thomas and Jane*, pp. 364–5.
75. Letter to Martha M. Lamont, 1 August 1849, quoted in Christianson, 'Private writing career', p. 239.
76. Letter to Miss Barnes, 24 August 1859, in Froude, *Letters and Memorials*, vol. 2, pp. 141–2.
77. P. Rose, *Parallel Lives: Five Victorian Marriages* (London, 1984), p. 253.
78. *Dictionary of National Biography* (1908).
79. Christianson, 'Rewriting herself', p. 52.
80. Letter to T. Carlyle, 30 July 1865, in Froude, *Letters and Memorials*, vol. 2, pp. 345–6.
81. Froude, *My Relations*, p. 9.
82. A. M. Skabarnicki, 'Two faces of Eve: the literary personae of Harriet Martineau and Jane Welsh Carlyle', *Carlyle Journal*, 11 (1990), p. 18.
83. A. Christianson, 'Jane Welsh Carlyle and her friendships with women in the 1840s', *Prose Studies*, 9–10 (1986–7), p. 286.
84. Skabarnicki, 'Two faces', p. 29.

2

Eliza Wigham: Religion, Radicalism and the Origins of the Women's Movement in Nineteenth-Century Scotland

ᐁ

Eliza Wigham was at the forefront of all the major campaigns to improve women's rights in Britain in the nineteenth century, and yet we know very little about her, indeed, much less than the other women covered in this volume. As she never kept a diary and, as a very private and humble woman, rarely spoke 'to others of her inmost feelings'[1], what documentation has survived of her life is fragmentary. However, from the anti-slavery agitation of the 1840s and beyond, through to the struggles for female education and the franchise, Eliza was an active and inspirational figurehead in a series of unpopular causes. The historian Clare Midgley has claimed that she was one of six women 'at the core of anti-slavery sisterhood in Britain'.[2] In spite of continued criticism and opposition, she never deviated from her mission. A belief that she was doing God's work sustained her in the face of censure, as did her humanitarian values and her pacifism. Eliza was a Quaker and the beliefs associated with her religion not only provided a theological basis for her activism, it also gave her access to a network of similarly-minded men and women. There were strong, close-knit family groupings, such as the Wighams, Smeals and Richardsons, within the Society of Friends and these familial connections, mainly created through marriage, provided the backbone of the radical reforming campaigns Eliza found herself involved in. Thus, when analysing the origins and development of the women's movement, particularly in Scotland, the role of religion and family is as important to discuss, as is the part of important individuals such as Eliza. Indeed, it is almost impossible to disentangle her story from these other influences.

The family roots lay in Coanwood, Northumberland, and it was from there that John Wigham left for Edinburgh in the early 1800s to join his cousin, John Wigham Junior, who was a shawl manufacturer in the city. While in Edinburgh he met and married Jane Richardson, of Whitehaven. There were several children, three of whom died in infancy.

In 1819, the Wighams took a house in South Gray Street on the south side of Edinburgh and it was there that Eliza was born on 23 February 1820, the third eldest daughter of what was to be a surviving family of three brothers and three sisters. Unfortunately we know little of her childhood other than it was 'bright and happy' and that she developed with her elder sister, Mary, and her younger brother, Henry, a love of botany that remained with her all her life.[3] However, when she was ten her mother died, only to be followed the next year by her eldest sister, Ann, at the age of sixteen, and a younger brother around this time.

In spite of the tragedy of family life, politics and a concern for the suffering of those in distant lands were never very far away. Eliza's uncle's home in Salisbury Road became a centre of much philanthropic and political interest in Edinburgh, where 'young people came in contact with some of the leading spirits of progress and philanthropy, and imbibed that enthusiastic love for truth and righteousness, and hatred of every form of wrong and oppression'.[4] The familial basis of protest was intensified when her father married Jane Smeal, secretary of the Glasgow Ladies Emancipation Society (GLES) and the sister of the main spokesperson of the Glasgow anti-slavery movement, William Smeal, in 1840; her sister, Mary, married Joshua Edmundson, of Dublin, in the same year. Her brothers, Henry and John, joined Mary in Dublin and they, along with Richard Webb and his sister, formed the backbone of anti-slavery activity in the south of Ireland. Writing to the American abolitionist, Maria Weston Chapman, Jane explained the family connections, saying, Eliza is:

> my husband's daughter and the other Eliza, is Eliza Nicholson the sister of Sarah Wigham who is the wife of John Wigham Jnr. My husband being John Wigham tertius – the two Johns are first cousins . . . We live within 5 minutes walk of each other and are on terms of the closest love & friendly intercourse.[5]

It was through these connections and gatherings that Eliza was introduced to the great radical issues of the day, with the most important being the abolition of slavery in the British West Indies. Quaker women had been active in William Wilberforce's campaign to end the slave traffic within the British Empire, which was abolished in 1808, and it was this constituency that joined in droves the Anti-Slavery Society which was formed in 1823 to bring about the gradual emancipation of slaves in the West Indies. They believed that a fundamental tenet of Christian life was a recognition that Christ died for all, and that all were equal in the sight of God. As such they believed in civil and religious liberties for all God's subjects regardless of race or colour.[6] In pursuit of this belief, the highly influential Edinburgh and Glasgow societies carried out propaganda campaigns against the purchase of slave produce, handing out pamphlets to women such as *What Does Sugar Cost?* and *Reasons for Substituting West Indian Sugar.*[7] However, in the 1820s, the main demand was for the gradual amelioration of slave conditions in the West Indies, rather than an outright call for the immediate abolition. This was left to the women abolitionists, including many Quakers. The Leicester Quaker, Elizabeth Heyrich, in her tract, *Immediate Not Gradual Abolition* (1824), called for a 'holy war' against slavery.[8]

It was not surprising the Quaker women spoke out so loudly in public against slavery since their position within the movement was qualitatively different to women in other religious organisations. While they were hedged in by social and theological constraints, Quakers were able to speak and preach freely in public and to hold offices within the movement, of which the minister – as Eliza became in 1867 – was the most important. They were also aware that while they enjoyed special rights within the Quaker movement it was not until 1896 that full equality was achieved with men. Prior to that, women were confined to the somewhat powerless Women's Yearly Meeting, while the Men's Yearly Meeting legislated for the movement as a whole. The daughters of the great Quaker proponent of free trade in Britain, John Bright, complained about 'the separation of the body into two parts, one which legislates, and another which, while amenable to any penalties in the power of the Society to impose, has no part in the conduct of its business'.[9] Thus, the freedoms they had gradually sensitised them to the need to relate their position within the Quaker movement to the larger claims of women outside religion; something that was reinforced by the struggles across the Atlantic ocean to end the plantation system.

The campaign to end slavery in the West Indies brought some British abolitionists into contact with groups in America opposed to the plantation slavery in the South. The interest was reciprocated as American abolitionists actively not only sought to replicate the strategy of the British women's anti-slavery societies, but also invited them to participate in their cause. This was made possible by the abolition of slavery in British colonies in 1833, and especially by the abolition of indentured slavery, or the apprenticeship system as it was known, in the West Indies in 1839. The women who had been active in these struggles joined the recently formed British and Foreign Anti-Slavery Society (BFASS) as auxiliaries to fight against slavery and the slave trade throughout the world.[10] The first act of the new society was to call for a World Anti-Slavery Convention to be held in London on 12 June 1840, an act that proved a turning point in the history of the women's movement in Britain.

   Female abolitionists in Britain rarely, if at all, challenged the right of
men to superior positions within the anti-slavery movement. The BFASS
only allowed for males to serve as officers and committee members.
Women were organised in separate organisations, whereas in the United
States most local anti-slavery societies included men and women.[11] As
early as 1839, the business and finance committees of the Pennsylvania
Anti-Slavery Society consisted of four women and three men.[12] The
American women were able to transform their ability to raise money for
the anti-slavery cause into some form of power, while British women
during the 1830s continued 'to define their anti-slavery involvement in
religious and moral terms, working through prayer and giving financial
aid to assist their American sisters'.[13] Even Jane Smeal and the Glasgow
Emancipation Society (GES) stressed that the women had 'no desire to
step beyond their appropriate sphere'.[14] Women in America, such as
Angelina and Sarah Grimke, were rejecting the idea of separate spheres
and beginning to link the issue of women's rights and the campaign
against slavery. In this political shift they were joined by William Lloyd
Garrison, whose journal – *The Liberator* – became the voice of American
radicalism. Garrison had a disproportionate amount of support in
Scotland, where his radicalism attracted Eliza and other women in
Edinburgh and Glasgow, and also in smaller places, such as Kirkcaldy
and Perth.[15] However, the linking of the women's question to the anti-
slavery campaign split the American Anti-Slavery Society (AASS). The
AASS divided into the 'old' and the 'new', with the latter under the leadership of Lewis Tappan opposing any attempt to link the anti-slavery
cause with other issues, including women's rights, and opposed full membership of women of the American and Foreign Anti-Slavery Society
(AFASS).[16] Thus, when the World Convention met, the American delegation was already deeply divided.
   It was also the question of women's rights that ended unity within the
British movement. The AASS had elected seven female delegates as representatives of the Massachusetts and Pennsylvania anti-slavery societies,
but when they presented themselves for seating they were refused a place.
The London Committee of Arrangements stated that their presence was
in conflict with established British 'customs and usage' and that if
breached it would subject the convention to 'ridicule'. It was clear that
they were being excluded as women and not as Garrisonians, since no
male Garrisonian delegate was refused a seat, indeed, a prominent fol-
lower of Garrison, Wendell Phillips, was appointed one of the convention secretaries.[17] Three hundred and fifty delegates debated the issue,
with the majority of British Quakers opposed to the seating of females.

Even George Thompson, who had done so much to push the idea of immediate emancipation and had converted many American and British women to the anti-slavery cause and Garrisonianism, showed the limits of male support for the women within the radical camp. Thompson called upon the female delegates to withdraw their application for seating at the convention.[18] When Garrison arrived at the convention six days late, he and three other male delegates from Massachusetts refused to sit or have their names added to the official register of attendance. The American schism divided the British abolitionists; however, it also dramatised the issue of women's rights more than any other event. As the American abolitionist Elizabeth Candy Stanton put it some years later: the exclusion of women delegates 'stung many women into new thought and action' and gave 'rise to the movement for women's political equality both in England and the United States'.[19]

In Scotland the abolitionists in the Edinburgh and Glasgow women's societies split over the issues articulated at the World Convention. In Glasgow, religious divisions further complicated a difficult situation. The Evangelicals within the GLES favoured the decision not to seat female delegates at the convention, since to act otherwise would have been contrary to divine teachings.[20] The pro-Garrison faction formed the Glasgow Female Anti-Slavery Society (GFASS), while the more conservative women remained within the fold of the GLES. The new organisation, unlike the GLES, was wholly independent and saw its role in fighting slavery as more than just raising funds for the male-dominated GES. It was also completely committed to the radical policies and the leadership of Garrison, attacking anyone who argued that he was responsible for the rift within the anti-slavery movement in Britain.[21] The GFASS also issued an *Appeal to the Ladies of Great Britain* calling for continued support for the AASS, but publicly avoided promoting the issue of women's rights. In contrast, the Edinburgh Ladies Society, under the strong leadership of Smeal and Wigham, remained in the Garrisonian fold. However, a rift developed between Eliza and her father who threw his support behind the BFASS, and by implication the AFASS, as did his cousin Anthony Wigham. When the men's Society in Edinburgh declared support for the new London organisation, the ELES remained steadfast, thanks to Eliza and Jane, in support of Garrison and the ASSS.[22]

Eliza and other Garrisonian women were also beginning to shift towards a policy of liberation, not just for slaves and women, but all of mankind who were oppressed, powerless and suffering. As Louis and Rosamund Billington point out, one of the reasons that the anti-slavery movement in Britain haemorrhaged support after the 1840 convention, was not simply due to religious and gender divisions, but also because of a broadening of the base of interest among women, such as Eliza, Elizabeth Pease (later Nichol), and Anne Knight, to include the Anti-Corn Law League, Chartism, temperance, and other reform issues.[23] The reason was also strategic however. Most anti-slavery societies were small in terms of numbers, if not influence. Both the Edinburgh and Glasgow Ladies Societies had less than thirty members in 1839,[24] with two-thirds being married women. They were also nearly all middle class, with only the GLES reporting some support from working-class women.[25] Thus, it made sense to reach out to other organisations, especially to the working-class Chartists, campaigning for a redistribution of political power in the hope that it might provide a larger platform in which to discuss the issue of women's rights. Some of the leading Chartists in Scotland and in England had after all drawn parallels between the oppressed poor in Britain and slaves in America. The Reverend Patrick Brewster, of Paisley, in his *Chartists and Socialist Sermons*, condemned those 'who refuse to deliver the White bondsman at home, [as being] worse than the guilty slave holder himself'.[26] Anti-slavery activists also reciprocated these concerns. The Garrisonian Elizabeth Pease criticised the upper classes for driving workers to 'desperation' by 'treating them as chattels made to minister to their luxury and add to their wealth'.[27] Among abolitionist women there was also an instinctive identification with the poor that derived from their philanthropic work among them. As Rinker points out, they had frequently visited the Glasgow slums and as such were 'eye-witnesses to the misery of these dark, filthy disease ridden urban ghettoes'.[28] Eliza herself took an active interest in philanthropic work among the poor of Edinburgh regularly visiting 'a district workhouse, reading to the poor women and bringing them extra comforts'.[29]

One of the other attractive features of the Chartist movement in Scotland as far as Eliza and other Garrisonians were concerned was its moral dimension. Unlike in England, a large number of Chartists were teetotal advocates. Total Abstinence Societies (TAS) flourished in lowland Scotland in the 1830s and 40s and the membership was mainly made up of Chartists and other radicals; indeed, Aberdeen TAS had 3,000 members most of whom were Chartists and a favourite song at gatherings was Neil Gow's *Farewell to Whisky*.[30] The abolitionists used the issue of temperance to create linkages with slavery. Garrison himself, since his editorship of the *National Philanthropist*, was committed to temperance and considered it 'one of the most popular subjects of agitation of the day'. Mary Carpenter, the British temperance reformer, stated that intemperance, like slavery, 'enslaved [the soul] as well as the body'.[31]

Eliza herself signed the total abstinence pledge and was the first vice-president of the Scottish Women's Christian Temperance Union and considered one 'of their foremost workers'.[32] She also campaigned in the Edinburgh municipal elections in the 1860s for councillors who 'advocated the temperance movement'.[33] On every occasion this linkage between slavery and temperance was pushed and stressed. For example, at a meeting held in the autumn of 1840 by the Paisley Temperance Society in honour of the abolitionists Charles Redmond and George Thompson, the former stated that while all anti-slavery groups supported the cause of temperance, the same could not be said for temperance societies. Abolitionists in the United States considered the causes to be 'almost synonymous', he declared.

However, while the concerns were analogous, Chartists and anti-slavery campaigners could only go so far in building alliances as differences quickly emerged on a series of issues. Firstly, and perhaps the most important obstacle in the way of unity, was the question of priority. The Garrisonians believed that the abolition of slavery in America should be prioritised over winning the franchise in Britain, while the Chartists held that the slavery question was a diversion from the real political struggle for the vote. Moreover, the refusal of the Garrisonians in America to take part in formal political life meant for many Chartists disparaging democracy itself, the very thing they were struggling for. This, of course, was not the only area of conflict. The issue of women's rights was not high on the Chartist agenda. Chartism was a campaign for male universal suffrage, and while women were a welcome part of the agitation, Chartists championed the ideal of domesticity for their wives in return for the badge of citizenship.[34] There was also a limit to how much the abolitionists could benefit from being identified with a movement that, under the leadership of Fergus O'Connor, was becoming increasingly aggressive and confrontational after 1840. Elizabeth Pease, echoing the sentiments of other sympathetic Garrisonians, warned against sacrificing their independence in return for Chartist support, and condemned the physical force elements within the movement.[35] The daughter of Elizabeth Fry wrote of her horror when Chartists, calling for the rights of English white slaves, broke up an anti-slavery meeting in Norwich.[36] Support for Chartism thus threatened to lose the abolitionists what backing they had among the enfranchised middle classes, particularly when Chartists began attacking the middle-class Anti-Corn Law League.

Secondly, there were class differences which provoked antagonisms between the largely working-class Chartists and the abolitionists. As we have seen the anti-slavery movement was largely the preserve of the middle classes, but it also had the backing and support of some highly influential aristocratic ladies, such as Harriet, Duchess of Sutherland, and her daughter, Elizabeth, Duchess of Argyll, the former of whom went on to issue a petition against slavery in 1853 that was signed by over 570,000 British women. Harriet's family had of course entered the pantheon of infamy in Scotland, as her family was directly associated with the Highland Clearances, in which families were evicted from the land to make way for sheep. Chartists in Scotland had spoken out against hereditary privilege and their opposition was endorsed by Karl Marx, when he angrily stated in an article in the *People's Paper*, that 'the enemy of British Wage Slavery has the right to condemn Negro-Slavery; a Duchess of Sutherland, a Duke of Athol [sic], a Manchester Cotton-lord – never!'[37]

The calculated appeal to the temperance movement also backfired over the same issue that had complicated relations with the Chartist movement: in a word, prioritisation. Richard Webb and others in the anti-slavery movement in Ireland had practically made slavery and temperance one and the same issue. But the 'Apostle of Temperance', Father Theobald Mathew, sidelined the Irish abolitionists by proclaiming that under no circumstances would he allow temperance to be part of any other reform movement.[38] When the movement spread to mainland Britain the same insistence on single issue reform was maintained. In Scotland, the Disruption of 1843 in the Church of Scotland had also siphoned off activists into the theological debates over the question of patronage and church and state relations. As Garrison and George Thompson attempted to awaken interest in Scotland in the anti-slavery cause, Elizabeth Pease noted that 'there the wave of religious feeling, which brought about the Disruption in 1843, was quickening the national conscience and predisposing the better part of the national conscience of such towns as Glasgow, Greenock, and Edinburgh, to a less lukewarm interest in matters affecting the larger community outside of Great Britain'.[39] Thus, all attempts to build alliances with movements of political and social reform had failed and by the end of the 1840s the anti-slavery cause and issue of women's rights, which was part of the radical Garrisonian platform, was almost moribund. As Richard Webb in Dublin gloomily noted in 1847: 'I am often really ashamed of the little we can do – Our influence contracts from year to year.'[40]

Religion also was a divisive factor within the anti-slavery societies in Scotland and elsewhere. Garrisonians, in questioning the concept of eternal damnation and the 'special inspiration of the Bible',[41] were becoming increasingly isolated from the mainstream Evangelicals in the United Presbyterian and Free Church in Scotland. Eliza conveyed to the

Boston Society the decision of the ELES to 'withdraw from connection' because 'leaders of that society (AASS) have given utterances to sentiments which . . . are infidel in their nature & blasphemous against the Most High God'. And while 'ardent tho' our love to the slave must ever be, there is still a higher principle than that of anti-slavery, viz. the honour of our God which we dare not compromise'.[42] The support Eliza and Jane gave to the ELES's opposition to the more radical strands of Garrisonianism, drew criticism from other supporters of Garrison in Scotland. Andrew Paton, of the GES, accused them of both compromise and cowardice, and sent a copy of the ELES report to Garrison, remarking that the 'Quakers are . . . a strange set, & beyond being fathomed in their motives and conduct'.[43] Paton's criticisms were a little unfair as privately Eliza had made clear that while she and her mother-in-law were 'united in their [ELES] feelings of uneasiness respecting the mode of argument in question', they did not think 'it right to withhold the little help we have been able to render to the slave through you'.[44] It was their pragmatism combined with an ability to compromise that held the ELES together. Despite all the pressures placed on it and against all the odds, the Society founded in 1833, did not disband until 1870, 'a record unmatched by any other anti-slavery society in Britain'.[45] Even at the lowest point of anti-slavery activity in Britain and Ireland in 1847 three Scottish women's societies were able to collect over 45,000 signatures in Glasgow and over 10,000 in Edinburgh for an address calling on American women to oppose slavery.[46]

The ebb and flow of support for the anti-slavery position was much conditioned by events in America itself and by the novelty value of visiting personalities, such as Harriet Beecher Stowe, the author of *Uncle Tom's Cabin*, who toured Britain in the early 1850s to much acclaim and interest. Flashpoints of tension in America, such as the Dred Scott case of 1857, which confirmed the legal status of slavery in the American South, or the doomed raid of the extremist abolitionist John Brown on Harper's Ferry, Virginia, in 1860 with the intention of starting a slave rebellion, also whipped up interest in Britain and stimulated anti-slavery societies. However, for much of the 1850s philanthropy dominated the activities of Eliza and other Quaker women. Eliza was active in the promotion of self-help schemes for the working class. She helped found the Penny Savings Bank for the poor of Causeway Side, Edinburgh, and managed it for over forty years. She offered advice to the savers on the benefits of using money wisely, counselling thrift rather than spending it 'for trifling purposes'.[47] Another initiative was the Women's Working Society (WWS), or Mothers' Meetings as they were also known, begun in the south side of the city in 1860 which lasted until 1897. It comprised mainly working-class women who would make items of clothing during the meetings of the Society from material supplied to them at a reduced price. Yet another institution that had a claim on her time was the Dean Bank Home for preventing neglected and destitute young girls from falling into crime. Eliza frequently visited the home and, in the summer, parties of the girls were invited to share tea with her in her garden. Of course, in all this there was an element of social engineering involved. The social contact between working- and middle-class mothers was seen to be beneficial in raising the level of domestic awareness in the former. As the annual report of the WWS remarked, 'The influence of this inter-course and exchange of feeling was seen in the increasing refinement and comfort of many homes.'[48] Religion, however, was never very far away. The penny banks had 'spiritual links' with the WSS and the Sabbath schools, which received 'recruits from the young depositors', and the WSS itself began and ended its meetings with a prayer.[49]

The outbreak of the American Civil War in 1861 saw interest shift towards events across the Atlantic. George Thompson was able to report to Garrison in 1863 that 'my meetings have all been on the American question – and such meetings! They have reminded me of those I was wont to hold in 1831, 1832 and '33 – densely crowded, sublimely enthu-siastic, and all but unanimous.'[50] In spite of the renewed fervour for abo-lition, the war in America was deeply troubling to members of a sect that felt warfare was 'incompatible' with the 'peaceable character of the Kingdom of Christ'.[51] Eliza wrote to Samuel May to express her pro-found abhorrence of the war and her continued support for the anti-slavery cause, saying:

> The matters in your country are of such intense interest that we are kept very close to you in sympathy & anxious watching & we eagerly read the news-papers from week to week – & grieve over the terrible losses in battle – the young hope & promise & all the broken hearts & desolated homes that these losses involve. It is dreadful to contemplate even from afar & what must it be to you! We sympathize with you very affectionately – & when there is cause for rejoicing we rejoice with you . . . we are very thankful that the slave is now recognised throughout the Republic as having certain rights, the withholding of which has brought down the vengeance of the Almighty in such calamities as have prevailed. I hope before long the nation will see a little further, & liberty to the slaves will be granted, not as a measure of self-preservation, but as a measure of justice & righteousness.[52]

Expressions of sympathy were bolstered by propaganda work, but Eliza's main political intervention was to publish an analysis of the events leading up to the civil war – *The Anti Slavery Cause in America and its Martyrs* – in the middle of 1863, which was widely circulated by both the Edinburgh and London ladies societies. Her book emphasised the contribution of the Garrisonians to the anti-slavery cause and in particular the service given by women. It also called on the British people:

> to guard our beloved country from any action, social or political, which may tend to ally her with a Confederacy having for its cornerstone American Slavery, the deadly enemy of the poor slave, and of Righteousness and Freedom throughout the world, and the impious rejecter and opposer of every law and attribute of Almighty God.[53]

She appealed to the British government to adopt a position of strict neutrality between North and South in the conflict and to proclaim itself on the side of the slave, arguing:

> Surely, it is the duty of Britain to refuse the right hand of political recognition and national friendship to a Confederacy avowedly, unblushingly, adopting for its corner-stone a system which degrades man to the level of merchandise, which has no respect for the virtues of woman, which robs the cradle, and denies the light of the Gospel to millions of immortal beings. The powers of darkness may be permitted to prevail for a season; but never let Britain be found arraying herself on their side, to her own degradation and to the injury of freedom throughout the world.[54]

However, her support for the North in the conflict posed a profound challenge to her pacifist beliefs. Eliza criticised Lord Brougham, in a letter to *The Scotsman*, for arguing that the slavery question must be resolved peacefully as was the case of British slavery in the West Indies, saying: 'The peaceful method of abolishing slavery was . . . wished for . . . by the Abolitionists, but . . . America would not listen to any overtures for emancipation while yet there was time to adopt them without bloodshed, they hardened their hearts.'[55] Thus, in the face of 'sin', force was an unwelcome but necessary part of the solution.

Lincoln's Emancipation Proclamation of 1863 assured the slaves of their freedom if the North prevailed in the civil war and this triggered the formation of Freedmen Aid Societies. This carried on the work of the Fugitive Slave programme, which had been supported by the ladies societies in Birmingham and Edinburgh in the 1850s. Eliza, as secretary of the ELES, wrote to the editor of the *British Friend* urging Quakers in Britain to emulate her society and send donations to assist in the process of educating the freed slaves in America.[56]

However, as Midgley points out, by the late 1860s feminists had moved away from the abolitionist issue to other questions; indeed,

for many leading British women abolitionists, feminism became the new focus
of their political energies, and concern for the suffering of enslaved and freed
black women abroad was displaced by growing awareness of the subordinate
position of women in British society.[57]

Her research shows that Quakers like Eliza grew increasingly concerned
with women's rights, particularly the issue of 'social purity'. This was a
coded term for the Contagious Diseases Acts of 1864 and 1867, which
were allegedly introduced in the interests of public health and were
enforced in military districts. The Acts allowed for the establishment of
a special corps of non-uniformed police who had the task of registering
women suspected of being prostitutes and subjecting them to periodic
medical examination. The leader of the campaign was Josephine Butler
who was appalled at the sexual bias of the legislation. As Elizabeth
Isichei points out, 'The Acts dealt with an evil in which both men and
women were by definition equally involved, but only women suffered the
penalties . . . they safeguarded the vices of men through the humiliation
of women.'[58] Eliza, it was claimed, 'laboured long and strenuously in the
cause of social purity, and, in conjunction with others, she waged a resolute war against the iniquitous laws for legalising vice'.[59] These 'iniquitous' laws were eventually repealed in the 1880s, but the importance of
the campaigns against them was the way in which they galvanised the
disparate range of women's groups and personalities into collective
action. Ten of the thirty-three leaders, including Eliza, of the Ladies
National Association against the legislation had been involved in anti-
slavery agitation. Seven of these ten were also involved in the women's
suffrage movement, four in promoting women's education, and two in
the campaign for a married woman's property act.[60] Eliza's house,
5 South Gray Street in Edinburgh, which she shared with her mother-in-
law until Jane's death in 1888, acted as one of the nerve centres of these
campaigns. She became secretary of the women's suffrage society in
Edinburgh and was found 'frequently pleading the justice of the claims
of women for Parliamentary franchise in public and private'.[61] Elizabeth
Pease was its treasurer and Priscilla Bright McLaren became its president.[62]

However, while Midgley argues that there was a decisive shift away
from anti-slavery activity to the question of women's right in the late
1860s, international affairs were never completely abandoned. As a
staunch pacifist Eliza opposed war and did her best to help the suffering
on both sides of the conflict. After the Franco-Prussian War of 1870 she
organised the sending of clothing to the poor in the most war-ravaged
districts. Again in the Bosnia troubles in 1876 aid was dispatched and an

orphanage established. The Turkish massacre of the Armenians in the late 1870s saw Eliza with others establish a relief committee, something which was personalised when she, in spite of her increasing infirmity due to rheumatic gout, received into her home a little Armenian girl whose mother had been a victim of the atrocities.[63] There was also an ongoing interest in the position of the emancipated slaves and the subordinate peoples of the Empire. Eliza and Elizabeth Pease established the Society for the Furtherance of Human Brotherhood in the mid-1880s to complete the work of the anti-slavery movement 'by securing, not mere declarations of emancipation, but the enjoyment of FREEDOM, EQUAL OPPORTUNITY, and BROTHERHOOD within the pale of the great human family'.[64] Although quite ineffectual, the Society not only attacked the US authorities for their failure to demolish racial barriers, but also called for justice for the peoples of the British Empire.[65]

With the death of Jane Smeal in 1888, Eliza lived alone, but gradually age and infirmity caused her to think of leaving Edinburgh to be with her family in Dublin. The death of her brother Henry in the autumn of 1897 made her mind up. Her house in South Gray Street was sold and, in May 1898, Eliza went to live with her widowed sister-in-law in the suburbs of Dublin. At a farewell meeting in her honour held at 5 St Andrew Square she spoke of the reasons behind her decision to sever ties with Edinburgh, saying:

> there are other ties which seem to call more insistently – the dear ties of affection and love, and I feel it best to go . . . sometimes when we look at the map we think the Irish Channel is but a narrow strip, and that we are very close to Ireland; but sometimes the Angel of Death comes and makes us feel what a very wide channel that . . . is. Then we feel we fain would bridge it when the Angel of Death comes in between and prevents the clasping of hands and the saying good-bye. That is the feeling . . . which induced me to decide to live among my precious kindred in Ireland, while there is still time, that when the hour comes for me to say good-bye I shall be among them. Love is a great thing.[66]

Unfortunately, for Eliza there was little time left. During the summer of 1899, her health began to deteriorate badly and in late October she was moved to her sister's home, where she died on 3 November of that year. In an obituary written in some obscure Edinburgh Christian paper, it was said of her that 'in all the moral and social movements Eliza Wigham took a large share in Modern Athens, and her influence was more potent in securing their advancement than any other in the city'.[67] However, although her importance was recognised by her contemporaries we know nothing of the woman herself. The lack of any personal papers, with the exception of a few literary fragments, has meant that others, who share her values and to an extent her faith, have constructed our perception of her. Thus, we know nothing of her doubts or fears, nothing of her anger or frustrations, nothing of her emotional attachments, outside of her love for her family and her devotion to her faith. What emerges from these constructed accounts of her life is an image of a kindly and saintly person, devoted to her fellow humans, especially those in pain or suffering, and to God. As her cousin put it, 'All who knew her will agree that a more beautiful character could be scarcely found on earth.' A young admirer went even further, claiming that her 'whole life was Christ-like and saintly'.[68]

There is no doubting Eliza's sincerity and her desire to improve the lot of suffering humanity, but like all those involved in philanthropic endeavour in the nineteenth century, there was an unquestioning acceptance of the economic and social basis of inequality. Socio-economic problems were individualised rather than treated as societal concerns. The initiatives such as the Penny Savings Banks, the homes for destitute girls, and so on, all had attached to them social values that were middle class in origin and designed to promote thrift, independence and self-help in the less fortunate. It was only later in the nineteenth century with the emergence of socialist parties that the 'social question', as it was known, came to dominate political discourse. In regard to the anti-slavery movement, as Midgley points out, initially, the 'majority of women represented their . . . activities . . . not as their *right* but rather as their *duty* to other women'. They saw themselves as extending the 'privileges' of British women to their enslaved sisters in the Empire and the USA, something that 'inhibit[ed] the development from anti-slavery to women's rights'.[69] There was little attempt to recruit working-class women into membership of the ladies anti-slavery societies in Britain; rather the strategy was to use them as campaigners in the 'great cause'. Eliza ministered to her social inferiors, but there is little evidence that she saw them as her equal.

However, notwithstanding these criticisms of Victorian philanthropy, Eliza remains a pivotal, but neglected, figure in the development of the women's movement. A movement that gradually, through the struggles over slavery, perceived the limitations imposed on women by the dominant ideology concerning gender relations and encouraged them to move from the private to the public sphere of activism. After Emancipation, challenges were made by women regarding their designated roles in society on a set of different, but connected, levels, from education to the franchise. This would not have been possible but for the pioneering activity of Eliza and other women who were not afraid to face hostility and ridicule. As Edinburgh anti-slavery activist Harriet Gardiner put it in a letter to the Garrisonian fund raiser, John Collins, in 1840:

> In this country a woman who holds really Liberal opinion is even more out of place than a man . . . the former had . . . to encounter the obloquy of being supposed to have both heart and head depraved, she is shunned as unfeminine and . . . obliged to constantly converse on only the most indifferent topics or hold one's peace.[70]

By 1912 these women, far from holding their peace, were battling the authorities and the police for their right to vote and already had achieved notable victories in the field of higher education and medicine. The public sphere of protest that Eliza and other radical women had occupied as a minority became in time the natural arena for women's political movements. And in spite of the unpopularity of the causes she was involved in she was able to rejoice and share in some of these outstanding successes for women at home, and also abroad in America and the West Indies in the abolition of slavery, although the ultimate goal of establishing the political equality of women with men was to elude her.

NOTES

1. Society of Friends, *Annual Monitor* (1901), p. 172.
2. C. Midgley, *Women Against Slavery: the British campaigns, 1780–1870* (London, 1992), p. 132. The other five were Harriet Martineau, Elizabeth Pease, Anne Knight, Mary Estlin and Anna Richardson.
3. Friends, *Annual Monitor*, p. 166.
4. Friends, *Annual Monitor*, p. 167.
5. Letter to Maria Weston Chapman, 1 April 1847, quoted in C. Taylor, *British and American Abolitionists. An Episode in Transatlantic Understanding* (Edinburgh, 1974), p. 313.
6. J. S. Rowntree, *The Society of Friends: its Faith and Practice* (London, 1901), pp. 50–7.
7. L. and R. Billington, 'A burning zeal for righteousness: women in the anti-slavery movement, 1820–1860', in J. Rendall (ed.), *Equal or Different: Women's Politics, 1800–1914* (Oxford, 1987), p. 85.
8. Billington, 'Burning zeal', p. 90.
9. E. Isichei, *Victorian Quakers* (London, 1970), pp. 108–9.
10. Billington, 'Burning zeal', p. 93.
11. K. K. Sklar, 'Women who speak for an entire nation: American and British women compared at the World Anti-Slavery Convention, London, 1840', *Pacific Historical Review*, (1990), p. 464.
12. Sklar, 'Anti-Slavery Convention', p. 490.
13. Billington, 'Burning zeal', p. 94.

14. Quoted in C. Midgley, *Women*, p. 158.
15. P. Rinker, 'Women and Garrisonian abolition, 1833–1860: with special emphasis on Scottish women', (unpublished Ph.D., University of St Andrews, 2001), p. 189; C. Duncan Rice, *The Scots Abolitionists, 1833–1861* (Louisiana, 1981), p. 54.
16. Sklar, Anti-Slavery Convention', p. 459.
17. Sklar, 'Anti-Slavery Convention', pp. 462–3.
18. Sklar, 'Anti-Slavery Convention', p. 470.
19. E. C. Stanton, *Eighty Years or More* (1898), pp. 82, 344.
20. Billington, 'Burning zeal', p. 97.
21. Rinker, 'Garrisonian abolition', p. 130.
22. Rinker, 'Garrisonian abolition', p. 116.
23. Billington, 'Burning zeal', p. 99.
24. Rinker, 'Garrisonian abolition', p. 60.
25. Rinker, 'Garrisonian abolition', p. 118.
26. Rev. P. Brewster, *Chartist and Socialist Sermons* (Glasgow, 1910), p. 4, quoted in Rinker, 'Garrisonian abolition', p. 155.
27. Letter to Anne Phillips, 29 September 1842, quoted in Taylor, *Abolitionists*, pp. 182–4.
28. Rinker, 'Garrisonian abolition', p. 184.
29. Friends, *Annual Monitor*, p. 175.
30. W. W. Knox, *Industrial Nation: Work, Culture and Society in Scotland, 1800–Present* (Edinburgh, 1999), p. 43.
31. Rinker, 'Garrisonian abolition', p. 177.
32. Friends, *Annual Monitor*, pp. 174–5.
33. *The Scotsman*, 11 November 1863.
34. Knox, *Industrial Nation*, p. 56.
35. Rinker, 'Garrisonian abolition', p. 173.
36. Midgley, *Women*, p. 150.
37. Quoted in K. D. Reynolds, *Aristocratic Women and Political Society in Victorian Britain* (Oxford, 1998), p. 127.
38. Rinker, 'Garrisonian abolition', p. 161.
39. A. M. Stoddart, *Elizabeth Pease Nichol* (London, 1899), p. 115.
40. Taylor, *Abolitionists*, p. 338.
41. Taylor, *Abolitionists*, p. 338.
42. Minutes of the ELES, 1 August 1850, in Taylor, *Abolitionists*, p. 346.
43. Letter to William Lloyd Garrison, 7 February 1851, quote in Taylor, *Abolitionists*, p. 362.
44. Letter to an unnamed person, 30 August 1850, in Taylor, *Abolitionists*, p. 348.
45. Rinker, 'Garrisonian abolition', p. 227.
46. Midgley, *Women*, p. 132.
47. J. Goodfellow, *The Print of his Shoe* (Edinburgh and London, 1906), p. 72.
48. Goodfellow, *Print*, p. 75.

49. Goodfellow, *Print*, pp. 73, 75.
50. Letter to William Lloyd Garrison, 5 February 1863, in Taylor, *Abolitionists*, p. 498.
51. Rowntree, *Society of Friends*, p. 52.
52. Letter to Samuel May, 16 January 1863, in Taylor, *Abolitionists*, p. 497.
53. E. Wigham, *The Anti Slavery Cause in America and its Martyrs* (Westport, CT, 1970 edn), p. iv.
54. Wigham, *Anti Slavery*, pp. 160–1.
55. *The Scotsman*, 11 November 1863.
56. Midgley, *Women*, p. 188.
57. Midgley, *Women*, p. 197.
58. Isichei, *Victorian Quakers*, p. 253.
59. *Annual Monitor*, p. 175.
60. Midgley, *Women*, pp. 172–3.
61. *Annual Monitor*, p. 175.
62. Midgley, *Women*, p. 175.
63. *Annual Monitor*, p. 177.
64. C. Midgley, 'Anti-slavery and feminism in nineteenth century Britain', *Gender and History*, 5 (1993), p. 358.
65. Midgley, *Women*, p. 196.
66. *Annual Monitor*, p. 186.
67. *Annual Monitor*, p. 179.
68. *Annual Monitor*, p. 183.
69. Midgley, *Women*, p. 203.
70. Quoted in Midgley, *Women*, p. 152.

3

Madeleine Smith: Sex and the Single Girl in Victorian Scotland

ℭ

Madeleine Hamilton Smith was twenty-one years of age, five feet two inches tall, of medium build, with deep-set large black eyes and long black hair, pretty but not striking, fashionably elegant in dress, and every inch the epitome of the daughter of a prosperous and successful Glasgow businessman. It would have been hard to imagine a less likely candidate for the title of the most notorious woman in Scotland in the second half of the nineteenth century. But Madeleine was just that. She was arrested and tried in 1857 for the murder of her lover, Pierre Emile L'Angelier, in a case that as one contemporary said 'deeply absorbed the interest and attention of a whole empire . . . [and] formed the central if not the exclusive topic of current popular speculation' during the nine days of its duration.[1] The jury's verdict of 'Not Proven' and the sensationalism surrounding the trial, with the revelations of pre-marital sex across the class divide, made the case a compelling one for contemporary essayists and subsequent biographers, all of whom have clearly been divided on the point of Madeleine's innocence or guilt. However, the search for truth in this case is one that is a fruitless exercise, since conclusive proof is not available to answer the charges one way or the other. What is of more importance is to consider what the case reveals in terms of contemporary attitudes in Scotland to class, gender and sex. Indeed, it could be argued that the case represented a crisis for Scotland's bourgeoisie since it threatened not only existing stereotypes of women as 'angels in the home' – here the angel is a potential murderer – but also assaulted in the most brutal way traditional mores and sexual codes of behaviour. As one commentator of the time put it, the trial

> has given to the world the rehearsal of a tragedy enacted in private life, where all was seemingly serene . . . It has tracked the footprints of vice and the dark shadow of a fearful crime among the sacred retreats of religion. The world has been awestruck by the discovery, and men reflect with trembling on the ominous and fierce volcano which suddenly sprung up at their feet.[2]

That 'volcano' was Madeleine's sexuality and the fear that other women may discover its meaning was what created the crisis for bourgeois society, and is the main subject of this chapter.

Magdalene, after her grandmother (later Madeleine), was born on 29 March 1835 in West Regent Street, Glasgow, the first child of five of James Smith and Janet Hamilton. The Smiths were extremely well connected in Glasgow society. James could number among his close friends and acquaintances the likes of John Houldsworth, cotton master and iron manufacturer, bailie and commodore of the Northern Yacht Club, and Andrew Orr, wholesale stationer and Lord Provost of Glasgow. In marrying Janet in 1833 – the daughter of David Hamilton, the most famous and respected architect in the west of Scotland and known for the 'Scottish baronial style' and landmark buildings such as the Royal Exchange, in Glasgow – Smith, son of a master builder from Alloa, was thought to have married above himself. James was a partner in his father's firm, but he also had interests in timber and was himself an aspiring architect. He was forced to declare himself bankrupt in 1843 when his father's insurance business failed, but with the assistance of friends and fellow freemasons, James had recovered and was clearly part of the Glasgow business elite in the early 1850s. He designed the McLellan Gallery in Sauchiehall Street and the city's Victorian Baths, and a number of other landmark buildings. The trappings of success included a town house in fashionable Blythswood Square, Glasgow, and a country retreat, Rowaleyn, overlooking the Clyde, near Helensburgh.

Wealth also bought privilege and Madeleine was sent to boarding school in London at the age of fourteen to 'finish' her off. As a pupil in Mrs Alice Gorton's Academy for Young Ladies in Clapham, Madeleine was taught 'godliness and good manners'.[3] The curriculum consisted of daily prayers, piano lessons, walking, discussions of current affairs, needlework, deportment, and elocution designed to rid her of her Glasgow accent: in short, everything consistent with making Madeleine enviable marriage fodder for a suitable member of her class. Mrs Gorton considered Madeleine to be 'diligent, attentive, and exceedingly bright', but also 'given to stubborn sulks which most alarm us'.[4] There was little in terms of intellectual stimulation included in the curriculum and the school's strict moral code meant that there was little relief from the tedium of the daily routine. The company of young men was forbidden with the exception of the clergy attached to the local St James Chapel, although the occasional closely supervised outing was permitted. As Mary S. Hartman suggests, the girls resorted to smuggling in to the Academy various proscribed romantic texts, which provided the basis for

amorous daydreaming, although it seems only Madeleine was destined
to 'act out her daydreams'.[5]

She returned to Glasgow at the age of seventeen to a life of idleness
and a constant round of social engagements to fill the void. Madeleine
was simply marking time until a husband could be found and she could
assume her 'natural' role as a wife and a mother. However, these ortho-
dox expectations failed to take account of her genuine sense of discontent with Glasgow and family life. After three years in London, the city
seemed highly provincial. She often wrote to Emile of her dislike of
Glasgow, the rain and the cold,[6] and the boredom of family occasions.
She never 'felt so tired as I am of Christmas Day. We have a large dinner
party, all old people';[7] and New Year's Day was 'a great bore' and 'a
horrid day'.[8] The only social occasions she seemed to enjoy were balls,
where she could be as flirtatious as her nature would allow; something
that was to be a constant source of irritation to Emile after they had
become lovers, and something that she constantly had to reassure him
over.[9] Her disenchantment with family life was also compounded by the
alienation Madeleine felt towards her parents. James Smith was the
undoubted stern, strict patriarchal head of household, whose word was
law, and who, as someone who had married above himself, was determined that his 'daughters would not marry below themselves'.[10] Like
most successful businessmen he was absent from home more often than
not, leaving for work at eight in the morning, while Madeleine rose at
nine, and not returning until the evening. He played little role in bringing up his children, save on Sundays when 'he presided over family
prayer sessions'. Madeleine remarked that he seemed estranged from her
and her siblings, and when on occasion she, 'appearing in low spirits',
looked to him for comfort, he 'never notices'.[11] While James seemed
strong, almost terrifyingly so, according to G. L. Butler,[12] Madeleine's
mother was the very opposite. From the sparse evidence we have, Janet
Smith was passive, submissive and frequently ill. She relied on her eldest
daughter to run the family home when she was at a low point; something
which Madeleine claimed in a letter to Emile in June 1856 that she had
done 'for the last two years'.[13] The mother's illnesses and the perception
of her as weak made her an unlikely confidante for Madeleine, and
although her sister, Bessie, was a possible substitute, it would appear that
they were, perhaps as a result of the age gap, never very close and she
was only mentioned in passing in letters to Emile.

Thus, by the time Madeleine met with Pierre Emile L'Angelier she was
bored, frustrated and looking for some adventure and/or diversion.
Emile was different. Born in Jersey on 30 April 1823, the son of an ambi-

tious French seed merchant, he was fluent in English and French. At the invitation of a Scottish landowner, Sir Francis Mackenzie, he came to Scotland at the age of eighteen to train as an estate manager. The death of his patron a year later saw Emile apprenticed to Dickson & Co., seed merchants, of Waterloo Place, Edinburgh until 1847 when he moved to Paris, where he claimed he served with the National Guard during the 1848 Revolution. On a promise of marriage he returned once again to Edinburgh in 1851, but his fiancée broke it off and he was left almost penniless. Emile was forced to live on the charity of the owner of the Rainbow Tavern, George Baker, for six to nine months, sharing a bed with his nephew, Robert, who was also coincidentally from Jersey. Towards the end of the year he found a new position in Dundee, but this proved only temporary. At the end of 1852 he again was on the move, this time to Glasgow where he found a work as a packing clerk with wholesale merchants, Messrs Huggins & Co. – a job he was to hold until his death in 1857.

Emile was small in stature, with a round face and a very large moustache. Henry Blyth, in his biography of Madeleine, described him as 'rather effeminate', and claimed he was immensely 'proud of his pretty little feet' and his 'small and dainty hands'.[14] In spite of this and his humble position and limited means, L'Angelier, because of his undoubted charm, was popular with the opposite sex and was considered to be something of a ladies' man by those who knew him. Giving evidence at the trial in 1857, William Ogilvie, bank clerk and secretary of the Dundee Floral and Horticultural Society, claimed that Emile's 'general subject of conversation was ladies . . . [and that] he had considerable success in getting acquainted with them'.[15] He was also dazzled by wealth and position and ingratiated himself through church connections with those on a higher social plane. Although baptised a Catholic, and then at the age of seven as an Anglican, Emile attended St Jude's Episcopal Church, Glasgow, and through the Reverend Charles Miles he was introduced to Peter Clark, curator of the Royal Botanic Garden, who found him a room in his house, where he lived for two years, and whose wife found him to be 'steady and temperate'. One might have expected that his boastfulness and his affectations might have exasperated and annoyed his colleagues, but the opposite seems to have been the case. L'Angelier was held in high regard by those he worked with, for example William Laird, who employed him in Dundee, said he was 'a very sober young man, and very kind and obliging'; and Thomas Kennedy, cashier in Huggins & Co., underlined the favourable image claiming that Emile was 'a well-behaved, well-principled, religious young man'.[16]

The outward show of charm and bravado, however, masked deep-seated feelings of insecurity and vulnerability that were manifested in his hypochondria and melancholia. Emile it seems was subject to extreme mood swings. Those he worked with commented on his 'variable spirits', of someone easily excited and just as easily depressed, almost suicidal at times. The cause of this was his failed marriage proposal. Robert Baker in his testimony spoke of his 'low spirits' and how he had 'often seen him crying at night'. Apparently just before he left for Dundee, Emile had said to him that 'he was tired of his existence and wished himself out of the world'. He went on to say:

> I rose out of my bed and went to him, and he said that if I had not disturbed him he would thrown himself out. The windows of the Rainbow are almost six stories from the ground . . . he had met with disappointment in a love matter . . . It was about a young lady in Fife.[17]

His friends and colleagues in Dundee also mentioned these feelings of melancholia and of general weariness in their statements to the court. When not obsessed with the idea of ending it all by throwing himself out of windows or over bridges, Emile was also consuming quantities of all sorts of medicines in order to deal with the variety of aches and pains, real or imagined, that he suffered from. Hunt says that in Glasgow he turned his stomach into a ' druggist's waste-pipe, and almost every quack remedy he could find was consumed', including arsenic.[18]

Thus, there were two Emiles, the self-confident public one, and the more melancholy private one. It was the former side of his character that Madeleine was drawn to. And yet if Emile had not moved his lodgings from the Clarks to his friend, the middle-aged spinster Mary Perry, of Renfrew Street, he may never have encountered her. As it turned out he lived only sixty yards from her home and it was in the street that he first spotted her and was immediately attracted to her. The problem lay in gaining an introduction. The middle classes had constructed an elaborate system of regulating private life to prevent undesirable social contact, particularly when it came to their daughters. A bad marriage could spell ruin for a family, and was a recurring fear, if not a nightmare, with parents. Therefore, calling cards, surveillance of the young and other methods of regulation were used by the propertied to limit connection to a known and safe world. To prise an opening into this closed society, Emile used the nephew of a colleague at Huggins' to procure an introduction to Madeleine while she was out with Bessie on an unchaperoned walk. As her defence council, John Inglis, disparagingly pointed out in his closing speech to the jury, the public nature of the meeting showed that Emile 'could not procure an introduction otherwise or elsewhere . . . [as] He was an unknown adventurer; utterly unknown'.[19]

The meeting proved to be electric for both parties and very soon after the initial encounter Madeleine wrote flatteringly to Emile, saying: 'I do not feel as if I am writing to you for the first time. Though our intercourse has been very short, yet we have become as familiar friends . . . One enjoys walking with a pleasant companion, and where could we find one equal to yourself?'[20] With that letter a clandestine relationship was begun that as it developed in intensity grew more fantastical by the month, eventually turning into a series of elaborate mind games played out by two increasingly desperate people – with only one winner. Emile had much to gain from the relationship if he could secure the right outcome – marriage and a certain passport into the elite section of Glasgow society. Madeleine for her part was carried away with naive ideas of love that no doubt were much influenced by the romantic novels she read in which love triumphs in the end no matter the barriers or difficulties. When a family friend informed her father that Emile was 'in the habit of walking with us', 'Papa', she said, 'was very angry with me for walking with a Gentleman unknown to him'. She naively declared: 'I don't care for the world's remarks so long as my own heart tells me I am doing nothing wrong.'[21] But within two weeks of this and considerable parental pressure she wrote to Emile saying that for the 'present the correspondence had better stop . . . By continuing to correspond harm may arise.'[22]

In spite of her early starry-eyed attitude to the relationship, Madeleine deep down realised that her father would not approve of her relationship with a lowly clerk, with a salary of only fifty pounds a year and little prospect of betterment. If it was to continue she had to display cunning and guile to engineer meetings and to ensure they were not found out: something that added an extra spice and element of danger to the affair and only furthered her passionate feelings for Emile. The solution was to meet late in the evening when her youngest sister, Janet, with whom she shared a room, was asleep. An accomplice, Christina Haggart, among the domestic staff was recruited to act as a go-between, posting and receiving letters, under an assumed name – Miss Bruce – when at Helensburgh, and leaving the back gate open for Emile to come in or Madeleine to go out without the Smiths knowing. With the help of Christina the relationship blossomed and within a fairly short space of time they had promised themselves to each other, and Madeleine was signing her letters to him as 'Mimi'.

The problem for Emile was that the more private the relationship became, the less the prospect of it becoming public, thus Madeleine, clearly besotted with him, was relatively quickly manipulated by him into speaking to her father about the idea of marriage. Her father, of course, refused to entertain the idea, and in what seems to have been a curt and condescending note, Madeleine passed on his decision to Emile. He reacted furiously, saying:

> I did not deserve to be treated as you have done. How you astonish me by writing such a note without condescending to explain the reasons why your father refuses his consent. He must have reasons, am I not allowed to clare [sic] myself of accusations . . . I warned you repeatedly not to be rash in your engagement and vows to me, but you persisted in that false and deceitful flirtation, and knowing at the same time that at a word from your father you would break all your engagement . . . Think what your father would say if I sent him your letters for a perusal. Do you think he could sanction your breaking your promises. No, Madeleine, I leave your conscience to speak for itself.[23]

Whether Madeleine broached the subject of marriage to her father is open to doubt, but having failed to achieve much with his moralising, in August Emile threatened to leave Scotland for Peru, a prospect that Madeleine claimed would 'break my heart', and she pleaded with him 'for my sake do not go'.[24] By December Madeleine is referring to Emile as 'My own darling husband', signing her letters to him as 'Mimi L'Angelier', and still entertaining, regardless of the opposition of her family, the fantasy that they would be married in the near future.[25] The events in the woods at Rowaleyn some six months later made that fantasy more real.

It is clear that Madeleine had decided to give herself to Emile before his arrival on Tuesday evening 6 May 1856. She wrote to him on the previous Friday to come to 'the gate . . . and wait till I come. And then, oh happiness wont I kiss you, my love . . . I don't think there is any risk.'[26] What took place that evening was a shock to Emile as it would appear from the letter written to him by Madeleine that not only did she initiate the lovemaking she was the dominant partner. As Sacheverell Sitwell in his *Splendours and Miseries* (1943) put it: 'She is so strong in character. She has urged him to this . . . She has chosen him . . . He is at her mercy.'[27] Madeleine herself expressed it rather differently, saying:

> Beloved if we did wrong last night it was in the excitement of our love. Yes, beloved, I did truly love you with my soul. I was happy, it was a pleasure to be with you. Oh if we could have remained, never more to have parted . . . I must have been very stupid in your eyes . . . But everything goes out of my head when I see you, my love . . . And you may rest assured after what has passed I cannot be the wife of any other but dear, dear Emile. No, now that

would be a sin . . . I did not bleed in the least last night – but I had a good deal of pain during the night. Tell me, pet, were you angry at me for allowing you to do what you did – was it very bad of me. We should, have waited till we were married. I shall always remember last night.[28]

There is some doubt as to whether the reply that Emile penned was ever received by Madeleine as it was found among his papers after his death in an envelope simply marked 'Mimi'.[29] But he used the situation to extend his control over her by making her feel regretful, even sinful, over what had happened, and in referring to her lack of bleeding suggesting that perhaps this was not the first time she had made love to a man. Such was the enormity of the event, and such was the level that she had descended to, he argued only marriage could restore her/them in the sight of God to moral probity:

> Since I saw you last night I have been wretchedly sad. Would to God we had not met that night . . . I am sad at what we did, I regret it very much. Why, Mimi, did you give way after your promises? My pet, it is a pity. Think of the consequences if I were never to marry you. What reproaches I should have . . . I will never again repeat what I did until we are regularly married. Try your friends once more . . . say nothing will change you . . . Unless you do . . . I shall have to leave the country; truly . . . I am in such a state of mind I do not care if I were dead. We did wrong . . . we have loved blindly. It is your parents' fault if shame is the result; they are to blame for it all. Though we have sinned, ask earnestly God's forgiveness and blessings that all the obstacles in our way may be removed from us . . . Mimi, unless Huggins helps me I cannot see how I shall be able to marry you for years . . . Mimi . . . you must take a bold step to be my wife . . . do speak to your mother . . . be bold for once, do not fear them – tell them you are my wife before God . . . My conscience reproaches me of a sin that marriage can only efface . . . I do not understand . . . your not bleeding, for every woman having her virginity must bleed. You must have done it some other time . . . I was not angry at your allowing me . . . but I am sad it happened. You had no resolution. We should have indeed waited until we were married. It was very bad indeed . . . No, nothing except our marriage will efface it from my memory. Mimi, only fancy if it was known . . . you would be dishonoured and that by me! Oh! Why was I born, my pet . . . You are my wife, and I have the right to expect from you the behaviour of a married woman – or else you have no honour in you; and more you have no right to go any where but where a woman could go with her husband. Oh! Mimi, let your conduct make me happy. Remember, when you are good how truly happy this makes Emile – but remember this, and if you love me you will do nothing wrong.[30]

Emile's resolve that the events of Tuesday evening were not to be repeated did not take account of what he had unleashed in Madeleine. As

Sacheverell Sitwell puts it: 'When he rises he is dead tired, and she has awakened into life.'[31] Madeleine's awakening made her less chaste and more predatory in her pursuit of sexual fulfilment and another letter later that month suggests that they went back to Rowaleyn woods; however, this time the act was not completed, as although she 'did burn with love . . . we were good and withstood all temptations'.[32] After this Madeleine talked quite freely about her body, although as Hartman points out, she never 'described lovemaking in anything but the most general terms, never referred to the sexual organs', and used a coded language to refer to intercourse – 'love' underlined – 'fondeling' – to refer to heavy petting. The nearest she gets to speaking explicitly about sex is in a letter to Emile in which she says, 'It is a pleasure, no one can deny that. It is but human nature. Is not everyone that <u>loves</u> of the same mind? Yes, I did feel so ashamed of having allowed you to see my (?). . .'[33] On another occasion she alludes to her ability to arouse Emile sexually when she says he is 'a naughty boy to go and dream of me and get excited'.[34]

So scandalised was the court at the sexual content of the letters that the judge ruled out the reading of certain passages, one of which he declared was written 'in terms which I will not read for perhaps they were never previously committed to paper as having passed between a man and a woman'.[35] The prosecutor and the defence council, as well as middle-class opinion in general, shared the judge's condemnation of the 'licentious' nature of Madeleine's letters. This would seem to confirm a popular impression of Victorian society as prudish and repressed when it came to the question of sex, particularly out of wedlock. Michel Foucault's massive study of the history of sexuality over the last three centuries shows that sex during the course of the eighteenth and early nineteenth century became 'carefully confined: it moved into the home'. A clear line, using the monogamous, legally married couple as the paradigm, was drawn between 'normal' and 'abnormal' sexual behaviour. Outside the parent's bedroom, illicit sex was condemned and 'abnormal' sex criminalised.[36] Thus, Victorian society was not silent on the question of sex; rather than a 'massive censorship . . . a regulated and polymorphous incitement to discourse' occurred.[37] Indeed, Victorians found it difficult to escape from sexual discourse as the clergy, educators and the medical profession continually pontificated on the subject as they became concerned with the 'need to keep it under close watch and to devise a national technology of correction'.[38] It was women, children and adolescents, who were the focus of surveillance and their sexual physiology the subject of study by doctors.

From these discourses and studies a model of sexuality was established, although throughout the nineteenth century it was subject to a

constant process of adjustment and refinement that reflected the changing context of class and power relations.[39] Males were assumed to be
active, aggressive and spontaneous, while females were seen as weak,
passive and responsive.[40] William Acton, a prominent and influential
physician of the time, argued that women were 'unsexed', and those who
believed that 'they could take pleasure in sexual intercourse courted the
danger of cancer of the womb, or even insanity'.[41] Females were held
responsible for taming the beast in men, as given encouragement men
could not be held accountable for their behaviour. Thus, Victorian
society went to great lengths to discourage spontaneous copulation.
Women's clothing consisted of quite a number of layers and even while
swimming or bathing in public they were required to cover up parts of
their bodies that might excite the opposite sex. Thus, the maintenance of
sexual propriety lay with women and as such female chastity was 'most
rigorously applied within the middle classes' and was central to bourgeois ideas concerning home and marriage.[42]

However, respectability was not only the cement that bound together
a class that was quite diverse in terms of income and occupation, it
was also what divided the bourgeoisie from those below them in the
social scale. To fall, as Madeleine did, was to join the ranks of the non-
respectable women, which equated with the Magdalene or the prostitute.
As Barbara Littlewood and Linda Mahood explain, in defining 'prostitute' or 'Magdalene' a representation of an 'ideal' female sexuality 'was
constantly incited . . . Assumptions were made, and solutions proposed,
which were not about women's sexuality in general, but more specifically
about the sexual and vocational status of working-class women.'[43] Since
young females in middle-class households were given the proper moral
instruction and training, it was inconceivable to the middle-class mind
that one of their own young women could fall, thus it was the 'lives,
behaviour and pleasures' of young working-class girls that came under
scrutiny, in order 'to define and discipline wayward sexuality'.[44] From
the point of view of the middle class Madeleine's behaviour was inexplicable. As one commentator put it: 'Her position in society, her education,
her prerogatives as a lady, make her offences fearfully aggravated.'[45]
Therefore, her actions could only be made intelligible through the construction of a victim scenario. Young and naive as she was, Madeleine,
as the *Saturday Review* later stated, had been seduced by a 'meaner and
more contemptible scoundrel it would be difficult to conceive . . . A prof-
ligate vain adventurer . . . this is what L'Angelier was.'[46]

Madeleine had fallen someway short of the 'ideal', but as long as her
affair with Emile remained private no one would be in a position to judge

her, and since they both considered themselves to be married in the sight of God they considered themselves to be acting morally. Indeed, according to the law in Scotland couples over the age of sixteen could marry (without parental consent) simply by declaring themselves man and wife in front of witnesses, and it was only in 1940 that it became a legal requirement to be married by a minister of religion or an authorised registrar. Madeleine worked hard to convince herself that she was prepared to give up her life of privilege for a more modest set of circumstances with Emile. She wrote to him, saying:

> What I meant when [I] said about the £50. I did think it was much too little for you to receive for your services. You told me you had £100, and I was quite satisfied with the sum and I tell you again it is quite enough. Yes, it is enough. I am satisfied with the sum – it is enough for all our wants. Emile, I knew you were poor, you told me yourself you were not rich. I am your wife. I shall love you as long as I live . . . I would not change you for anyone I ever saw. . . . You love me – and that is worth gold. We shall love and be happy.[47]

In spite of her protestations of love and her wish to be married Madeleine, suddenly aware that Emile had even less than she thought, began to procrastinate, although her main fear was incurring the wrath of her family and the judgement of society. When he suggested seeing the local minister and publishing the banns of their intending betrothal, she tried to deflect the move by claiming they could get married without them:

> About those horrid Banns – love, I wish we could do without them, for they go on Friday, why my old father will be there at church on Sunday to stop them . . . Emile, my sweet love, I have often heard of clergymen in Glasgow marrying people without banns . . . Just go to their house and ask them to marry us. If not that sweet love why not the J.P.? And you say that a marriage by a J. of Peace is binding, why not do it'.[48]

She wrote a few days later that it would not be possible to be married without publishing the banns, but by that time her father had other ideas concerning her future.

William Minnoch was a successful thirty-seven-year-old Glasgow merchant, a partner in the firm of Houldsworths, cotton spinners, and a friend of Madeleine's father. He lived in the apartments above the Smiths and although Madeleine knew him socially, attending a concert with him in early December, she showed little interest in him, claiming that 'I have no regard for him'.[49] Until, that is, her father encouraged Minnoch with the idea of marriage. The first time she mentioned Minnoch in a flattering light to Emile was in a letter in mid January 1857, when she said: 'Mr M. dined with us to-night – do you know I think if you knew him you would like him, he is most kind. I like him very much better than I used to.'[50] By the end of the month Madeleine had accepted a proposal from Minnoch that was symbolised by the gift of a necklace, although there was no signed formal agreement to marry until 12 March. The letters written to Emile thus became crucial to her future. She demanded that Emile hand them over to her servant, Christina Haggart, saying:

> I trust to your honour as a Gentleman that you will not reveal any thing that may have passed between us. I shall feel obliged . . . [if you] bring me my letters and Likeness on Thursday eveng. At 7 . . . C.H. will (take) the parcel from you. On Friday I shall send you all your letters, Likeness, &ca. I trust you may be happy, and get one more worthy of you.[51]

She also explained why she had cooled on the relationship and the prospect of marriage to him:

> You may be astonished at this sudden change – but for some time back you must have noticed a coolness in my notes. My love for you has ceased, and that is why I was cool. I did once love you truly, fondly, but for some time back I have lost much of that love. There is no other reason for my conduct, and I think it but fair to let you know this. I might have gone on and become your wife, but I could not have loved you as I ought . . . It has cost me much to tell you this – sleepless nights, but it is necessary you know.[52]

When Emile refused to comply with her wishes and threatened to expose their affair to her family, the superior tone of the last letter gave way to a desperate pleading. She wrote: 'For God's sake do not bring your loved Mimi into open shame . . . for God's sake do not send my letters to Papa. It will be an open rupture. I will leave the house. I will die.'[53] In the following letter it is clear that Madeleine has become even more frantic, pleading:

> Emile, my father's wrath would kill me; you know little of his temper. Emile, for the love you once had for me, do not denounce me to my P/. Emile if he should read my letters to you he will put me from him, he will hate me as a guilty wretch . . . On my bended knees . . . for the mercy at the Judgement Day do not inform on me – do not make me a public shame . . . do not bring my father's wrath down on me. It will kill my mother (who is not well). It will forever cause me bitter unhappiness. I am humble before you and crave your mercy . . . Oh, will you not, for Christ's sake, denounce me. I shall be ruined. Who would trust me. Shame would be my lot – despise me, hate me – but make me not the public scandal . . . I could stand anything but my father's hot displeasure. Emile, you will not cause me death. If he is to get your letters, I can not see him any more. And my poor mother. I will never more kiss her – it would be a shame to them all. Emile will you not spare me this . . . do not expose me.[54]

In a society were reputation was everything, and women were completely dependent on men, Madeleine recognised the extreme seriousness of the situation: she was literally staring into the abyss. The realisation of this provoked a new strategy. As part of the process of cooling she had begun to address her letters not to 'her darling husband', but simply to 'Emile'. The former style of address was resumed and he was once more her 'dear, and ever beloved sweet, little Emile', and she was 'longing to meet again sweet love. We shall be so happy.'[55] At the same time she was writing to William Minnoch and speaking of beginning 'a new life – a life which I hope may be of happiness and long duration to both of us. My aim in life shall be to please you and study you.'[56] Emile had realised that Madeleine and William had formed some kind of relationship and he wrote to her asking is 'there any foundation in your marriage with another . . . And is it true that you are, directly or indirectly engage to Mr. Minnoch or to any one else but me?'[57] Eighteen days later his landlady, Mrs Jenkins, found him early in the morning doubled over with a burning pain in his stomach and bowels; it was the third attack of this kind in less than two months. By 11 a.m. that day the doctor had pronounced L'Angelier dead and he was buried in St David's Church, Glasgow on 26 March. Madeleine's letters were found by a colleague of Emile's, who had been entrusted with disposing of the belongings, and he alerted his employers, Huggins & Co, to the suspicion that his death was not from natural causes. They forced a post-mortem carried out by Drs Steven and Thomson, which led to the discovery of eighty-two grains of arsenic in his body, enough to kill fifty people. The fact that Madeleine had recently purchased large amounts of arsenic, and given the contents of the correspondence, led the police on 31 March, in the presence of Archibald Smith, the Sheriff-Substitute of Lanarkshire, to charge her with the murder of her former lover.[58]

The trial that followed on 30 June was part of a theatrical, almost carnivalesque, experience for those who witnessed it as part of the crowd and who turned up in their hundreds every day. Within the courtroom itself there was a

> scene . . . as the High Court of the Justiciary has never presented before in the present century. The whole of the Faculty of Advocates would seem to be there . . . a goodly array of Writers to the Signet appeared in their gowns; upwards of a score of reporters . . . moustachioed scions of the aristocracy; ministers of the Gospel . . . civic dignitaries are in abundance. A few women . . . Lords Cowan and Ardmillan, after they are relieved from their duties elsewhere, come and sit . . . so does the Hon. Lord Murray, and Lords Wood, Deas, and others.[59]

The social structure of urban Scotland was represented in a trial that, as Blyth recognised, was designed to counter any suggestion 'that there was one law for the rich and another for the poor'.[60] Thus, the importance of the trial goes way beyond the actual establishment of innocence or guilt. In a society in which the working classes had been effectively denied political rights, in spite of the Chartist campaigns in the 1840s, the enfranchised middle and upper classes had to display an even-handedness in administering the law that would convince the former of the legitimacy of their ability to speak and legislate for all, even if meant the execution of one of their own.

The Smiths hired John Inglis, Dean of the Faculty of Advocates, one of the most skilful and eloquent members of the Scottish legal profession, at a reputed one hundred guineas a day, to make sure that death was not the outcome. The prosecution case rested on one main piece of evidence and a self-evident motive: the purchase of arsenic, which was subsequently administered in late-night cocoa to Emile, and the desperation of her position, which forced Madeleine to go to extraordinary lengths to stop him revealing the contents of her letters to her father. Inglis, in a final speech lasting four hours, effectively countered the case for the prosecution by arguing that if the motive for murder was to silence Emile then it was flawed since during the investigation her letters would be uncovered and her relationship to and intimacy with him would be uncovered. As he said, 'what possible advantage could she expect from L'Angelier ceasing to live, so long as the letters remained?' Inglis also painted Emile as an unstable adventurer 'never to be depended upon', indeed, a man whose race and class marked him as criminal, who took advantage of a naive young girl. As he put it: 'Influence from without – most corrupting influence – can alone account for such a fall.' Rather than Madeleine, it was Emile, he argued, who had been 'in the habit of using arsenic', and who was increasingly desperate when it was apparent he had failed a second time to gain access to society through marriage, who took his own life as an ultimate act of revenge.[61] *The Scotsman*'s editorial underscored this view when it stated: 'In his massive pride, he took too much of the drug (arsenic) and, in a bizarre twist of fate . . . he died.'

Madeleine for her part sat in court, flanked by two policemen and the matron of Edinburgh Prison, looking the epitome of middle-class respectability, although her parents, who had taken to bed, were conspicuous by their absence. She was modestly but elegantly dressed in a 'well-cut, brown silk frock with black silk cloak, a small fashionable bonnet, trimmed with white silk riband, which showed the whole front of her head, lavender kid gloves on her small hands, and holding in the right a silver-topped bottle'.[62] Most of those present were struck by her self-possession and near indifference to the proceedings as correspondent for *The Examiner* remarked:

> to Madeleine Smith alone his [Emile] death seems to have been no shock, no grief, and she demeaned herself . . . as if L'Angelier never had a place in her affections. If it had been a trial for poisoning a dog the indifference could not have been greater.[63]

Perhaps Madeleine's composure was the consequence of knowing something of the social psychology of her class. Certainly, she understood the importance of sartorial appropriateness in the creation of a demure and vulnerable image. The all-male, predominantly middle-class jury saw in her their daughters, and although they faced the uncomfortable possibility that Madeleine had 'criminalized the private' sphere of domestic life,[64] they dismissed it as untenable and bought into the victim theory of the defence council as the only acceptable explanation of her conduct. C. J. Watt, the biographer of John Inglis, summed it up brilliantly when he said:

> The pale but fresh firm face, set in the curtained bonnet of the day, the graceful figure, its lines traceable through the lace of a black mantilla, the lustrous eyes and full quivering lips as she sat in the seat whence so many had gone to the scaffold, caused even strong men to quail at the mere apprehension of her doom. Guilty or innocent, she made them think, not of the crime or the possibility that her hand had poisoned the fatal cup, but of their own sisters and daughter. To hang her was impossible![65]

On the first count of attempted murder she was found not guilty, on the other two counts of attempted murder and murder, the jury – by a vote of thirteen to two – found the charges against Madeleine 'Not Proven', that peculiar verdict that the Scottish novelist Wilkie Collins said 'is not permitted by the law of any other civilised country on the face of the earth'.[66] She walked from court a free woman to the acclaim of the crowd who had gathered in thousands to cheer the verdict. Indeed, such was the excitement that Madeleine had to be smuggled out of the High Court to a waiting cab and driven to Slateford station, where she boarded a train for Stepps, near Glasgow, and from there was driven to Rowaleyn.[67] From the moment the verdict was delivered public opinion divided on the question of her guilt or innocence. The Dean of the Faculty left the court with 'averted eyes, refraining the customary, congratulatory handshake', so convinced was he of her guilt.[68] Jane Welsh Carlyle in a letter to her husband described her as 'a little incarnate devil'.[69] Madeleine herself recognised, in a letter to Miss Aitken written shortly after the trial, that her support was regionally divided, with the east more favourable to her than the west of Scotland, where 'the feeling . . . is not so good towards me as you kind Edinburgh people'.[70] The press was also supportive, although the English newspapers were more qualified, with *The Times* reminding its readers that she 'goes forth free from the penalties of the law – that is all'.[71] Pamphleteers and biographers have been equally divided. An anonymous pamphlet, *The Story of Minnie L'Angelier, or Madeleine Hamilton Smith* (1857), was the first in a long line of partisan publications. The author excoriated the character and reputation of Madeleine, referring to her as a 'woman experienced in shameless intrigue – a woman degraded and caught in her own snare'.[72] *Who Killed L'Angelier*, written by Scrutator later in the same year, was a scathing riposte in defence of Madeleine and did much to amplify the suicide thesis suggested by Inglis at the trial. The lines of debate laid down in these publications have influenced all further writings on the subject. Geraldine Butler in her biography – *Madeleine Smith* (1935) – saw her as 'a liar and an expert in deception', and was convinced that she had poisoned Emile;[73] a view shared by Nigel Morland in *That Nice Miss Smith* (1950), by P. Hunt in *The Madeleine Smith Affair* (1950), and by Henry Blyth, although more qualified, in his study of the affair – *Madeleine Smith* (1975). Mary S. Hartman in *Victorian Murderesses* (1985) was convinced of her guilt and felt attending a performance of the opera *Lucrezia Borgia* gave her the idea of poisoning Emile. The most recent publication, however, by Douglas MacGowan – *Murder in Victorian Scotland: the Trial of Madeleine Smith* (1999) – returns, after exhaustive research, an open verdict.

Whether she did or didn't do it can never be satisfactorily answered, but most writers have argued that if she had been tried in an English court Madeleine would have been found not guilty since the prosecution's case was fatally flawed on the two most important points: possession and intention. Although she unintentionally created an industry round her personality, it is clear that far from her life coming to an end as a result of the trial, it could be argued that it was simply moving to a different level of experience. Because of her notoriety she recognised almost immediately, in her letter to Miss Aitken, that she would have 'to leave Scotland for a few months'.[74] Her family's reputation was destroyed and the Smiths were forced to change address three times in their desperate search for obscurity. Rowaleyn was sold and the family moved to Bridge of Allan, Stirlingshire, and, finally, to Polmont, Edinburgh. Madeleine changed her name to Lena and moved to Plymouth where she met the artist and business manager of William Morris, George Wardle. The couple were married on 4 July 1861 at St Paul's Church in Knightsbridge, London. Her father and brother attended the wedding, although her sisters, Janet and Bessie, were absent. Madeleine and George, with the help of a generous dowry from Mr Smith, set up home in Bloomsbury near the British Museum. However, when her father died in 1863 he left her nothing in his will.

As a result of her husband's artistic connections, Madeleine moved freely among the Pre-Raphaelites and the Morris set. As a result, she and her son, Tom, later became involved in socialist politics as members of Morris' Socialist League, established in 1884. In fact, Tom was arrested in Edgeware Road, London, in September 1886 for making 'violent speeches'.[75] Her daughter, Kitten, was quite bohemian, and did not believe in marriage and scandalised polite society by being one of the first women to smoke in public.[76] George and Madeleine drifted apart and he went to live in Italy in 1890, coincidentally the year in which a junior clerk, Malcolm Nicholson, at the High Court of Justiciary was tried and sentenced to twelve months' imprisonment for stealing her letters and attempting to sell them to an Edinburgh bookseller,[77] an event that re-stimulated press interest in the Madeleine Smith affair. With the help of her brother-in-law, the silk manufacturer Thomas Wardle, Madeleine at the age of seventy set up home in the village of Leek, Staffordshire. The death of Thomas Wardle in 1909 and George the following year in a Plymouth nursing home led to the income stream being shut off and at the grand old age of eighty she emigrated for America to be near her son and his family. While there she married again and became Lena Wardle Sheehy – the name she took to her grave in New Hope Cemetery, New York, where she was buried in April 1928.

Madeleine Smith found obscurity in the twentieth century on another continent, but for most of the second half of the nineteenth century she was one of the most notorious and controversial women in Scotland and Britain. That she has remained more than a ten-day wonder is testimony not only to the ambiguity surrounding the case, and the manner in which the openness of the verdict has beguiled succeeding generations of historians and writers, but also because of the valuable insights that are to be gleaned from the relationship between Madeleine and Emile regarding issues of sex, gender and class at this time. The revelations of female pleasure in sex shocked contemporaries and challenged current stereotypes of the 'unsexed' woman. The ease with which the couple were able to plan their assignations and find pleasure in each other's company also raised questions as to how many other middle-class girls lost their virginity before marriage and how controlling was Victorian society since they managed to evade, with little effort, the surveillance of adults. Madeleine's alleged poisoning of her lover seriously disturbed middle-class society as her actions constituted a full-scale attack on the idea of the 'angel in the house'; she was not so much an angel, more like a malevolent presence. She represented a darker side of Victorian domesticity: an antidote to the idealisation of the private sphere. Although some would like to interpret her actions as some kind of proto-feminist challenge to male constructions of femininity and female sexuality[78] – after all it was Madeleine who found passion across the class divide, drove the relationship towards full blown sex, revelled in it, wanted more, and when tired of it poisoned her lover, not for romantic reasons but purely for status – in reality she saw herself as subordinate to men and, indeed, at times obsessively craved submission. She wrote to Emile in July 1856, saying:

> I will do anything, I will do all you mention in your letters to please you . . . be my guide, my dear husband . . . I promise I will not go about the streets, Emile, more than you have said. We went about too much, I shall not go about much . . . I shall take lessons in water colours . . . I shall love and obey you . . . I shall do all you want of me.[79]

At no time, even in passing, did she criticise the highly patriarchal nature of bourgeois society and a woman's place within that system of subordination. If she held a grievance against her place in society, her protest was simply an individual act of defiance. Thus, her opposition to conventional social mores was not meant to galvanise other women, or shock the complacency of the Glasgow middle classes, it was simply a dangerous pursuit of pleasure that had been crafted in her imagination by reading romantic fiction and by her arrogance that privilege would shield her if found out. It was only later after her marriage to George Wardle and her involvement with the Socialist League that some kind of critique of society emerged. In the end, it was a doomed affair borne out of boredom and frustration with the narrow confines of a world where place and position were everything; it dramatised the symptoms of female discontent, but had no cure to offer for women similarly situated.

NOTES

1. Anon., *The Story of Minie L'Angelier or Madeleine Hamilton Smith* (Edinburgh, 1857), p. 1.
2. Anon., *The Story*, p. 4.
3. H. Blyth, *Madeleine Smith* (London, 1975), p. 11.

4. Quoted in M. S. Hartman, 'Murder for respectability: the case of Madeleine Smith', *Victorian Studies*, 16 (1973), p. 385.
5. Hartman, 'Murder', p. 386.
6. Letter to Emile, postmark illegible, but probably September 1856, Anon., *The Story*, Appendix XIII, p. 328 (all future references to letters are from this publication).
7. Letter to Emile, 26 December 1856, p. 345.
8. Letter to Emile, no date, p. 348.
9. Letter to Emile, 7 June 1856, pp. 312–13.
10. Blyth, *Madeleine*, p. 4.
11. Quoted in Hartman, 'Murder', p. 387.
12. G. L. Butler, *Madeleine Smith* (London, 1935), p. 9.
13. Letter to Emile, p. 315.
14. Blyth, *Madeleine*, p. 31.
15. All trial evidence from www.amostcuriousmurder.com
16. www.amostcuriousmurder.com
17. www.amostcuriousmurder.com
18. Blyth, *Madeleine*, pp. 33–4.
19. C. J. Watt, 'Speech in Defence of Madeline Smith', in *John Inglis . . . a Memoir* (Edinburgh, 1893), Appendix B.
20. Letter to Emile, February 1855, p. 302.
21. Letter to Emile, 3 April 1855, p. 302.
22. Letter to Emile, 18 April 1855, p. 303.
23. Letter to Madeleine, 19 July 1855, p. 305.
24. Letter to Emile, 4 September 1855, p. 307.
25. Letter to Emile, 3 December 1855, p. 308.
26. Letter to Emile, 3 May 1856, p. 311.
27. Quoted in P. Hunt, *The Madeleine Smith Affair* (London, 1950), p. 73.
28. Letter to Emile, 7 May 1856, p. 312.
29. Blyth, *Madeleine*, p. 65.
30. Quoted in Blyth, *Madeleine*, pp. 65–8.
31. Quoted in Hunt, *Madeleine*, p. 73.
32. Quoted in Blyth, *Madeleine*, p. 69.
33. Quoted in Hartman, 'Murder', p. 390.
34. Quoted in Blyth, *Madeleine*, p. 81.
35. A. Duncan Smith, *The Trial of Madeleine Smith* (Edinburgh, 1905), p. 273.
36. M. Foucault, *The History of Sexuality*, vol. I (London, 1978), p. 3.
37. Foucault, *Sexuality*, pp. 34, 69.
38. Foucault, *Sexuality*, p. 120.
39. J. Weeks, *Sex, Politics and Society* (London, 1994 edn), p. 23.
40. L. Nead, *Myths of Sexuality: Representations of Women in Victorian Britain* (Oxford, 1989), p. 6.
41. Hartman, 'Murder', p. 391.
42. Nead, *Myths*, p. 6.

43. B. Littlewood and L. Mahood, 'Prostitutes, Magdalenes and wayward girls: dangerous sexualities of working-class women in Victorian Scotland', *Gender and History*, 3 (1991), p. 172.
44. Littlewood and Mahood, 'Prostitutes', p. 172.
45. Anon., *The Story*, p. 38.
46. *Saturday Review*, 11 July 1857.
47. Letter to Emile, December 1856, pp. 336–7.
48. Letter to Emile, 13 December 1856, pp. 340–1.
49. Letter to Emile, 14 December 1856, p. 336.
50. Letter to Emile, 16 January 1857, p. 353.
51. Letter to Emile, February 1857, p. 356.
52. Letter to Emile, February 1857, p. 356.
53. Letter to Emile, 10 February 1857, p. 357.
54. Letter to Emile, February 1857, p. 358.
55. Letter to Emile, February 1857, p. 360.
56. Letter to William Minnoch, 16 March 1857, p. 368.
57. Letter to Madeleine, 5 March 1857, p. 365.
58. Anon., *The Story*, p. 7.
59. Anon., *The Story*, p. 14.
60. Blyth, *Madeleine*, p. 131.
61. Watt, *Inglis*, Appendix B.
62. J. Forster, *Studies in Black and Red* (London, 1896), pp. 45–6.
63. Quoted in Butler, *Madeleine*, p. 165.
64. S. Sullivan, 'What is the matter with Mary Jane? Madeleine Smith, legal ambiguity, and the gendered aesthetic of Victorian criminality', *Genders*, 35 (2002), p. 32.
65. Watt, *Inglis*, p. 85.
66. W. Collins, *The Law and the Lady* (London, 1988 edn), p. 95.
67. Anon., *The Trial of Miss Madeleine Hamilton Smith . . . Special Verbatim Reports* (Edinburgh, 1857), p. 17.
68. Butler, *Madeleine*, p. 165.
69. Letter to T. Carlyle, 26 July 1857, in A. J. Froude (ed.), *The Letters and Memorials of Jane Welsh Carlyle*, vol. II (London, 1883), p. 83.
70. Letter to Miss Aitken, 19 July 1857, quoted in Anon., *The Trial*, p. 293.
71. *The Times*, 10 July 1857.
72. Anon., *The Story*, p. 10.
73. Butler, *Madeleine*, p. 99.
74. Letter to Miss Aitken, 19 July 1857, p. 293.
75. Butler, *Madeleine*, p. 179.
76. Butler, *Madeleine*, p. 180.
77. Anon., *The Story*, pp. 288–91.
78. See Hartman, *Victorian Murderesses*, and Sullivan, 'Mary Jane'.
79. Letter to Emile, 11 July 1856, p. 324.

4

Sophia Jex-Blake: Women and Higher Education in Nineteenth-Century Scotland

ॐ

Sophia Jex-Blake, Scotland's first female doctor, was arguably the most important figure in the women's movement in Britain in the second half of the nineteenth century. As her biographer, Margaret Todd, put it: 'She *was* the movement . . . she stood . . . for women.'[1] What justified that large claim was her (ultimately successful) struggle for women to be admitted to universities in Britain on the same basis as men. The ground on which she chose to fight was the right of women to matriculate as students in the Faculty of Medicine at the University of Edinburgh. Indeed, much of the hopes of women rested on this struggle, since if the closed doors of medicine could be unlocked, then it was reasonable to expect that other doors, such as parliament and the professions, similarly tightly shut in the face of women would be thrown open. As Lady Frances Balfour said, 'There were three great fights . . . First Education, then Medicine, then the Suffrage.'[2] However, the campaign waged by Sophia and her supporters against one of the mostly deeply ingrained misogynist institutions in the country not only profoundly challenged male stereotypes concerning a woman's capabilities both physically and mentally, it also divided the women's movement itself. The policy of confrontation favoured by Sophia when dealing with the medical profession was opposed as adventurism and seen as wrong-headed by those women activists, such as Elizabeth Garrett Anderson, who wished to prove by example that they were equally as capable as men given the opportunity. The tactical disagreement between Anderson and Jex-Blake over direct action and peaceful persuasion in many ways pre-empted the division between the Suffragettes and the Suffragists over attitudes to law and order in the early 1900s, and also women's organisations and their struggles for equality throughout the twentieth century. Thus, the debate concerning how to deal with and (eventually) overcome male prejudice is as important to discuss, as it is to detail the actual struggle waged by Sophia in respect of university entrance, for it remains at the centre of an ongoing feminist discourse.[3]

However, given her somewhat privileged background, Sophia seemed an unlikely figure to spearhead the struggle for higher education for women. She was born in Hastings on 21 January 1840 to Thomas Jex-Blake, retired barrister, and Maria Emily Cubbit, the youngest of three surviving children; the first three Jex-Blake siblings had died. The family name had only been used since 1837, when Sophia's grandfather obtained a Royal Licence to change the family name from Blake in honour of his grandmother.[4] Sophia's mother and father were Evangelical Anglicans and their deeply held religious beliefs and, perhaps, also their advanced years, ensured that the children were brought up in a highly protected environment. From an early age they were encouraged to read serious books by (mainly) religious writers. Light fiction and popular magazines of the time, such as *Punch*, were considered vulgar and forbidden, as were dancing and theatre-going.[5] One might have considered her upbringing somewhat restricted, if not repressed, but at no time did Sophia ever express any reservations regarding her childhood, and at no time did she consider her parents to have been unduly harsh in their childrearing practices. As she claimed: 'No one ever had a happier childhood than I.'[6] Although she was extremely fond of her father, it was with her mother that Sophia, or Sophy as she was known, had the strongest and most compelling bond. She once wrote in her diary, 'I could not live without her love.'[7]

Her parents home-educated her until she was eight years old; after this Sophia went on to attend six schools in the next eight years. Teachers found her a determined and headstrong girl, good at Latin and maths, but equally 'wilful, insubordinate, [and] often regrettably unladylike'. One teacher wrote to her when she heard that she was to receive Confirmation in the Anglican faith, saying: 'Confirmed! – in what? – in following your own foolish ways? There needs no confirmation in that . . .'[8] Their failure to cope with her 'wildness' and 'disobedience' saw Sophia packed off to boarding school at the request of her mother, whose health was poor, and who equally was finding it difficult to manage her unruly behaviour.[9] Her father wrote to her asking, 'Do you think, darling, that by divine grace you are less self-willed day by day?'[10] One of her classmates provided an assessment of the young Sophia's character, which proved uncannily accurate. She said of her, that '[she] is . . . excessively clever but unfortunately knows it, and makes a point of showing off upon every occasion. She is truthfulness itself and can really be trusted. Very passionate but very penitent afterwards. Affectionate.'[11]

Although her schooldays were not the happiest of times for Sophia, her love of learning did not diminish. While staying with cousins in

London she enrolled in Queen's College in the spring of 1858, where she followed a varied curriculum that included maths, English, French, philosophy, theology and church history. Within a fairly short space of time she was offered a tutoring position in mathematics that carried with it a salary of £100 per annum. Her father, who was already providing Sophia with an allowance of £200 a year, was outraged at the thought of a paid position and wrote to Sophia that she would 'degrade' herself hopelessly; only working-class women went out to work.[12] Sophia retorted by asking her father why it was perfectly acceptable for her brother to earn a salary from teaching but not her? He replied that 'Tom was a man . . . and could command a salary of £1,000 a year'.[13] The double standards employed by her father ensured that his rather utilitarian argument would be lost on Sophia, and ignoring his request she took the salary.

Financial independence and a demanding occupation saved Sophia from the pampered, but utterly empty and routine, lifestyle that was usual for a young woman of her social standing until, that is, a suitable husband could be found. In her diary, Sophia laid out a daily 'plan' of activities, which provides some clues as to why women who possessed the same restless intelligence as her found it vital to breakout from this rather pointless way of life:

> 8.30am Rise, breakfast with the rest of the world. Have walk till 11. Then . . . some . . . writing, painting, etc., till dinner at 1. Afternoon will be taken up with driving. Come in at 4. Then read till tea. After tea, write, or read out downstairs. And go to bed with the rest of the world. That would be rather more rational than my present programme: Rise and breakfast at 11 or later. Dawdle till dinner. Drive. Read till tea. Read or write to 2 or 3am.[14]

It was while tutoring at Queen's College that Sophia met the housing reformer, Octavia Hill, who was perhaps singularly to make the most intense and significant emotional impact on her life. Their meeting was wholly fortuitous and was the result of Sophia's need for tutoring in bookkeeping methods before she embarked on voluntary work on behalf of the Society for the Employment of Women. She described Octavia after their first meeting as a 'clever, pleasant girl – much nicer than I thought'.[15] For her part Octavia, in a letter to her sister, described Sophia as 'a bright, splendid, brave, generous young lady living alone in true bachelor style'.[16] The two women could not have been more different: Octavia was working-class, artistic, reserved and sensitive, while Sophia was privileged, domineering, passionate and outgoing. It is difficult to judge whether the relationship they formed was a romantic friendship or a full blown sexual one. There are hints however that it may have been the latter. Sophia in her diary speculated on a number of occasions about the prospect of love and marriage. At the age of eighteen she stated that 'I did not fancy that I should ever marry, for I though I should require too many qualities to meet in the man I could think of as my husband'.[17] On another occasion, she declared that 'I love women too much ever to love a man'.[18] Indeed, it is only when she thinks of a relationship with a woman that Sophia's passionate nature emerges. In her diary she recorded her feelings towards another (anonymous) woman, whose friendship and/or love she had dispensed with, saying:

> My . . ., my beautiful, whom I used to think mysteriously close to my soul . . . [now] Every action, every word of her's seems to anger me unreasonably, – I feel the fiend on me and yet the wild resistless love will not quite be swept away, and comes back in floods of passing tenderness for a moment. And I can't tell her, make her understand, and she will lose her love for me . . . I am very miserable . . . I feel such a wild maddening love now, as if I knew it would soon be out of my power to love her.[19]

The one time she refers to physical intimacy between herself and Octavia is when on holiday in Wales: 'She sunk her head on my lap silently, raised it in tears, and then such a kiss!'[20] The feelings were reciprocated. When Sophia went abroad for a short time, Octavia missed her acutely. She wrote to her saying that 'London feels strangely desolate, the lamps looked as they used to, pitiless and unending as I walked home last night, and knew I could not go to you'.[21]

The opportunities for intimacy increased when they decided to share a house together along with Octavia's family at 14 Nottingham Place, but the opportunities for disagreement also grew. Mrs Hill resented Sophia's domineering ways and the frequent clashes they had over a whole range of household issues began to tell on the fragile health of Octavia. To preserve her sanity and to retain her mother's love, Octavia decided to end the relationship with her 'darling child'. Sophia was devastated. As one longstanding friend later put it: 'She was never the same again . . . it cut her life in two.'[22] The break was decisive and they were never reconciled, although Sophia never gave up hoping that their relationship could be mended. As Margaret Todd said:

> Till the close of her life the friendship on her side remained unbroken . . . in reported wills she left the whole of her little property to Miss Hill . . . until the eve of her last illness she would not extinguish the hope that even in this life the friendship might be renewed.[23]

With the emotional scars of a failed relationship still quite evident Sophia left London for Germany and an English teaching post in the

Grand Ducal Institute at Mannheim, working only on a bed and board basis for six months. The teaching regime was intense, the hours were long, and there were few days off. It appears that Sophia did not enjoy a good rapport with all her pupils, and she was subject to ridicule by them for an inability to sing, paint and embroider. They also laughed at her for crying during church services.[24] In spite of this, Sophia found the experience rewarding and returned home towards the end of January 1864 determined to continue with her teaching career. She visited a number of schools in England, investigating girls' education, with a view to opening a college for females. Although nothing came of this, she realised that there was much more to discover on the subject, and it was this awareness that prompted her to take a more comparative approach. Sophia, in the company of a family friend, Isabel Bain, decided to visit America to carry out research into educational opportunities for girls in a country less hidebound by tradition and more open to new ideas, particularly as regards the position of women. The decision was to prove to be a life-changing one.

She arrived in Boston on 8 June 1865 and was soon introduced to twenty-eight-year old Dr Lucy Sewall, resident physician to the New England Hospital for Women and Children, and later she was guest in the house of the philosopher Ralph Waldo Emerson. She also travelled around the country amassing material on girls' education, which eventually was published in book-form in 1867 – *A Visit to some American Schools and Colleges* – and was fairly well-received in Britain. Sophia was generally supportive of the more egalitarian approach to schooling in America and the mixing of the sexes, but was concerned that if 'we . . . mingle different classes of children in such proportions and under such conditions . . . [we have to] ensure that the higher standard shall prevail over the lower'. In practice, this meant that the 'refined speech of the more fortunate children' should be adopted, as there was a 'risk that the uncouthness of the labourer's children would prevail'.[25] The strong belief Sophia had in the values and virtues of the upper middle class produced an innate and unthinking elitism even when expressing socially progressive sentiments. For example, in discussing the issue of co-educational classes in universities in Britain, she felt that 'it is both possible and right for ladies and gentlemen to study in the same classes . . . [but] I am equally certain that boys of a low social class, of small mental calibre, and no moral training, are utterly unfit to be admitted to a mixed class'.[26]

Thus, in spite of the more openness of American culture, Sophia's sense of class superiority was always apparent. Even her growing perception that medicine might be her true vocation was partly founded on the idea of helping her less fortunate sisters, and consistent with the middle-class concept of public service. She wrote to her mother saying: 'I say a dozen times a day – Were I not a teacher, I would be a doctor . . . I find myself getting desperately in love with medicine.'[27] From her observations at the Dispensary, Sophia also perceived the need for women, especially poorer ones, to be treated by their own sex, since they would not only feel more comfortable, but their peculiar medical problems would be dealt with with more sensitivity by a female rather than a male doctor. As she declared:

> I think that anyone who passed a couple of mornings in this dispensary would go away . . . convinced of the enormous advantage of women doctors; and one sees how clearly the poor women feel it by the crowds that come . . . when the lady physicians are in charge, and the handful that come . . . when a man presides.[28]

This conviction remained with Sophia all her life and she wrote to *The Times* thirty years later, saying:

> I have now been in practice for nearly twenty years, and during the whole of this time I have been receiving fresh evidence that there are a very large number of women, especially poor women, who will not accept the necessary treatment from a man, and who have in many cases endured years of continuous suffering before they had the opportunity of obtaining relief from their medical sisters.[29]

Indeed, there was much ignorance among medical practitioners on matters concerning women's health. Even into the twentieth century women were still being told that the 'safe' period for sex was during the middle of the cycle, that is, during ovulation.[30]

However, by the time she had returned to Britain in June 1866, Sophia had made up her mind to become a doctor, and with the support of her parents she returned to America in September to achieve that goal. She, along with another young woman, Susan Dimock, applied for entry to Harvard Medical School 'on the same terms and conditions as other students', only to be informed that there was 'no provision for the education of women in department of this university'.[31] The two women obtained some limited clinical training at Massachusetts General Hospital, but Sophia, after a protracted and unsuccessful campaign against the intransigency of Harvard, was encouraged by Dr Elizabeth Blackwell and her sister Emily to try New York in March 1868 for further instruction. The Head Demonstrator of Anatomy of Bellevue Hospital, Dr Moseley, was persuaded to give her private lessons in dissecting and practical anatomy, and after a brief holiday in England with Lucy Sewall, Sophia returned to New York to enrol in the Women's Medical College of New York Infirmary, which had been established by the Blackwell sisters in the autumn of 1868. Sophia had found her vocation in life and though she 'never had worked so hard', she had 'never been in such good health . . . I eat and walk and sleep perfectly, have no pains and aches, and the sweetest of tempers'.[32] However, that feeling of blissful content-ment was shattered with the news of her father's illness. In spite of a 'rush' across the Atlantic and through Dublin, she arrived back in England too late. Her father had died on 6 November and although Sophia was heart-broken, she consoled herself with the thought that it could have been worse: it might have been her mother.[33] Despite entreaties from Lucy Sewall, she refused to return to America to finish her training, fearing that if her mother should fall ill she would again be too late to say her fare-well; instead she took Lucy's advice to 'open the profession to the women in England'.

Sophia articulated the case for women's entry to medicine in an influential essay in Josephine Butler's edited publication *Women's Work and Women's Culture* (1869). Her argument rested on four main prem-ises: firstly, that women had historically a recognised and renowned place in the healing process, and that could be proven as far back as ancient civilisation; secondly, that women would not suffer, as argued by some in the medical profession, either mentally of physically, from protracted study of anatomy or have their morality degraded; thirdly, the claim that there was no demand for women doctors and no demand from women to become doctors was statistically wrong as evidence from America showed 'there was a large amount actually waiting for them'; and, fourthly, that women were 'arbitrarily' prevented from studying medi-cine by the self-interest of men who feared unreasonably that their live-lihoods would be threatened by an influx of female practitioners. Women were not motivated simply by the prospect of widening their sphere of employment, most of the pioneers in any case were, like Sophia, from well-to-do families, who were in little need of a salary. They saw entry into medicine as not only speeding up reform in other areas of social and political life, but also as a means to change current medical practices. It is significant that the first female doctors were interested in 'patient centred care, preventive medicine, family medicine, child sexual abuse and sexual education'.[34] In rejecting male prejudices and raising the ambitions of women to a higher moral plane, Sophia pleaded not for any special treatment for her sex, only that they be permitted a level playing field and 'be admitted to the examinations already established for men, and . . . [to] receive their medical degree on exactly the same terms'.[35] The essay raised public consciousness regarding the 'deliberate exclusion of women from the medical profession' and 'made women determined not to be bought off with an offer of limited entry: they were asking for no favours' only ' a reinstatement of traditional rights'.[36]

Having diagnosed the areas of contention, Sophia, in characteristically determined fashion, set about resolving them. The problem was that the barriers to the successful entry of women to the medical profession in Britain were even more formidable than those that existed in America and Western Europe. Before the Medical Act of 1858 anyone could attain the status of a medical practitioner in Britain; it was simply an exercise in nomenclature. What the Act did was to regulate the profession by insisting that only those holding appropriate qualifications awarded by one of nineteen awarding institutions – the universities, the Colleges of Physicians and Surgeons, the London Society of Apothecaries and Apothecaries' Hall, Dublin – could be registered annually as approved practitioners. Degrees given by foreign institutions were not recognised unless they had been awarded prior to 1858 and the person could prove that he or she had been practicing medicine before that year. The state further enhanced the professionalisation of medicine by only allowing qualified doctors to sign medico-legal documents, or take legal action to recover unpaid medical fees, and by only appointing registered practitioners to government service.[37] The legislation did not expressly exclude women from the medical profession: those practitioners such as Elizabeth Blackwell and Elizabeth Garrett Anderson, who held qualifications from overseas institutions and who satisfied the regulations, were placed on the annual register. What effectively barred other women from following in the footsteps of Blackwell and Anderson was the inclusion of a set of regulations governing the structure of medical degree courses that had to be followed by the awarding institutions; this included lectures and practical training under the supervision of approved teachers, and the award of signed certificates proving the successful completion of a part of the course before entry to the examination was permitted. Since universities in Britain at this time were men-only clubs, the legislation effectively prevented women's entry to medicine.

Women only had limited access to university education in Scotland through the Ladies' Educational Associations (LEA), which had been established while Sophia was in America at Edinburgh and St Andrews, indeed, the latter introduced the Lady Licentiate in Arts in the year 1876–7;[38] in Glasgow there were courses of lectures open to women, but no formal organisation until the formation in 1877 of the Glasgow

Association for the Higher Education of Women.[39] Thus, women could attend public lectures on subjects as varied as botany, mathematics and biblical criticism, sit examinations and receive certificates, but it was clear that there were no links with this kind of study provision to the possibility of a career; it was simply another layer of decoration and refinement. As the Edinburgh Association made clear in its first annual report: its aim 'is not . . . [to] train [women] for the professions, but to give them the advantages of a system acknowledged to be well-suited to the mental training of the other sex'.[40] Sophia wanted much more than this and after trying a number of universities, including Cambridge, London and St Andrews, she decided to focus her energy on gaining entry to the medical faculty of the University of Edinburgh, because of 'its freedom from ecclesiastical influence and other constraints'.[41] However, it was less to do with tolerance, and more to do with the fact that there was a thriving LEA in existence at Edinburgh, and the encouragement she received from some of the senior staff, particularly David Masson, Professor of Rhetoric and English Literature, who provided a letter of introduction to the Dean of the Faculty of Medicine.

After successfully canvassing all the members of the Faculty and Senate, the university approved as an 'experiment' her entry into Natural History and Botany classes, but, as Moberly Bell points out, 'the admission was hedged around with provisos – she might prepare for matriculation but there was no undertaking that she might sit the exam'.[42] An appeal was lodged against the decision, which was upheld by the university court in April 1869; however, interestingly, the decision to end the 'experiment' was not based on principle, but on the practicalities of arranging teaching for the 'convenience' of one woman. To Sophia this was an open invitation to reapply: this time in greater numbers. There was no shortage of volunteers, some of whom were outstanding individuals, but four were selected: Isobel Thorne, who was married, and three single women, Helen Evans, Edith Pechey and Mathilda Chaplin (later another two joined and they became known in popular terms as *Septem contra Edinam* – the seven against Edinburgh). Sophia again approached the Faculty of Medicine offering to guarantee to pay the fees of her fellow students, which were set at double the rate for males, and to accept separate teaching arrangements. This arrangement was agreed by the Faculty, and ratified by the Senate, and eventually by the University Court in July 1869. The five women, the first in Britain, were allowed to matriculate for a medical degree and sit the relevant examinations. Sophia recorded in her diary: 'Won after all! – and I do think this must be at last . . . the beginning of the end'; and further reflected that 'a university in Britain may be literally open to women – if so, won't that have been worth doing?'[43] The victory, however, was to prove short-lived.

What undermined the position of the women was the refusal of Professor Crum Brown in Chemistry to award the Hope Scholarship to Edith Pechey, in spite of the fact that she was the top student in her year. This was justified on the basis that women were taught separately and therefore were not considered to be 'members of the class' and as such could not be granted certificates of attendance allowing them to take the examination. Sophia and the others opposed the decision and lodged an appeal. Their appeal was upheld by the Senate, but by only one vote, although the decision not to award the scholarship to Pechey was also, and somewhat contradictorily, affirmed.[44] This event was the beginning of a protracted legal battle to drive women from the University of Edinburgh, which was spearheaded by Professor Robert Christison, the Queen's surgeon, an elder in the Church of Scotland, and a widower of twenty years, with three sons and no sisters, who 'worked with men and played with men'.[45] Christison believed that while women could, and should, be midwives, they were not suitable material for doctoring. The other main opponent was the Professor of Surgery, Joseph Lister, Quaker, who believed that anything lowering the barriers separating the sexes would lead to a decline in moral standards.[46] Other professors in the opposition camp also stressed the issue of morality, claiming, as Professor Thomas Laycock did, that women who sought an education in medicine might be 'basely inclined', and that unless their references were carefully scrutinised, teachers might be harbouring 'Magdalenes' (that is, prostitutes) in their classes.[47]

These misogynist and, in the case of Laycock, quite scandalous views were supported by others in the medical profession. Dr Henry Bennett, articulating the views of many practitioners, argued that men, Caucasian men in particular, were superior on all levels to women, claiming:

> The principal feature which appears . . . to characterise the Caucasian race . . . above all other races, is the power that many of its *male* members have of advancing the horizon of science . . . I am not aware that the female members of our race participate in this power, in this supreme development of the mind; at least I know of no great discovery changing the surface of science that owes its existence to a woman of our or of any race. What right have women to claim mental *equality* with men?[48]

However, the fact that all the women passed the examination and that Edith Pechey had come top in the chemistry class did much to undermine the views of Bennett and others who felt that women had smaller brains than men and, thus, would not stand up to the mental rigours of a degree course in medicine. The realisation of this only intensified the attempts to remove them from the Faculty of Medicine by fair means or foul. As Sophia herself recognised:

> the results in the class examinations aroused in our opponents a conviction that the so-called experiment was not going to fail of itself, as they had confidently hoped, but that if it was to be suppressed at all, vigorous measures must be taken for that purpose.[49]

The women were not without support. They had the backing of sympathetic figures in the Medical Faculty, the university, the wider profession, and in the national press. The *British Medical Journal* had spoken out against the injustice of the university's stand on Edith Pechey, as did *The Times*, the *Manchester Guardian*, the *Spectator*, and, nearer to home, *The Scotsman*. They had, however, little assistance when it came to coping with the day-to-day incidents of bullying and harassment, or the invidious, unspoken attempts to deny them teaching in crucial areas. Sophia catalogued the terms of abuse: her doorbell was 'wrenched off' and her nameplate damaged five times; a Catherine wheel was attached to her door; smoke was blown in their faces; filthy letters were sent; they were waylaid in quiet streets; obscenities were shouted at them in public.[50] In the lecture rooms doors were shut in their faces, horse laughs and howls were uttered when they approached classes, 'as if a conspiracy had been formed to make our position as uncomfortable as might be'.[51] Edith Pechey, in a letter to *The Scotsman*, also spoke of being followed in the streets and having 'the foulest epithets', such as 'whore', shouted at her.[52] Although it was fairly clear that the perpetrators of these acts were male students, since many of the epithets used medical terms, the women were powerless to complain as the university took the view that the students were only under its control during class hours. The sustained campaign of harassment reached a climax in the Surgeons' Hall Riots in November 1870.

Sophia and the others had been granted permission to enter classes on anatomy and surgery in October 1870 conducted by qualified lecturers under the auspices of the Edinburgh Extra Mural School. Permission had also been granted by the Committee of Management of the Edinburgh Royal Infirmary to allow the women to receive clinical instruction on designated wards, in spite of a petition signed by 500 male undergraduates opposing such a course of action. However, when Sophia and the others attempted to sit the anatomy examination on 18 November they faced a hostile crowd of around 200 male undergraduates, who blocked the entrance to the Royal College of Surgeons. As Sophia put it: 'We walked straight up to the gates . . . when they were slammed in our faces by a number of young men, who stood within, smoking and passing about bottles of whisky, while they abused us in the foulest possible language.'[53] After some further jostling the university janitors managed to obtain access to the anatomical classroom for the women, who by this time were mud-splattered, and the exam proceeded. At the close some Irish students, known as the 'Irish Brigade', escorted them out of the Royal College to safety.

The actions of the male undergraduates brought nationwide condemnation. *The Scotsman* summed up the general feeling of the public towards the Riots when it declared that

> a certain class of medical students are doing their utmost to make the name of medical student synonymous with all that is cowardly and degrading, it is imperative upon all . . . men . . . to come forward and express . . . their detestation of the proceedings which have characterised and dishonoured the opposition to ladies pursuing the study of medicine in Edinburgh.[54]

For her part Sophia remained convinced that the events were less a spontaneous celebration of male prejudice, and more 'a plan deliberately made in the university'.[55] She saw the professors as the main instigators of action as male undergraduates even in mixed classes were on the whole reasonably well behaved except 'when a difficulty was *suggested* to the students'.[56] Sophia was prepared to voice these opinions in public, even if meant risking legal action. At the meeting of subscribers to elect the new Committee of Management of the Edinburgh Royal Infirmary on 2 January 1871 in St Giles' Cathedral, Sophia was incensed at the decision of the meeting not to elect six managers known to be sympathetic to the women's position proposed by the Lord Provost. In an intemperate and over-wrought speech, she claimed that 'Dr Christison's class assistant was one of the leading rioters and the foul language he used could only be excused on the supposition I heard that he was intoxicated'.[57] During the course of her speech she was shouted at, yelled at and had peas thrown at her, and to cap it all the next day she was issued with a writ of libel brought against her by Christison's assistant.

The libel case, which both 'disturbed' and 'shocked' Elizabeth Garrett Anderson,[58] united Sophia's supporters in the Committee for Securing the Complete Medical Education of Women in Edinburgh (CSCMEWE), of which the Lord Provost, Duncan McLaren, was chairman, and included the editor of *The Scotsman*, friendly members of the Medical Faculty, and other 'distinguished' persons, and totalled around a thousand members.[59]

Although the jury found in favour of the 'pursuer', only after the casting vote of the foreman, they awarded the derisory sum of one farthing in damages, but Sophia was forced to bear the legal costs of the trial set at just over £900; a sum that was paid by the Committee after a successful appeal to the public. That was not the end of legal proceedings or attempts by Christison and his allies within the university to expel the women. At a meeting of Senate a motion to recommend to the Court that the 'existing regulation in favour of female students be rescinded' was carried by one vote. A storm of protest was unleashed both by professors in other faculties and the medical and national press whose ferocity forced the Court to reject the recommendation. However, Christison refused point-blank to provide clinical instruction for the women. To overcome this considerable barrier they appealed to the Senate to appoint special university lecturers paid for out of their purses to provide what Christison declined to, or alternatively relax the regulations allowing them to take more classes in the Extra Mural Department than the pro-scribed number of four. The Senate took legal opinion, which found against the women and their demands, and on this advice decided to take no action against Christison or provide alternative arrangements. Sophia and the CSCMEWE challenged the decision and the Lord Advocate and Sheriff Fraser upheld the position of the women and their right to sit pro-fessional examinations and insisted that 'the Professors are bound to teach all persons who present Matriculation tickets to them'.[60]

After receiving a note from the Secretary of the University that she and the others were not permitted to sit the professional examinations in October 1871, Sophia threatened the university with legal action and the authorities caved in. However, an attempt to ensure that the univer-sity 'render it possible for those women who have already commenced their studies to complete them' was lost at Court by a small majority. A few days later the Senate, by a margin of one vote, decided to recom-mend to the Court that the 'existing regulations in favour of female stu-dents be rescinded'.[61] It was not, however, all negative as in 1872 there was one notable landmark victory. After a protracted legal battle with the Edinburgh Royal Infirmary, the women were admitted to the wards on condition that they would be taught separately from males, and only go to those wards to which the physicians invited them. The training was distinctly inferior to that received by male undergraduates, with only three hours set aside for instruction, and few more that were dependent on the whims of the physicians involved, but at least the principle had been accepted. This was unacceptable to the CSCMEWE who began legal proceedings to reverse the decisions arrived at by the university Court and Senate and to put the women on an equal basis with men. If the women were not provided with the necessary instruction to prepare them for their final examinations the Committee stated that it would bring an Action of Declarator against the university. This pushed the university towards a compromise: if the women passed up the right to graduate, they would be provided with instruction and 'certificates of proficiency' should they pass the examinations. Since only possession of a university degree allowed one to practice medicine, these certificates were useless. There was no other course left to Sophia and her supporters other than to bring an Action of Declarator forcing the Senate to 'allow the women to present themselves for a medical degree'.[62]

The Action was heard by the Lord Ordinary, Lord Clifford, in the Court of Session in July 1872 and after hearing the submissions from counsel he declared in favour of the women. Sophia recorded in her diary: 'Substantially the whole cause won for all women, I believe.'[63] Although the women knew that the university was appealing Lord Clifford's decision, they simply concentrated on their work for their final examinations. Then disaster struck in June 1873 when by a majority of seven to five the Inner Court declared that the action of the Senate in 1869 of permitting women to matriculate was illegal. Added to this was a personal catastrophe for Sophia. All the women who sat the final examinations passed – except for her! The failure was in many ways not unsurprising given the weight of canvassing, organisation and petitioning carried by her. This activity was not simply confined to establishing the right of women to receive higher education, but extended also to the issue of political enfranchisement. At the height of the struggles in Edinburgh, Sophia, as one of the finest orators of her time, was invited to address a suffrage meeting in April 1871 in London, to espouse a cause that she was associated with all her life.[64]

At a meeting of the CSCMEWE in October it was decided not to appeal the case to the House of Lords. The doors of the University of Edinburgh had been firmly bolted against women at least for the time being. Although unsuccessful the episode in Edinburgh had not been entirely fruitless, as Sophia pointed out:

There was no 'failure' . . . it was the seed sown in tears in Edinburgh that was reaped in joy elsewhere . . . in view of then prevalent attitude of the [medical] profession, and the underdeveloped state of public opinion at large, it was absolutely requisite that the battle should be fought out somewhere, and that no mere passive policy would have secured (at any rate for many years) the results that have now been won.[65]

The battle had been lost, but as far as she was concerned, not only did she believe the war would eventually be won, but on a personal note she felt that she had been unfairly treated by her examiners and wrote sometime later in 1874 to *The Times* saying so; an action that brought condemnation down on her head from all quarters, including her close allies, such as Isobel Thorne, who wrote to her concerning the 'irreparable' damage done to the cause.[66]

Sophia had already divided her supporters and the women's movement in general with her attack on Elizabeth Garrett Anderson. Elizabeth believed that the Edinburgh years were a 'disastrous failure', and she feared that a similar catastrophe might occur in London should Sophia be allowed her way. Sophia's experience in Edinburgh had convinced her that one of the ways round male prejudice and opposition was to establish an all-women's hospital that would not only care for female patients, but provide the necessary clinical instruction for women to complete their degrees, and she began to raise interest in the project. In a letter to *The Times*, Elizabeth opposed any scheme that might lead women to be educated separately from men as it would inevitably mean separate degrees being awarded and separate registration procedures being implemented, that, she argued, would prejudice the public in favour of male doctors and convince society of the inferior status of women. Women doctors under this scheme would simply be consigned to the bin-end of the medical profession. A far better plan was have women take their degrees abroad and set themselves up in practice as unregistered doctors. Gradually opposition would melt away as the women showed themselves to every bit as capable as men.[67] Sophia poured molten oil on such a suggestion, arguing that studying abroad was more expensive thus putting medicine out of reach for those women from less well-off backgrounds, and that foreign degrees had no legal status in Britain. In contrast, to the gradualism preached by Elizabeth, she advocated a more radical approach that included women teaching women, confrontation with opponents, and a full-scale political campaign to persuade parliament to open the doors of the universities to women.[68]

In many ways this clash over strategy was as much one of character as of ideology. Elizabeth's gradualist approach was in keeping with her reserved and introspective personality, which provided her with few close friends, while Sophia's policy of confrontation was the product of an impulsive, outgoing and warm-hearted personality, which some found over-bearing, but many admired. Elizabeth's influence in the women's movement traded on her own iconic status and success, while Sophia took risks on behalf of others, and suffered public humiliation in

Edinburgh as a result. Elizabeth, who married in 1871, was also convinced that it was possible to have a career and run a home, while Sophia believed that one had to choose between these roles, saying that 'it [is] in most cases undesirable to "serve two masters" . . . and [I] consider those women most wise who deliberately take their choice *either* to marry or devote themselves to a learned profession'.[69] Women obviously took note of Sophia's views since 80 per cent of female doctors in 1911 were unmarried.[70] Moreover, these bruising encounters radicalised Sophia to the point where detachment and patience were rendered impossible, as she made clear some years later:

> when we came in contact with such unexpected depths of moral grossness and brutality, we had burnt into our minds the strongest possible conviction that if such things were possible in the medical profession women must . . . force their way into it, for the sake of their sisters, who might otherwise be left at the mercy of such human brutes as these.[71]

As the action moved from Edinburgh to London that fire was focused in a political direction.

Not all men were 'brutes', and Sophia generously acknowledged from time to time the support given to the cause by men such as Professor Masson, without whose support, she declared, 'our struggle . . . would have been impracticable'.[72] Important cross-party contacts were also developed with sympathetic MPs, such as Russell Gurney, James (later Sir James) Stansfeld and William Cowper-Temple. Sophia worked tirelessly behind the scenes supplying arguments, facts, and even at the request of Cowper-Temple a draft bill,[73] to grant powers to Scottish universities to admit women as students and award them degrees. The bill, which was introduced in the early months of 1874, received tremendous support from the town councils of Aberdeen, Edinburgh and Linlithgow, as well as from 16,000 women who signed a petition pleading for women's rights to medical education, and 471 graduates of London University. Some thirteen professors in the University of Edinburgh gave their support. In all sixty-five petitions in favour of the bill were presented to parliament.[74] As expected Robert Christison and his supporters on the Court and Senate petitioned against the bill, as did the University of Glasgow. The parliamentary opposition used delaying tactics, but the real reason for the failure to make progress was the fall of the Liberal government, which saw the bill sidelined until July 1875 when it was defeated by 196 votes to 153.[75]

Although she received one blow after another, which might have completely demoralised even the most committed members of the cause, each defeat only seemed to strengthen Sophia's resolve. Her faith was important here: the belief that she was 'fighting the battle of the Lord' and that defeat only meant that 'God intended her to try again' helped to steel her will for the conflicts to come.[76] Thus, while parliament procrastinated, Sophia pushed on with her plans to open a hospital for women in London. After a long search for suitable premises she settled on 'a very old fashioned house' in Henrietta Street (later Handel Street), off Brunswick Square, which George IV had kept for one of his many mistresses. Sympathetic medical staff had been recruited prior to this and the London School of Medicine for Women (LSMW) was duly opened on 12 October 1874, with Elizabeth Blackwell and Elizabeth Garrett Anderson 'reluctantly' joining the provisional management committee in order to avoid the public becoming aware of a 'split in the camp'.[77] Of the first fourteen students, twelve had been together in Edinburgh, and although the new hospital faced a number of financial difficulties, its immediate problem was one of recognition. The LSMW had to affiliate to a teaching hospital in order that the students could receive clinical training and they had to be admitted to professional examinations in order to comply with registration requirements. Attempts by the Dean to procure recognition from the nineteen London Examining Bodies were met with one rebuff after another.

However, the drawn-out political wrangling in parliament bore some success with the passing of an Enabling Bill for the United Kingdom and Ireland introduced by Russell Gurney in August 1876, which had the approval of the General Medical Council. The legislation was permissive rather than compulsory in as much as it allowed a university to instruct and examine women for medical degrees, but did not compel them to open their doors to them. Dublin was the first institution to examine women and Edith Pechey successfully passed in September 1876. Better still, the Irish College of Physicians and the Queen's University of Ireland recognised the LSMW in February 1877. In the October of that year both Edith and Sophia, who had already taken the Masters Degree of the University of Berne, Switzerland, successfully presented themselves for examination and along with three other of the Edinburgh women were added to the Register of the General Medical Council. On passing her degree examinations at Dublin, Sophia became a Licentiate of King's and Queen's College of Physicians, Ireland and immediately wrote to her mother appending her victorious signature 'Sophia Jex-Blake, M.D.L.K.Q.C.P.I.'[78] However, their clinical training was completed while in Edinburgh; for those students of the LSMW such instruction was still proving problematic and this had a demoralising impact on them and the staff. It was only due to the perseverance of James Stansfeld that a solution was found to break the impasse. In February 1877 at a chance meeting he convinced the chairman of the governing body of the Royal Free Hospital to accept the women students for clinical training on payment of an annual income of not less than £400 and a subsidy of 300 guineas.[79] The following year the University of London agreed to admit women to all degree courses, including medicine.

However, as in the aftermath of most struggles when victory has been all but won, differences become more apparent than solidarities, and in this sense the battle for medical education suffered no different an outcome to that of many other social and political movements. Sophia, whom James Stansfeld recognised as making the 'greatest of all contributions to the end attained',[80] desired the newly created position of organising secretary in the LSMW, but at the executive meeting to discuss the appointment, Elizabeth Garrett Anderson was also proposed for the position. To avoid a split Isobel Thorne was selected, an outcome that Sophia accepted with good grace, saying she was 'about the best possible, with her temper and excellent sense, so much better than I'.[81] But the sense of disappointment, although well hidden, was obvious and she left London and the LSMW in 1878 for, of all places, Edinburgh, where she took a house in Manor Place and set up a practice and a small dispensary with beds for five patients. Insult was added to injury when in 1883 Elizabeth was appointed Dean of the LSMW and Sophia's nominee, Edith Pechey, failed to find anyone to second her nomination. Given that Elizabeth had strongly argued and canvassed against Sophia's proposal for an all-woman hospital it was a hurtful and insensitive appointment that paid little respect to the heroic efforts of Sophia in establishing the LSMW. The final parting of the ways came in 1897 when she resigned as a trustee of the hospital, after an acrimonious exchange of letters with Isobel Thorne, over re-building plans that she argued had been approved of by the executive council without proper costing and without the financial resources to underwrite the scheme.[82]

By this time Sophia's practice in Edinburgh was thriving. She wrote to her mother saying that after only a short time in practice 'I just completed my first £50 – earned in . . . less than three months . . . I have had 23 patients (nearly 100 visits) at my private house, and about as many more at my Dispensary which has only been open a fortnight.'[83] By the end of the year she had treated 574 patients. However, the practice had to be given up temporarily. In the spring of 1881 her mother's health began to deteriorate and in late June it took a turn for the worse. For ten days and nights Sophia was in constant attendance at her bedside in

Rugby, where her son Tom was headmaster. She passed away on 8 July and the impact of this on Sophia was profound. As she put it: 'No human being loses what I do in her.'[84] Attempts to commune with her dead mother were made by Sophia, lying awake at night 'concentrating every faculty on the effort. But I got no response.'[85] The house in Manor Place, where her mother had spent half her time since 1878, was sold and she bought a 'roomy, rambling old house', Bruntsfield Lodge, on the south side of the city, with her constant companion, Ursula Du Pré, and from there built up her practice once more. Sophia also became involved in local political activity, organising a few large suffrage meetings and taking part in canvassing and propaganda work on behalf of women candidates for poor law guardianships. In 1884 she wrote a book, *The Care of Infants*, which laid the basis for her more ambitious work, *Medical Women*, published in 1886. Work had become a surrogate for continuing grief, and the volume of activity was greatly increased with the decision by the Edinburgh and Glasgow Colleges of Physicians and Surgeons to admit women to examinations (Edinburgh in 1884 and Glasgow in 1885). This led Sophia to embark on an equally bold plan for the establishment of a similar hospital to the one she had played a leading role in founding in London – the Edinburgh School of Medicine for Women (ESMW).

During the early 1870s Louisa Stevenson and Ursula Du Pré had bought the old medical school in Surgeons' Square, which was where Professor Robert Knox (infamous in the late 1820s for buying corpses from the murderers Burke and Hare for his anatomy class) and several other medical luminaries had lectured. It was quickly restored to its old purpose and became the new ESMW. Arrangements were also made with Leith hospital to provide the women students with clinical training and the School opened its doors to students in the autumn of 1886. From the outset the School's financial position was unstable and, in spite of a resident secretary and a caretaker, the day-to-day running fell increasingly on Sophia, who was not only running her practice, but also was lecturing in the Extra Mural School of the University of Edinburgh, the first woman to do so, on midwifery. 'For a year or two everyone was happy', wrote Margaret Todd, 'then the clash of temperaments came.'[86] Sophia's fiery temper and single-mindedness were well known, but over time she added a splash of authoritarianism, particularly in her dealings with students, and an autocratic attitude to those whom she considered below herself. Sophia's quite old-fashioned understanding of discipline and deference brought her into conflict with some of her older and more outspoken students, which led to the Cadell sisters, Grace and Martha, who were among the first students to enrol, bringing an action for breach of contract against the ESMW in 1889.

Under the agreement with Leith hospital the women were allowed on the wards in the afternoon but had to clear the premises by 5 p.m. Four of the women contravened this regulation by staying on a little longer and this produced a letter of complaint from the hospital's Lady Superintendent. Sophia ordered them to apologise, which they all did, but two days later thirty-year-old Martha Cadell withdrew her apology, although she promised not to infringe the regulations again. Sophia warned Martha that unless she changed her course of action she would not admit her to the School in the 1888–9 session. According to Sophia, Martha and Grace continued 'to show a spirit of insubordination and discontent in a variety of ways' and concluded that if 'the good discipline and order of the school were to be maintained' they 'must cease attendance at the school'.[87] The action for £500 in damages was heard in the First Division of the Court of Session and the outcome did not reflect well on Sophia. The judges remarked on her high-handedness and her demand of unquestioning obedience, and that she 'had forgotten that . . . [she] could not treat grown up people as . . . [she] might treat children'.[88] They also found that in her dealings with one student, Miss Sinclair, who had been humiliated in front of the class and charged by Sophia with 'improper and dishonourable conduct' for merely asking an examiner to review her failed paper in the light of her illness, she was unreasonable and unjust. Lord Kyllachy found in favour of the sisters and awarded them £50 in damages plus costs.

The dissatisfaction of the Cadell sisters and some other students, including Elsie Inglis and Moira Geddes, the niece of Elizabeth Garrett Anderson, led to the foundation of a rival school for medicine for women – the Scottish Association for the Medical Education of Women – in January 1890 funded mainly by Elsie Inglis' father and his friends. Sophia's attitude to the rival school was nothing less than hostile and her dealings with it showed her to be bitter and spiteful: the radical had turned reactionary. Sophia use her influence to prevent Leith hospital from providing clinical training for the students of the Scottish Association, which prompted the chairman to remark at the first general meeting:

> The Scottish Association applied for permission for its pupils to study in the Leith hospital, and the application was opposed by Miss Jex Blake's school . . . What a delightful comment this is upon the denunciation of doctors, indulged in by Miss Jex Blake herself, long years ago . . . She has now a monopoly in the Leith hospital, and though there are women studying medicine in another school than hers, who wish to have access to that Hospital

for clinical training, she refuses to let them have admission to it. The consistency of this is not remarkable; still less prominent is the desire it shows for helping women to the services of women doctors, and helping women to become women doctors. Years ago, the demand for this was based, partly on philanthropic considerations. Now these are to be set aside, and a monopoly being established at the Leith Hospital, it is maintained against sisters who are knocking at the door and seeking for admission.[89]

The Scottish Association's students achieved what Sophia failed to: admittance to the wards of the Edinburgh Royal Infirmary. The rival school's numbers swelled as the ESMW's dwindled. A bequest from Dr Henry Muirhead in 1889 to Queen Margaret College, Glasgow, for the 'education of women by women' in medicine put even more pressure on the School by siphoning off students from the west of Scotland.[90] In 1892 an act of parliament opened the universities to women and after twenty-five years of struggle the Court of the University of Edinburgh in October 1894 declared its determination to admit women forthwith to graduation in medicine. By 1898, with little or no students, Sophia had no option but to close the school doors and admit defeat.

After a driving tour during the autumn of 1898 of around 1,100 miles through the south-east counties of England in search of a retirement home, Sophia finally found one – Windydene – near the village of Mark Cross, on the Forest Ridge of Sussex, five or six miles south of Tunbridge Wells. It was here that she spent the next fourteen years of her life. She busied herself in her garden and dairy, but still found time to write and campaign on behalf of women's suffrage. She never, according to Todd, became 'restless or impatient over the long delay', but was uncomfortable with the militancy of the Suffragettes and plans for tax-resistance, although she 'admitted that they had given the cause a prominence that nothing else could have'.[91] In July 1910 she wrote a stiff reply to a letter by Octavia Hill in The Times opposing the extension of the franchise to women, although the paper refused to publish it. She passed it to Octavia in any case, but it was greeted with stony silence.[92] Sophia also wrote letters intended to raise public awareness of the dangers of the motor car. She complained about the 'reign of terror' inflicted on the law-abiding majority by a minority with a 'craze for rapid motion'. She called, quite presciently, for the building of special roads 'at the expense of the motorists, where the risks would be limited to their own fraternity'.[93]

All this was carried on despite evidence of failing health. In the letter to Octavia she referred to her lameness and rheumatism that confined her pretty much to Windydene. Indeed, since she had suffered her first heart attack in Edinburgh (sometime in the late 1890s) her health had been increasingly giving cause for concern. The heart attacks began recurring and in 1901–2 she suffered from a mysterious growth which was life-threatening and involved an operation. She had a new lease of life and went on for another ten years until her death on 7 January 1912. Sophia was buried in Rotherfield Church, in Sussex, coincidentally just a few yards from her former ally, James Stansfeld.

Prior to her departure from Edinburgh a farewell reception had been held, which included the great and the good of Edinburgh society. Professor Masson moved a resolution that mentioned her pioneering work in opening up the medical profession to women and congratulated her 'on the present success everywhere of the cause'.[94] Four years earlier the women of the defunct National Association for the Medical Education of Women met in November for the last time and in an address signed by, among others, Eliza Wigham, Elizabeth Pease Nichol and Louisa Stevenson, expressed their 'appreciation of the great sacrifice you have made of time, and strength, and money, to win for younger women . . . a complete medical education crowned by a degree'.[95] The triumphalism of these farewells to Sophia implied that the struggle was over and that victory had been achieved. There is some compelling evidence to support this optimistic assessment of women's position at the turn of the century. The number of women matriculated in medicine at Glasgow University doubled in twenty years, from 58 in 1893–4 to 109 in 1913–14,[96] and by 1914 over 1,000 women had graduated from the University of Edinburgh.[97] For the Scottish universities as a whole, research shows that the number of females as a percentage of the total number of undergraduates was growing at a remarkable rate:

Table 4.1 *Women as a percentage of the total number of undergraduates in Scottish universities at selected dates*

University	1894–5	1907–8
Aberdeen	4.5	31.0
St Andrews	17.5	40.0
Glasgow	9.1	24.0
Edinburgh	8.6	18.0

[Source: L. Moore. 'The Scottish universities and women students, 1862–1892', in J. J. Carter and D. J. Worthington (eds), *Scottish Universities: Distinctiveness and Diversity* (Edinburgh, 1992), p. 145]

However, in spite of strong evidence of progress, it has to be remembered that the legislation of 1892 was 'enabling' rather than 'compulsory' and that none of the Scottish universities made provision for women in divinity or law. Even in medicine barriers still existed to full recognition, in spite of the legislation. The University of Edinburgh held out against recognising medical women as full members of the university until 1916; before this date they were forced to attend most of their classes in the School of Extra-Mural Studies. They were also prevented from experiencing the total range of social activities. For example, female medical students were classed as 'visitors' when attending the Edinburgh University Women's Debating Society, as the Senate would only recognise the Society if membership was restricted to matriculated students.[98] There was also the issue of mixed classes. By the end of the first decade of the twentieth century women at the University of Glasgow were still being taught in separate classes in chemistry, anatomy, embryology, surgery, the practice of medicine and all clinical subjects.[99] The voluntary hospitals, particularly in Glasgow, remained equally discriminatory. The Western, Royal Infirmary and the Victoria Infirmary all refused to accept female residents; in fact, the only voluntary hospital in the city to accept women was the Royal, although not until 1899. The Western only accepted women to clinical instruction in 1920, and did not appoint them to resident posts until the Second World War.[100] Thus, women doctors were farmed out to the less prestigious Poor Law hospitals and maternity units. Even here in matters of promotion women were discriminated against with none achieving the coveted position of Parochial Medical Officer, who was responsible for the distribution of outdoor relief.[101] The principle of equality may have been established, but the attitudes of male doctors remained less egalitarian and more misogynist. Even after the Second World War the London teaching hospitals were still closed to women. Any success women achieved in hospital medicine after 1914 was, as Wendy Alexander pointed out, 'in female or female dominated institutions or in . . . female specialities',[102] and it was really only in the 1960s that a notable and significant change in perceptions in medicine and society as a whole began to occur.[103]

Sophia Jex-Blake and her determination to succeed where others had failed made possible what progress occurred in the field of medical education for women. It was her sacrifices, her hard work, and single-mindedness that galvanised sympathetic opinion and support in the country, and which finally convinced the government that a change in the law was both necessary and essential. None of this would have been possible if she had not had the money to pursue this aspiration. It was money supplied to her by her mother, and by influential women in Edinburgh society, that allowed Sophia and the others, some of whose fees she paid, to undertake the long and rocky road to graduation and qualification as a doctor. On the way, she made a great many friends, but an equal number of enemies, and not just among the males of the medical profession. Her self-righteousness, her uncompromising manner, her lack of consideration for human frailty,[104] annoyed, divided and frustrated even her most loyal supporters, and Sophia ended up an overlooked and somewhat isolated figure. In spite of the fact that she achieved more for women in the field of medicine than Florence Nightingale did, it is 'the Lady with the Lamp' that has been awarded heroic status in national popular consciousness. The difference lay in the fact that Sophia challenged in a fundamental way perceived notions of femininity, while Florence as ministering angel merely confirmed them.

Sophia's attempts to revolutionise medicine were also linked to other demands for civil and political rights for women and this also brought opposition from a wide range of opinion. However, although she consistently campaigned for the franchise for women, she did not always support social reforms in the interest of women. Her relationship, for instance, with Josephine Butler reached breaking point in 1869 when she refused to support her campaign against the Contagious Diseases Act of 1864, which allowed for the compulsory medical examination of women suspected by non-uniformed police of being prostitutes, in spite of the fact that Butler's petition tied the issue to the need for women doctors.[105] Sophia argued that repeal might be detrimental to public health and this was more important an issue than an increase in the arbitrary powers of the police over women.[106] She was also opposed to married women becoming doctors and as such in an unintended way promoted domesticity and underscored the traditional role of women as wives and mothers. It was never clear as to how women from less affluent backgrounds were to become doctors, as far as Sophia was concerned they only benefited from the struggle by being allowed treatment by their own sex. Her position in the social structure prevented her from embracing more egalitarian policies based on the redistribution of wealth. Sophia looked down on men from the lower rungs of the social ladder, describing those students who took part in the Surgeons' Hall Riots as of 'a low social class',[107] and labouring men and their children as 'uncouth'; at the same time, she dismissed the 'programme of socialism' as 'unworkable' and contrary to human nature.[108] Her beliefs were driven by her experience of gender in its most discriminatory form and, perhaps, her sexuality. Female emancipation lay in the construction of a gender-free meritocracy in which power and privilege was amended but fundamentally unchallenged. In spite of its shortcomings as a social philosophy, its articulation put Sophia somewhat in advance of middle-class opinion and led to disputes within the women's movement (which in the case of Elizabeth Garrett Anderson was as much personal as ideological) over what was the best way forward in dealing with the intransigency of a misogynist society. This dilemma between direct action and passive resistance has continued to divide and disunite feminist movements throughout the world, but it is clear that without that bold and fearless step into the socially unknown by Sophia, women in Britain would have waited much longer to achieve some form of parity with men in the field of higher education. Thus, for all her faults and limitations, one can hardly disagree with Edith Pechey when she said that 'all we have done in opening up the medical profession to women was mainly due to Sophia Jex-Blake, who had got all the abuse because she had done all the work'.[109]

NOTES

1. Todd, *The Life of Sophia Jex-Blake* (London, 1918), p. vii. Almost all references to letters and extracts from her diary are taken from Todd, since all the personal papers were destroyed on Sophia's instruction after the biography was published.
2. F. Balfour, *Ne Obliviscaris. Dinna Forget*, vol. I (London, 1930), p. 120.
3. N. Walter, *The New Feminism* (London, 1998); N. Walter (ed.), *On the Move: Feminism and the Next Generation* (London, 1999); A. Coote and B. Campbell, *Sweet Freedom: the Struggle for Women's Liberation* (Oxford, 1987); L. Segal, *Is the Future Female? Troubled Thoughts on Contemporary Feminism* (London, 1987).
4. S. Roberts, *Sophia Jex-Blake: a Woman Pioneer in Nineteenth Century Medical Reform* (London, 1993), p. 6.
5. Roberts, *Sophia*, p. 8.
6. Todd, *The Life*, p. 2.
7. Diary extract 26 January 1858, quoted in Todd, *The Life*, p. 58.
8. Quoted in Todd, *The Life*, p. 48.
9. E. Moberly Bell, *Storming the Citadel: the Rise of the Woman Doctor* (London, 1953), pp. 62–3.
10. Quoted in Todd, *The Life*, p. 30.
11. Quoted in Todd, *The Life*, p. 33.
12. Moberly Bell, *Storming*, p. 64.
13. Quoted in Moberly Bell, *Storming*, p. 65.
14. Diary extract 10 January 1858, quoted in Todd, *The Life*, p. 56.
15. Diary extract 26 January 1860, quoted in Todd, *The Life*, p. 84.
16. Quoted in E. Moberly Bell, *Octavia Hill: a Biography* (London, 1942), p. 52.

17. Diary extract 10 January 1858, quoted in Todd, *The Life*, p. 56.
18. Quoted in Todd, *The Life*, p. 65.
19. Diary extract 26 January 1858, quoted in Todd, *The Life*, p. 58.
20. Quoted in Todd, *The Life*, p. 86.
21. Quoted in Moberly Bell, *Octavia*, p. 54.
22. Quoted in Todd, *The Life*, p. 95.
23. Todd, *The Life*, p. 94.
24. Roberts, *Sophia*, p. 42.
25. Quoted in Roberts, *Sophia*, p. 59.
26. S. Jex-Blake, *Medical Women: a Thesis and a History* (Edinburgh, 1886 edn), pp. 157–8.
27. Letter 24 November 1866, quoted in Todd, *The Life*, p. 173.
28. Letter to Mrs Jex-Blake, 27 November 1866, quoted in Todd, *The Life*, p. 174.
29. *The Times*, 22 September 1896.
30. Roberts, *Sophia*, p. 95.
31. Quoted in Todd, *The Life*, p. 190.
32. Letter to Mrs Jex-Blake, 13 November 1868, quoted in Todd, *The Life*, p. 205.
33. Todd, *The Life*, p. 208.
34. J. Geyer-Kordesch and R. Ferguson, *Blue Stockings, Black Gowns, White Coats: a Brief History of Women Entering Higher Education and the Medical Profession in Scotland* (Glasgow, 1996), p. 22.
35. S. Jex-Blake, 'Medicine as a profession for women', J. Butler (ed.), *Women's Work and Women's Culture* (London, 1869), pp. 80–120.
36. C. Blake, *The Charge of the Parasols: Women's Entry to the Medical Profession* (London, 1990), p. 94.
37. Roberts, *Sophia*, p. 36.
38. L. Moore, 'The Scottish universities and women students, 1862–1892', in J. J. Carter and D. J. Worthington (eds), *Scottish Universities: Distinctiveness and Diversity* (Edinburgh, 1992), p. 140.
39. Geyer-Kordesch and Ferguson, *Blue Stockings*, p. 37.
40. Quoted in S. Hamilton, 'The first generations of university women', in G. Donaldson (ed.), *Four Centuries: Edinburgh University Life, 1583–1983* (Edinburgh, 1983), p. 102.
41. Blake, *Parasols*, p. 97.
42. Moberly Bell, *Storming*, p. 68.
43. Diary extracts 1 and 4 July 1869, quoted in Todd, *The Life*, p. 258.
44. Moberly Bell, *Storming*, p. 73.
45. Roberts, *Sophia*, p. 96.
46. Roberts, *Sophia*, p. 99.
47. Roberts, *Sophia*, p. 95.
48. *Lancet*, 18 June 1870.
49. Jex-Blake, *Medical Women*, p. 83.

50. Jex-Blake, *Medical Women*, p. 111.
51. Quoted in Todd, *The Life*, p. 298.
52. *The Scotsman*, 13 July 1871.
53. Jex-Blake, *Medical Women*, p. 92.
54. *The Scotsman*, 22 November 1870.
55. Jex-Blake, *Medical Women*, p. 94.
56. Jex-Blake, *Medical Women*, p. 158–9.
57. *The Scotsman*, 3 January 1871.
58. Moberly Bell, *Storming*, p. 86.
59. Moberly Bell, *Storming*, p. 79.
60. Quoted in Todd, *The Life*, p. 332.
61. Quoted in Moberly Bell, *Storming*, pp. 80–1.
62. Moberly Bell, *Storming*, p. 81.
63. Quoted in Todd, *The Life*, p. 373.
64. Todd, *The Life*, p. 297.
65. Jex-Blake, *Medical Women*, pp. vii–viii.
66. Todd, *The Life*, p.418; *The Times*, 20 June 1874.
67. *The Times*, 5 August 1873.
68. *The Times*, 23 August 1873.
69. Jex-Blake, *Medical Women*, p. 212.
70. Blake, *Parasols*, p. 160.
71. Jex-Blake, *Medical Women*, p. 136.
72. *The Times*, 12 October 1907.
73. Anon., 'Sophia Jex-Blake', in *Dictionary of National Biography, 1912–1921* (London, 1927), p. 298.
74. Jex-Blake, *Medical Women*, pp. 172–3.
75. Roberts, *Sophia*, p. 149.
76. Todd, *The Life*, p. 398.
77. Letter to Elizabeth Garrett Anderson, 21 August 1874, quoted in Roberts, *Sophia*, p. 146.
78. Blake, *Parasols*, p. 185.
79. Moberly Bell, *Storming*, p. 102.
80. *Nineteenth Century*, July 1877.
81. Quoted in Todd, *The Life*, p. 448.
82. Letters, 2, 25, 30 June 1897, Sophia Jex-Blake Collection, Royal Free Hospital Archive, London.
83. Quoted in Todd, *The Life*, p. 460.
84. Quoted in Todd, *The Life*, p. 473.
85. Quoted in Todd, *The Life*, pp. 474–5.
86. Todd, *The Life*, p. 499.
87. *The Scotsman*, 9 March 1889.
88. *The Scotsman*, 24 October 1889.
89. *The Scotsman*, 7 February 1891.
90. Geyer-Kordesch and Ferguson, *Blue Stockings*, p. 45.

91. Todd, *The Life*, p. 532.
92. Todd, *The Life*, p. 538.
93. *The Times*, 25 September 1909.
94. Todd, *The Life*, p. 524.
95. Quoted in Todd, *The Life*, p. 510.
96. W. Alexander, *First Ladies of Medicine: the Origins, Education and Destination of Early Women Medical Graduates of Glasgow University* (Glasgow, 1987), p. 11.
97. Hamilton, 'First generations', p. 113.
98. Hamilton, 'First generations', pp. 103–9.
99. Alexander, *First Ladies*, p. 28.
100. Alexander, *First Ladies*, p. 41.
101. Alexander, *First Ladies*, p. 54.
102. Alexander, *First Ladies*, p. 63.
103. Geyer-Kordesch and Ferguson, *Blue Stockings*, p. 54.
104. Todd, *The Life*, p. 490.
105. A. Bashford, *Purity and Pollution: Gender, Embodiment and Victorian Medicine* (Baskingstoke, 1998), p. 97.
106. Moberly Bell, *Storming*, p. 88.
107. Jex-Blake, *Medical Women*, p. 157.
108. Quoted in Todd, *The Life*, p. 534.
109. Quoted in Todd, *The Life*, p. 424.

5

Lady Frances Balfour: The Radical Aristocrat

Frances (née Campbell) Balfour, the tenth child of the Duke and Duchess of Argyll, was a snob, albeit a very courageous one, but a snob nevertheless. Her breeding and education instilled in her a strong sense of social superiority that manifested itself in her disdain for those below her and in the many acid comments made to both friends and enemies alike. As her daughter, Blanche, once remarked: 'She lived on her friendships . . . and by her letter writing she killed them more than once.'[1] But her insensitive and overbearing manner was in reality a cloak that hid a deep sense of inferiority. This derived from her physical appearance. Short, with a limp, Frances was acutely aware from an early age that she would never have the physical stature expected of females of the upper classes. Indeed, if anything she looked more like a rather bad-tempered female head teacher than a member of the patrician class. She also failed to conform to the social and political roles laid out for women of her class, acting as a proselytiser in elite circles for a very unpopular cause in the late nineteenth and early twentieth century – women's suffrage. Frances was one of a small band of brave women of privilege who were prepared to face social ostracism by actively engaging in the female suffrage campaign, speaking at meetings, lobbying her influential male relatives, such as her brother-in-law and Tory prime minister, Arthur J. Balfour (1902–5), writing to the press and generally haranguing anyone prepared to debate the issue with her. She was also a Liberal married (unhappily) into one of the leading Conservative families in Britain. Thus, in spite of her impressive social pedigree and political connections, Frances was never quite at ease with her surroundings. Even her presence on the platform of the women's suffrage movement was of ambiguous benefit: bestowing, on one level, a measure of respectability and, on the other, confirming in the minds of many working-class men and women that the struggle was essentially one concerned with votes for rich women, of further privileging the already privileged. However, regardless of how one views her impact on the suffrage campaign, there is no doubt that in many ways her experiences personalise the unfolding drama of the long quest for women's political rights in nineteenth- and early twentieth-century Britain.

Frances was born at Argyll Lodge, Kensington, London in 1858, and although raised in comfort, she had a miserable childhood. Emotionally repressed and physically disabled, she endured many years of pain. Frances speaks bitterly of her childhood being 'blighted' by a disease of the hip that left her strapped up in heavy wooden splints and prostrate for long periods. For fear of having her leg 'cut off', she was uncomplaining in spite of the 'great physical pain'. Her stoicism was seen as heroic by parents who barely comprehended their child's torture. But, then again, the Argyll children were not expected to cry or show emotion except for a 'real cause', and since most causes were false, tears were only permitted at the death of a loved family pet.[2] The emotional repression of her childhood meant that as an adult Frances was unable to express her deeper sentiments verbally to anyone. Only through letter writing could she 'reveal depths of feeling and sympathy'.[3] However, gradually the lameness began to disappear, but she was left with one leg longer than the other, which resulted in her having to wear a built-up shoe to prevent her walking on tiptoes. Frances freely admits that her pugnacious character was born of these early struggles and suffering.[4]

Her parents were deeply religious. The mother, Lady Elizabeth Leveson Gower, was the daughter of the Duchess of Sutherland and, although brought up in the Anglican Church, when she married Argyll she joined the Church of Scotland and took her first 'Scotch communion' at Roseneath in 1844. As time wore on she became rather otherworldly, associating herself with all sorts of weird and wonderful religious causes and divines. As Frances says, 'My mother and her family were essentially in the world, but not of it.'[5] Her father, George Douglas Campbell, the eighth Duke of Argyll, was equally devout, but less drawn to mysticism. As a result of the Disruption of 1843 in the Church of Scotland, he moved his political allegiance from the Tories to the Whigs.[6] Brought up in such circumstances it came as no surprise that the older Frances embraced Christianity and the Church of Scotland with an almost Jesuit-like enthusiasm. In a letter written in May 1894, she described herself as the 'handmaiden of the Church of Scotland'.[7] As Dr Norman MacLean perceptively noted in his obituary, for Frances the 'one great, all-controlling love in her life to which everything was subservient . . . was her love for Scotland and the Scottish Church', and to her the 'Church of Scotland was . . . the very soul of Scotland'. Such was her devotion to the church that she never missed a General Assembly, ensconced in her reserved seat in the Throne Gallery.[8] On a practical note, she personally collected money for the restoration of the Crown Court Church in London, which formerly was the place of worship of the Scottish Ambassador prior to the Union of the Crowns in 1603. Her husband, Eustace, a trained architect, oversaw the work. Frances' devotion was also shown in the education of her children: the only aspect of it that she personally saw to on a systematic basis was the 'learning by heart of the metrical version of certain psalms and paraphrases of the Church of Scotland'.[9] Although devout, it was a highly sectarian form of Presbyterianism she practised with little tolerance of other faiths. Arthur Balfour had to use his considerable powers of persuasion, when she presented *The Last Sleep of Argyle* to the General Assembly of the Church of Scotland, not to have the martyr's last words inscribed on the frame: 'I die not only as a Protestant, but with a heart hatred of Popery, Prelacy and all superstition whatsoever.'[10] Her religion was matched by her morals. When she caught Blanche playing backgammon with Hugo Elcho at Whittingehame, the family home of the Balfours in East Lothian, for half-a-crown, she 'shook with fury, and unleashed an epic scene, culminating in a peroration about the wages of sin'.[11] Frances loathed gambling and any other vices that were condemned morally by the church. Rather eccentrically, she refused to attend the theatre or read a play; even Shakespeare was avoided as morally dubious.[12]

Her upbringing also instilled in her a strong sense that the role of the landed elite in society was to inspire the lower orders by exemplary social conduct and to provide them with political leadership; something that centuries of breeding and experience, she felt, had especially equipped them to do. As Frances put it: 'Great territorial wealth implied great responsibilities towards those who lived on the land . . . they (the landowners) were the recognised leaders in many spheres of life, and leadership and statesmanship was in their blood and race.'[13] In response to Labour's demands in the 1920s to nationalise the land, she defended the right of hereditary ownership, saying:

> To be the owner of land, is to be 'useless' in the eyes of Labour today. They will soon have destroyed ownership, and it will become a thing of the past, but what they divide among those who clamour to despoil and possess, will lack all that has built up this great and unique country. It is because the Patriarchs had traditions and inherited a sense of the responsibilities of their position that the traditions as yet hold together.[14]

This principled society did not have any regard for 'American dollars or . . . the charms of the chorus girl' and '"*Noblesse oblige*" was the unspoken code of its manner'.[15] Although rooted in Tory paternalism, in which the rich had a duty to the poor, it was nevertheless an extremely snobbish and exclusive society as the only point of entry was genetic. Frances heavily criticised new, mainly American, wealth for introducing crass forms of materialism into polite society, claiming it had turned Cannes, her holiday destination, 'into a vast Casino, crowded with painted harridans and loafing foreigners: the parasite Americans in those days kept to Nice and Monte Carlo'.[16] Even her political allies in parliament were looked down on. Balfour described the Liberal MP for Coventry from 1874–84, H. M. Jackson, later Lord Allerton, as 'a rough, self-made man, no gentleman and his women folk are absolutely common'.[17] She was equally dismissive of the lower classes, frequently referring to them as the 'mob' and highly critical of their manners and dress. She once snobbishly remarked on 'the ungainly carriage of the multitude', and argued that what distinguished them from their betters was 'deportment': 'a way to behave which differed from the mob'.[18]

Balfour's belief in the superiority of landed society over other forms of social organisation was also influenced to a large extent by her disdain for city life. Although she spent a great deal of her adult life in London, Balfour viewed the city and its inhabitants as essentially corrupt and degraded. Poverty and squalor and disease were rife, young people, particularly from the Highlands, were led astray and social relationships had degenerated into impersonal and brutal forms. Glasgow for her encompassed in one chaotic and sprawling space the extremes of the social consequences of rapid and unplanned urban growth, as she put it:

> Glasgow the greatest and most noisome of the cities of Scotland. There, even thirty years ago, Labour and Capital were in ceaseless antagonism, there great wealth and the most abject poverty were in visible contrast . . . The best of our Highland blood has for generations poured into Glasgow, only to fall victims to whisky and TB, and the people bred in pure air and decent conditions, have not long stood in crowded dwellings of this pestilential city.[19]

Her Christianity and social ideals were given political expression in her membership of the Liberal party. As we have seen, the Argyll family had transferred its political allegiances from the Tories to the Whigs after the Disruption and their home became the haunt of Liberal politicians and radical thinkers. Frances remembers as a child William Gladstone, leader of the Liberals, David Livingstone, the famous missionary, Garibaldi, the Italian nationalist, and John Bright, one time leader of the Anti-Corn Law League and Liberal MP, all visiting the family home and endlessly discussing politics with her father. This highly charged political atmosphere consumed the young Frances and, notwithstanding her religious devotion, politics became her abiding passion. As Blanche remarked: 'Conversation, especially on politics, was to her like brandy to a drunkard.'[20] However, her first formal contact with the political world was knitting woolly garments for children of freed slaves in America. Emancipation of the slaves was the great radical cause of the nineteenth century: 'A passion of the purest and highest belief in the heart of my home,'[21] claimed Balfour. Legions of men and women in Britain had for some time campaigned to end American slavery, but only after a bloody and brutal civil war was this achieved in 1863. Although radicals everywhere heralded Emancipation, its achievement simply reinforced the views of female activists that the issue of political rights was not simply a question of colour but also of sex. The political connection was all too obvious. As Balfour stated,

> the subjection of any race or nation, be they black or white, male or female, was a thing against the laws of God and man. I hold the belief that the American Civil War . . . set the civilised world seriously to think, whether the inequality of sex, could be as little defended as slave-holding.[22]

However, serious engagement with the world of politics was placed to one side for the moment. There were far more important things to do, such as come out, find a husband and have children. In this quest, Frances was somewhat at a disadvantage given her disability, confessing in her memoirs, that she had a 'morbid belief that my lameness . . . would prevent my ever marrying'. As such Frances could not dance and she hated the 'coming out' balls that only served to emphasise her disability, although she realised this was the only possible way of finding a husband.[23] And find a husband she did. At a ball given by Lord and Lady Goschen at their home in Portland Place, London, she met Eustace Balfour. The courtship and marriage was rushed through at such a pace that even her father was shocked. The wedding took place at Frances' insistence in St John's Presbyterian Church in London in 1879. The whole affair was modest and somewhat dowdy out of respect to the memory of Balfour's mother who had died the year before. There was no best man's speech and no sit-down meal, although Gladstone did attend. There was also no honeymoon and the couple simply retired to the Balfours' family home before spending their first year of married life on Arthur's Strathconan estate in Ross-shire. This was the first time Frances had stayed for any length of time in a Highland county outside Argyllshire. Perhaps, the rather sad affair of the wedding was symptomatic of what was to come. The marriage was unhappy, in spite of producing five children (three boys and two girls). Eustace had a liking for strong drink and by 1910 he was a confirmed alcoholic. He died shortly after this in February 1911. Neither Balfour, in her autobiography, or her daughter, in her memoirs, makes very much of their relationship with Eustace. Blanche mentions her father on only seven occasions in a book that runs to 190 pages. All she reveals is his profession, architect, and his friendship with the Pre-Raphaelite artists, William Morris and Edward Burne-Jones. Eustace it seems played very little part in his children's upbringing and, for Blanche at least, he remains a distant, shadowy figure. He fairs little better in Frances' rambling account of her life and times, only his architecture and funeral being referred to towards the end of the second volume; indeed, he is almost airbrushed out of her life as she spends page after page detailing her relationship with his brother Arthur, whom she 'far preferred to Eustace'.[24]

Frances found married life unstimulating as there was very little to do outside the domestic and the normal philanthropic work expected from rich women. She enjoyed her relationship with Burne-Jones and his wife, Georgina, declaring that she had 'fallen a complete prey to the Pre-Raphaelite Art', but it was not enough for Frances. As she put it:

> When I first wished to take up some form of work there was very little in England that was outside the scope of what used to be called 'Church work'. Women were not asked to do any political work, there were no Local Bodies on which they might sit, they were not even permitted to be guardians of the poor, only men were capable of dealing with the nurseries of the State and the poverty or lapses of young women.[25]

Her first foray into organised political life, rather surprisingly given her Liberal beliefs, was to join the Primrose League established by the Conservatives to interest women in politics. However, she soon left to become a member of the Women's Liberal Unionist Association (WLUA). Balfour was also involved in various charitable bodies, which doubled as forums for discussing women's issues and building up invaluable social networks of similarly minded upper- and middle-class women on the suffrage question. The first committee she served on was the Working Ladies Guild, an organisation dedicated to alleviating poverty among 'gentle women', that is, women of the middle class that had been left unprovided for and could only look forward to low-paid employment as a governess and an impoverished old age. Balfour's interest in the position of women was further enhanced by her involvement with the Traveller's Aid Society (TAS). Its establishment was influenced by the Evangelical revival of the mid-1880s in London. Under the leadership of the social reformer William Stead, the TAS offered protection to young women who might have otherwise fallen into prostitution. Another organisation she was associated with all her life was the National Council for Women (NCW) formed in 1895 to look after the care of young working girls. However, realising that their poverty was associated with the kind of employment they took and the high levels of exploitation and danger they were exposed to, small groups – Unions of Women Workers – were formed to improve their situation in the workplace. By 1918 there were 126 branches and 156 affiliated societies of the NCW.[26] While working with TAS, Balfour came in contact with Miss Jenner, the daughter of William Jenner, Queen Victoria's physician, and her friend, Miss Dimock, who were both early suffragists. In 1887 after a conversation with Miss Vernon, she joined the Central Committee for Women's Suffrage. This was a very courageous act on the part of Balfour as for women of her social class to be involved in such a movement was considered 'shocking – ridiculous', more often 'wicked, immodest and unwomanly'. There was also a risk of social ostracism in high society as a 'Woman's Rights woman was one who had marked herself as being something "nice people did not know"'.[27]

Balfour argues very strongly that she became part of the suffrage campaign by inclination, rather than through conversion. As she put it:

> People used to ask me who had made me a Suffragist, under what influence had I come. The influences of my time and Society were all without exception against the Freedom of Women. I can truly say that no one of my social class had the least feeling for, or wished to know, more about these unwomanly women. Personally, I knew that the idea was there, and as the years passed and knowledge grew, I was entirely convinced that it was a Cause which would make the world a place of more equal justice, and that the position of women was one that could not last, because it was supported by prejudice and by arguments which could be defeated by a child.[28]

The suffrage movement, of course, can be traced back into the late eighteenth century, but it was really kick-started into life in 1867 after J. S. Mill's women's franchise amendment to the Second Reform Bill was thrown out by parliament. Three local societies were formed in response – Edinburgh, London and Manchester – and another two followed in Bristol and Birmingham. The early societies campaigned on the platform that women of property be granted the vote and on other issues such as higher education for women, women's property rights, and so on. In Scotland two million signatures were collected in 1867–8 in favour of women's enfranchisement and branches of the National Society for Women's Suffrage were formed in every city and town of note.[29] Little progress was made and frustration created various splits in the movement. Millicent Fawcett formed the moderate National Union of Women's Suffrage Societies (NUWSS) at the turn of the century, and Charlotte Despard formed the Women's Freedom League (WFL). A more significant development was the founding of the Women's Social and Political Union (WSPU) by the Pankhurst family in 1903 with the motto 'Deeds not Words'. From this point there were two identifiable tendencies within the suffrage movement: the suffragist and the suffragette. Generally, suffragists preferred to work through existing political channels and use traditional forms of exerting pressure on parliament for change: petitioning, writing letters to the press, demonstrations and public meetings. Militants were defined as those women who were prepared to use violence and risk imprisonment in support of the cause, and were members of the WSPU. From 1906 the campaign began to become more militant and in attempts to raise public awareness acts of civil disobedience, such as throwing stones, breaking windows, chaining to railings and setting fire to pillar-boxes, escalated and many women were arrested and imprisoned. In Scotland the WSPU did not adopt a militant stance until 1913. Having done so, there occurred a wave of acts of civil disobedience, dubbed by the *Glasgow Herald* as the 'Scottish outrages'. Glasgow's pillar-boxes were attacked and set alight, the mansion house of Farrington Hall in Dundee was fire-bombed, causing damage estimated at £10,000, and even in and near the dormitory town of St Andrews there were several arson attacks, most notably on Leuchars Station.[30] As the campaign intensified, especially after the passing off the Cat and Mouse Act in April 1913, increasing numbers of women were arrested. In gaol hunger strikes were undertaken by some of the militants and this led to force-feeding. The campaign of direct action culminated in June 1913 when Emily Davidson committed suicide by throwing herself under the King's horse in the Epsom Derby. For the British public this was one act of defiance too much and from this point the suffrage issue lost ground among women. The outbreak of the First World War in August 1914 saw the movement mothballed for the duration of hostilities and suffragettes and suffragists mainly fell into line behind the war effort. Patriotism, it seemed, proved a far more potent force among women than the franchise.

Balfour's role in the suffrage campaign was varied, but chiefly limited to influence and propaganda. As she freely admits, she was useless as an organiser: 'I was no good at organisation, bad at committee work, and a shockingly bad Chair of the London Society.'[31] This was mirrored in her domestic life. Blanche claims that her mother 'had no faculty for organisation' and thus had to rely heavily on her servants.[32] Lacking administrative

skills, Balfour's contribution lay in her role as a 'liaison' officer between the
suffrage movement and the Commons and as a public speaker. Although
she rarely spoke outdoors and abhorred going on demonstrations, Balfour
delivered speeches on the franchise on platforms the length and breadth
of the country, 'from Sunderland to Torquay, from Norfolk to North
Wales'.[33] During one autumn in the years 1910–12 she recorded that she
had spoken at sixty meetings. She also found time to write two books in
this hectic period – *Lady Victoria Campbell* (1910) and *Life and Letters of
the Reverend James McGregor* (1912) – as well as serve on a parliamentary commission investigating the divorce laws.

As her role might suggest Balfour was a constitutional suffragist rather
than a militant suffragette. She opposed the militants for a number of
reasons. Firstly, she disapproved of law breaking, saying: 'I did not believe
that any law breaking would show that women were fit to take part in
any law making.'[34] Secondly, she felt that the strategy of co-operation
with any politician willing to endorse an extension of the franchise, as
advocated by the WSPU, would mean 'supporting what were then called
Socialists, and later when they grew in numbers and importance, the
Labour Party'.[35] If one adds to this her political concerns over suffragette
attacks on Liberals and issues of respectability, there existed a chasm too
wide to bridge between Balfour and the WSPU.

But there never existed such an obvious dividing line within the suffrage movement. The militants may have been condemned for their
aggressive tactics by the constitutionalists, but there was a genuine admiration expressed, even among the most law-abiding members of the
movement, for their bravery and courage. Balfour movingly wrote on
hearing of the death of her sister-in-law Constance Lytton:

> the greatest part of Con Lytton's Life and Death . . . was the revolution it
> created in the minds of many, those who knew her, had lived in the family
> beside her, and those even in circles that did not know her, were compelled to
> look into the *Common Cause* as our newspaper was called, and study what
> had turned this gentle woman into a fearless heroine. All her family were con-
> stitutional Suffragists, neither did she attempt to turn them to Militancy, but
> she inspired and led many to give the best in them to the constitutional Cause.
> Some felt it was the only way in which Militancy could be proved wrong,
> others, among them myself, felt how shamelessly little we had hitherto given
> to show the double faith in us. The faith that the Cause was a just one, and
> the faith that our country would at last be convinced that this Reform was
> needed.[36]

Again on hearing of the suicide of Emily Davidson, she underlined her
admiration for the 'spirit that animated some of the Militants', saying:

I consider that for sheer courage few deeds equal that of Emily Davidson . . . this 'fanatical' young person gave her life for Women's Suffrage. I never saw Emily Davidson, but I always feel as if I had known her . . . I was due to speak in Hertfordshire that day . . . There was little time to prepare any speech for the occasion, and we said what was in our hearts and minds. When I asked the meeting, which of us would have the courage to do that deed, I was met with a silence that was better than words.[37]

However, Frances was also opportunist and craftily used the threat of militancy to pressurise those in power who were sympathetic to the cause to do more to introduce legislation on the suffrage question. In a letter to the Home Secretary, Herbert Gladstone, she wrote: '[T]he strength of the movement grows. If we are to keep the whole thing constitutional among thousands of women we must have help.'[38] She also recognised that the militants by their actions generated tremendous publicity for the movement and stimulated debate and interest. Speaking at Northampton in July 1912 Balfour admitted that 'but for the action of militant suffragists they would not have [had] such a large meeting'.[39]

Thus, although the line between the suffragists and suffragettes could be fuzzy at times, the involvement of Balfour and other women of privilege in the suffrage campaign raises the question of representation: was it all encompassing or was it limited to upper- and middle-class ladies? If the movement was, indeed, only representative of a small, although wealthy, section of society then it might explain its failure before 1914 to achieve maximum impact on the government. As one NUWSS organiser in Edinburgh put it:

To the man in the street all those working for the Suffrage appear to be rich women or women of the leisured classes. They find it difficult that we want the vote for the benefit of our country and in order to help our poorer sisters.[40]

For Scotland, Leah Leneman shares the perception of the activist and has argued that although 'no one can doubt that there must have been a working-class component to the movement: the difficulty is in finding it'.[41] Martin Pugh, in his revisionist history of the women's suffrage campaign, comes to a similar conclusion to Leneman. Although recognising the part played by individual women in the movement, Pugh found that of thirteen branches of the more working-class-friendly WFL only one could be shown to have had a 'substantial working-class membership'.[42] Pugh sees the absence of working-class women in the movement as unsurprising given their domestic and family responsibilities, which were too onerous to allow for active participation; only the well-to-do had the means and the familial support to become committed members.

Moreover, imprisonment, which in working-class eyes was the equivalent of entering the poorhouse, posed such a significant threat to notions of respectability that few women were prepared to dare it.

On the other hand, a number of feminist historians have stressed the importance of the franchise in working-class political discourse and the active roles played by working women, such as Annie Kenney, in the movement. The classic study – One Hand Tied Behind Our Backs – by Jill Liddington and Jill Norris of female textile workers in Lancashire demonstrated convincingly the extent of working-class women's involvement in the struggle for the vote in that part of Britain. By shifting the focus of the historian away from London, Liddington and Norris were also influential in drawing a portrait of the movement as above class and party, tensions notwithstanding, and stressing the unifying issue of the franchise for women.[43] Even Leneman admits that in Glasgow the socialist and suffrage movements were 'closely intermingled', with prominent Labour leaders, such as Tom Johnston, editor of Forward, strongly supporting the enfranchisement of women. Indeed, as early as 1893 the Scottish Women's Co-operative Guild had sent a petition to the government in favour of an extension of the franchise.[44] It is clear also that women as privileged as Balfour saw enfranchisement in broader terms than simply votes for rich women. As she states: 'I don't remember any date in which I was not a passive believer in the rights of women to be recognised as full citizens of this country.'[45] However, while there is compelling evidence to question the middle-class image of the suffrage movement articulated by Leneman and Pugh,[46] the fact remains that working-class women were clearly thought of by their better-off sisters as mere foot soldiers in the struggle. As Eustance et al. state, working-class activists 'were denied real power in many suffrage societies'.[47]

However, when the trumpet sounded in August 1914 all shades of the women's movement, with the exception of the WFL, supported the call to arms and Balfour was an enthusiastic patriot. Indeed, patriotism proved a more potent symbol for women than the franchise, as former militants handed out white feathers to conscientious objectors. As a consequence of their involvement in the war effort and as a reward for the sacrifices they made, the vote was granted to those women over the age of thirty in the Representation of the People Act of 1918. Frances, therefore, considered the job only half-finished and continued the struggle for women to qualify for the franchise on the same basis as men. Her first contribution was to write a fine biography of a fellow suffragist, Dr Elsie Inglis, in 1918 and in this new phase of the movement's history join the London Society for Women's Service, which succeeded the London Society for Women's

Suffrage, in 1919. In 1922, to raise awareness among women of the need to stand as parliamentary candidates, she joined the Committee of the Million Shilling Fund. Women were finally placed on the same electoral footing as men when the voting age was reduced from thirty to twenty-one in 1928; however, the equal rights campaign went on much longer.

Although Balfour played a prominent role in this epic struggle, there remains an outstanding question to address in respect of the impact the movement had on her political consciousness. Did her experiences in the suffrage movement make her a feminist and/or a radical? The answer is somewhat contradictory in that she was a feminist in spite of herself. Her daughter takes the view that it was hard to reconcile Frances' views on the suffrage question with her dismissive attitude to other women. As Blanche puts it, 'My mother [had an] avowed contempt for most women's opinions' and viewed their company with 'obvious boredom'.[48] On one occasion Frances had asked several bishops to lunch at her home in Addison Road, London, and one had thought to bring his wife along uninvited. She simply turned to the poor woman and said: 'All right, you sit there . . . but don't open your mouth or you will spoil the whole evening.'[49] It was also clear that Frances rarely acted without first seeking the approval of Eustace. She saw marriage as 'the greatest event' in a woman's life. Anyone disagreeing with this view was dismissed as 'a con-genital idiot'.[50] It was an institution that was 'dear to all who care for the good of the state and the well-being of the race'.[51] Even with the widen-ing of political opportunities after enfranchisement in 1918, Frances was still of the opinion that women 'have to be the centre and the shrine of the home, to be mothers, the educators of the race that was to carry on the Empire, Church and State'.[52] She, thus, accepted a family set-up that was patriarchal in structure. As such she was careful to reassure her husband that as far as participation in suffrage demonstrations were con-cerned – or appeals to the 'mob' as Frances described them – there was 'nothing militant about our looks, our dress or our intentions'.[53] Indeed, militancy was not an option for her as even if she had the inclination 'a prior claim would have withheld me'.[54] Women, therefore, were unfairly denied political rights, but it was not envisaged by her that the resolution of this inequality would fundamentally lead to a restructuring of family and household relationships. Political empowerment had few social repercussions as far as she was concerned. Men and women would still conform to traditional stereotypes with the former as breadwinners and the latter in a state of economic, if not political, dependency. When the WFL campaigned in the 1924 general election for women to vote for women candidates regardless of party label, Frances opposed the strategy as irresponsible and instead called on women to 'let their ruling purpose be to establish righteous government amongst a free people'.[55]

However, she did feel that there were new possibilities for women after 1918 and that it was possible to combine family and a career in politics or in some other sphere of activity. Women had attained full citizenship and that for her meant that there could be no areas in public life in which women could not be represented. The creation of women elders in the Church of Scotland was part of the new dawn of possibility and she initiated an unsuccessful campaign to break this particular bastion of male authority. In a speech given at Govan Town Hall, Glasgow, Frances declared:

> She would like to see women elders in our Churches. She could not see why that should not be, except for the conservative nature of ministers – of all men . . . in our Churches today. Women who had got full citizenship of a free country knew that the State and the Church could not think of the State not acknowledging the organisations of the Church. Civil citizenship brought them into closer touch with great organisations, and women now feel more and more the great importance of Christian work in their midst.[56]

Her plea for a greater role for women in the church became ever more radical as she began to demand that they be allowed into the ministry. Since women had been granted the 'rights and responsibilities of free citizenship' why, she asked, could they not 'go and minister'? She believed it was only the entirely erroneous 'belief that the ministry is a priestly office' that prevented women from moving out of their male-allotted place. In other words, it was a Romanist and not a Presbyterian doctrine, and had little relevance in a world where women 'are proving that they have all the male attributes'.[57]

Frances also campaigned for a considerable period of time for women to be free from state interference in the labour market; a phenomenon that advertised her feminist credentials, but exposed the contradictions and weaknesses in her thinking. She was actively involved with the anti-trade-union Freedom Defence League, which was set up to 'assert the right of every individual to their own labour'.[58] Her view was that interference by the state in the labour market to protect the interest of women workers would price them out of employment. Thus, Balfour opposed legislation aimed at trying to ameliorate the long hours shop assistants had to be on their feet by providing them with seats, arguing that smaller employers faced with the cost of introducing them would either take the cost of installing them out of their workers' wages, or economise on labour. For women in general 'it would make it more difficult to procure honest work'.[59] Her views did not go unchallenged and the chairman of the Early Closing Association, A. Cameron Corbett, reminded her that 'all attempts for improved conditions of labour . . . [since] the Factory Acts have been met with the argument that workers would be thrown out of employment'.[60] However, Balfour's belief in the beneficence of the free market blinded her to such criticism and led her to oppose the campaign against sweating, that is, women who worked from home and were subject to long hours and very low pay. Speaking in opposition to legislation designed to protect women in these sweated occupations, she argued: 'It was an absolute fallacy to contend . . . that the suppression of home industry would destroy all sweated labour . . . there were many people who were only too ready to put every restriction they could upon women's labour.'[61] After the war Frances continued her efforts in the sphere of women's work. She joined the Open Door Council (ODC) in 1926 and was a member of its executive council along with Lady Rhonnda, Emmeleine Pethick-Lawrence and some other notable female activists. The ODC's objective was to campaign for women's opportunities, the rights to work and to protection at all stages of their lives on the same basis as those of men. As an equal-rights organisation it was very active on the issue of gender inequalities in working conditions and wages, earning it the opposition of the trade unions who 'damned it as a middle-class feminist body'.[62] As such the ODC was never in a position to mobilise the support of those women it sought to influence.

If her position as a feminist was open to equivocation, Frances' other political activities constituted a bewildering mass of contradictions. Her views on free trade and trade unionism might have marked her out as a right-wing Tory, but nothing could be further from the truth. She was equally opposed to the Tories, which was a difficult political position to hold given that she was married into the Balfour family, and, through them, related to the Cecils (a Conservative dynasty on a par with the Churchills – Lord Salisbury the three-times British Prime Minister in the nineteenth century was a Cecil). In a letter to her close friend, Professor George Saintsbury, she proudly proclaimed: 'I always thank Heaven that no creature belonging to our name has ever been in the Tory camp!'[63] She also thought of herself as a nationalist, something that was evident from early childhood. Frances recalled that when she and her siblings passed the 'Solway [Firth] we duly cheered, and when returning to England we hissed like ganders'.[64] However, she did not favour separation. Asked if she wanted Home Rule for Scotland in 1922, she replied: 'How can Scotland want Home Rule, when England and Scotland have one flag and one country?'[65]

It was her strong links with the Church of Scotland that encouraged her sense of national identity and this led her to sympathise in the 1890s with the cause of Irish Home Rule and its leader Charles Stuart Parnell. The home rule question had come to the top of the political agenda in 1884 when William Gladstone signalled his support. His endorsement of home rule split the Liberal party in two, with a rebel faction under the leadership of Joseph Chamberlain forming the Liberal Unionist party. Initially, she was opposed to Irish Home Rule on two counts: firstly, because of the ferocity of Fenian violence and, secondly, on the basis that success might well presage the collapse of Empire. Balfour stated that 'if ever the Home Rule policy were carried out such things would happen that every right-minded person would ask whether he or she had done all in his or her power to stop the horrors'.[66] She joined the WLUA to defend the Union, but she quickly grew disenchanted with the Liberal Unionist position on Ireland, something that owed much to her distrust of Chamberlain, whom she considered as 'little better than Beelzebub'.[67] Balfour found herself supporting Parnell – a 'man essentially made to govern Ireland' – and the Irish nationalist group in parliament, writing: 'It may be my Celtic blood, but I frankly say my sympathies are with the Irish in Ireland, and in the House [of Commons].'[68] Perceptively, she realised that a united Ireland was impractical given the antipathy of Protestant Ulster to the rest of Ireland; thus she advocated and by doing so anticipated the Treaty of Partition of 1921, that 'what we ought to do is to build a wall (like the Roman wall) round Ulster and leave the rest of Ireland to him [Parnell]'.[69] Parnell's fall from grace and the opposition from all sides of the House to Irish Home Rule saw the bloody struggle continue, culminating in the 1916 Easter Rising, an event that more than anything else paved the way for the 1921 Treaty.

Her shifting position on Ireland did not mean that Frances was any less committed to the Empire. Her imperial loyalties were impressively demonstrated during the Boer War. Along with other leading suffragists, Millicent Fawcett and Mary Arnold Foster, she wrote to *The Times* complaining of a conspiracy in the international press to place Britain's actions in South Africa in a poor light while, at the same time, applying a noble gloss to the activities of the Boer rebels. She called with the others for a public subscription in order to combat this pernicious propaganda campaign against Britain, claiming that the international press corps 'see nothing but rapacity on our part and a valiant defence of their independence by the Boers . . . this view is absolutely misleading and erroneous'.[70]

The Liberal Unionist position on the Empire was a strong attraction for Balfour, although as in the case of Ireland and, of course, the suffrage question, she was gradually becoming disenchanted with the party. These frustrations climaxed with the party's conversion to protectionism. Again Joseph Chamberlain was the catalyst. By rejecting the idea of free trade in favour of tariffs, he overthrew one of the great inviolable economic doctrines of Liberalism and this was one step too far for Balfour. She wrote of her disenchantment thus:

> In 1904 I severed my alliance . . . with the Liberal Unionist Association, we had reached days in which the party were following political doctrines, quite different from those which formed the faith on which Liberal Unionism was founded . . . I shall end by coming out after a speech in which I will give the Liberal faith that is in one. This consists of distrust of Fiscal Reform, Colonial Preference or any of the new terms for Protection . . .[71]

Thus, Frances once more embraced Gladstonian Liberalism and found herself back in the party fold. But her politics remain impossible to define in terms of an ideology or an 'ism'. She was a contradiction in many ways, but, outside of religious devotion, two themes seem to stand out among all the confusion and incoherence: the importance of birth and place, and the desire for political equality between men and women. These were in contradiction to each other; one implied a deferential and hierarchical society, while the other implied a dynamic and democratic social structure. Balfour was able to reconcile them in her own mind only because she failed to comprehend the linkages between what she considered mutually exclusive political positions. She failed to appreciate that each step forward in the politicisation of the nation undermined the traditional role of landed society as the natural governing elite. Furthermore, each blow for democracy undermined the social role of the landowners as the state became increasingly responsible for welfare and the 'mob' more dependent on its beneficence. Deference was impossible as a means of social control in this more fluid and dynamic society that Frances and other women of privilege had helped to create. Although she did her best to deny the socio-political changes taking place in Britain, particularly after the First World War, even to the point of refusing to have electric light installed in her home at Addison Road in London,[72] there was little she could do except to bemoan the rise of a plebeian culture and extol the out-of-date virtues of landed society. She remained unrepentantly, until her death in 1931 from bronchial pneumonia, a snob.

The roots of her snobbery, of her bluff-and-bluster manner, lay in Frances' sense of not quite fitting in, of never quite being in the right place

socially or politically. Two extracts from her diary written at the beginning and at the end of 1912 show the extent to which she felt an outsider:

> Tonight I am again alone in my room. The gale has died away. Downstairs
> they are again complete, with Arthur added. It will be best tonight to note the
> blessings of the year. Not to forecast my fears . . . feel very lonely . . . much
> failure in myself of loving kindness. That is what I need in great abundance . . .
> I watched the year in alone in my room. I hear the child . . . singing *Auld Lang*
> *Syne* . . . The pain and weariness are very heavy, and I feel so alone among
> them. It is best to sing little, and write less, to ask for the over shadowing
> strength and courage.[73]

In spite of all this, Frances Balfour and other courageous women in
the suffrage campaign lived to witness the triumph of their 'just and fair
cause' and in doing so fundamentally altered the political landscape of
Britain, maybe in ways they would not have anticipated, but nevertheless in ways beneficial to women every where.

NOTES

1. B. E. C. Dugdale, *Family Homespun* (London, 1940), p. 76.
2. F. Balfour, *Ne Obliviscaris. Dinna Forget*, vol. I (London, 1930), p. 9.
3. Dugdale, *Family*, pp. 75–6.
4. F. Balfour, *Ne Obliviscaris*, vol. I, p. 12.
5. Balfour, *Ne Obliviscaris*, vol. I, pp. 33–4, 37, 49.
6. Balfour, *Ne Obliviscaris*, vol. I, p. 35.
7. Balfour, *Ne Obliviscaris*, vol. I, p. 22.
8. *The Scotsman*, 26 February 1931.
9. Dugdale, *Family*, p. 149.
10. Obituary, *The Times*, 26 February 1931.
11. Dugdale, *Family*, p. 72.
12. Dugdale, *Family*, p. 142.
13. Balfour, *Ne Obliviscaris*, vol. I, p. 50.
14. Balfour, *Ne Obliviscaris*, vol. II, p. 257.
15. Balfour, *Ne Obliviscaris*, vol. I, p. 50–1.
16. Balfour, *Ne Obliviscaris*, vol. 1, p. 364.
17. Letter to Mrs Henry Fawcett, 16 December 1891 (Autograph Letter
    Collection: Female Education, 1850–1951, Women's Library, GB01069/4).
18. Balfour, *Ne Obliviscaris*, vol. I, p. 94.
19. Balfour, *Ne Obliviscaris*, vol. II, pp. 106–7.
20. Dugdale, *Family*, p. 106.
21. Balfour, *Ne Obliviscaris*,vol. I, p. 91.
22. Balfour, *Ne Obliviscaris*, vol. I, pp. 91–2.

23. Balfour, *Ne Obliviscaris*, vol. II, pp. 149–50.
24. J. Ridley and C. Percy (eds), *The Letters of Arthur Balfour and Lady Elcho, 1885–1917* (London, 1992), p. 19.
25. Balfour, *Ne Obliviscaris*, vol. II, p. 117.
26. C. Law, *Women: a Modern Political Dictionary* (London, 2000), pp. 20, 172.
27. Balfour, *Ne Obliviscaris*, vol. II, p. 114.
28. Balfour, *Ne Obliviscaris*, vol. II, p. 127.
29. L. Leneman, 'A truly national movement: the view from outside London', in M. Joannou and J. Purvis (eds), *The Woman's Suffrage Movement: New Feminist Perspectives* (Manchester, 1998), p. 38.
30. E. King, *The Scottish Women's Suffrage Movement* (Glasgow, 1994), p. 24.
31. Balfour, *Ne Obliviscaris*, vol. II, p. 172.
32. Dugdale, *Family*, p. 118.
33. Balfour, *Ne Obliviscaris*, vol. II, pp. 173–4.
34. Balfour, *Ne Obliviscaris*, vol. II, p. 141.
35. Balfour, *Ne Obliviscaris*, vol. II, p. 137. She later came to the conclusion that with the benefit of hindsight this was the correct strategy and that some Labour leaders, such as Philip Snowden, were not so bad.
36. Balfour, *Ne Obliviscaris*, pp. 162–3.
37. Balfour, *Ne Obliviscaris*, pp. 164–5.
38. Letter to Herbert Gladstone, 6 November 1908, quoted in D. Morgan, *Suffragists and Liberals: the Politics of Woman Suffrage in England* (Oxford, 1975), p. 55.
39. *The Times*, 1 July 1912.
40. *Common Cause*, 5 May 1910, quoted in L. Leneman, *A Guid Cause: the Women's Suffrage Movement in Scotland* (Edinburgh, 1995 edn), p. 93.
41. Leneman, 'Truly national', pp. 46–7.
42. M. Pugh, *The March of the Women: a Revisionist Analysis of the Campaign for Women's Suffrage, 1866–1914* (Oxford, 2000), p. 213.
43. S. S. Holton, 'Reflecting on suffrage history', in C. Eustance et al., *A Suffrage Reader: Charting Directions in British Suffrage History* (2000), p. 23.
44. Leneman, *Guid Cause*, pp. 35, 43.
45. Balfour, *Ne Obliviscaris*, vol. II, p. 115.
46. C. Eustance et al., 'Writing suffrage histories – the "British" experience', in Eustance et al., *Suffrage Reader*, p. 5.
47. Eustance et al., 'Suffrage histories', p. 5.
48. Dugdale, *Family*, p. 116.
49. Percy and Ridley , *Arthur Balfour*, p. 19.
50. Balfour, *Ne Obliviscaris*, vol. I, p. 235.
51. *The Times*, 6 June 1913.
52. *Glasgow Herald*, 23 May 1919.
53. Balfour, *Ne Obliviscaris*, vol. II, p. 169.

54. Balfour, *Ne Obliviscaris*, vol. II, p. 141.
55. *The Times*, 23 October 1924.
56. *Glasgow Herald*, 14 March 1920.
57. F. Balfour, 'The ministry of women', *The Scotsman*, 16 January 1931.
58. Balfour, *Ne Obliviscaris*, vol. II, p. 172.
59. *The Times*, 8 August 1899.
60. *The Times*, 10 July 1912.
61. *The Times*, 19 May 1906.
62. Law, *Women*, p. 172; M. Pugh, *Women and the Women's Movement in Britain, 1914–1959* (Basingstoke, 1992), p. 69.
63. Balfour, *Ne Obliviscaris*, vol. II, p. 189.
64. Balfour, *Ne Obliviscaris*, vol. I, pp. 16–17.
65. *Glasgow Herald*, 5 December 1922.
66. *The Times*, 12 November 1891.
67. Dugdale, *Family*, p. 151.
68. Letter to George Saintsbury, 3 December 1890, quoted in Balfour, *Ne Obliviscaris*, vol. II, p. 187.
69. Letter to George Saintsbury, 14 December 1890, quoted in Balfour, *Ne Obliviscaris*, vol. II, p. 190.
70. *The Times*, 14 March 1900.
71. Balfour, *Ne Obliviscaris*, vol. II, p. 398.
72. Dugdale, *Family*, p. 114.
73. Diary of Frances Balfour, 31 December 1911, 31 December 1912 (National Archive of Scotland, Edinburgh, GD4/33/2/427).

6

Mary Mitchell Slessor: Serving God and Country

༄

In a letter written a few years before her death, Mary Mitchell Slessor, in a typically self-effacing manner, described herself as 'just an insignificant wee auld wifey'.[1] History, however, has used a different vocabulary in delivering a verdict on her extraordinary life. Since 1915, this humble and unassuming Dundee weaver and, later, missionary, has become perhaps the most celebrated Scotswomen of the last century. W. P. Livingstone, her first biographer, wrote: 'She will be remembered . . . and each generation will hand down to the next the story of the Great White Mother who lived and toiled for their good.'[2] That verdict has been sustained over subsequent decades in the various publications of the Church of Scotland and (mainly Christian) historians. James Buchan, in the early 1980s, citing the late historian Margery Perlam, stated that she was 'one of the greatest women of her generation'.[3] The work of these and other writers has conferred iconic status on Mary, as witness the recent issue of a ten-pound note by the Clydesdale Bank bearing her face and a map of her mission stations. Although there is much that is fascinating about Mary and her story, these historical constructs of her life have created a one-dimensional and almost mythological character. The narrative in their accounts is fairly standardised, indeed, virtually a cliché: drawn from the slums of Dundee, Mary is called through her love of Christ to undertake the most hazardous missionary work in a part of Nigeria – Calabar – where literally no white man would go, and endure the most appalling dangers to her life and well-being. The result is little short of hagiography, but that is the image that has been handed down to generations of Scottish children since her death in 1915. Fortunately, reappraisals taking place in the writing of imperial history, particularly in regard to gender, allow us to move from hagiography to more intellectually stimulating ways of assessing Slessor and her work in Africa. Research on the experiences of women travellers and female missionaries in the 'Dark Continent' and in India, has opened up new possibilities for evaluating Mary's relationship to the imperial project, and in interpreting the role of missionaries in this respect.[4] However, before discussing her in this context, it is necessary to explore the background of her early life through to womanhood, since much of this serves to provide an explanation of her desire to become a missionary and her relationship with the peoples of West Africa.

She was born at Gilcomston, Aberdeen, on 2 December 1848, the second-eldest child in what became a family of seven. Her father, Robert, was from Buchan and was a shoemaker to trade. His family was reasonably well-to-do and of farming stock. Some of the scions of the Slessors were educated and had a church connection. Mary recalled many years later that 'two sons were at Cambridge' and one of them had become a clergyman in Aberdeen.[5] Similarly, her mother was from a respectable background and raised in a 'home of refinement and piety'.[6] Thus, Mary's origins and connections were far removed from the poverty-stricken condition that characterised her family life in Dundee. That situation was brought about by her father's over-fondness for strong drink, which cost him his job in Aberdeen and plunged his wife and children into poverty. Consequently, when Mary was eleven, the Slessors moved south to Dundee to a 'bare and comfortless' house[7] in an effort to find Robert employment: firstly, as a shoemaker and, latterly, as a labourer in the jute mills. This attempt at a new start, however, proved only temporary. Her father took to drink again and became increasingly abusive. In common with the experience of many families in Scotland, Saturday night for Mary and her mother became one to dread. On a number of occasions they were driven from their home and forced to spend the night on the streets until Robert had sobered up.

Perhaps just as damaging as the physical scars of alcoholism on the women was the threat of losing face in the community. Respectability was a social value that the middle class and the skilled working class shared, although they might have interpreted it in different ways.[8] For the working class it was staying clear of the Poor Law and that meant subscription to sobriety and thrift. Robert Slessor's drinking, thus, seriously compromised not only the women's concept of respectability, but also that of the community they worshipped in. Both mother and daughter constantly feared that 'church friends should come to know the secret', thus, according to Livingstone, a great deal of effort went into 'hiding the skeleton in the house'.[9]

As her father spent every penny he earned on drink, the burden of providing for the family fell more and more on the shoulders of Mary's mother, and eventually upon Mary herself after the death of three of her siblings. From the age of eleven Mary was a half-timer in Baxter's Mill and from the age of fourteen she graduated to full-time work putting in twelve hours a day at the power loom. Her father's death around this time, as well as that of her brother John, further burdened Mary to provide for her family. The long hours in the mills left her with very little leisure time, and what she had was devoted almost exclusively to the church and its activities. She graduated from Sunday School to Bible Class, later becoming part of the Home Missions and a teacher in the Sabbath School of the United Presbyterian Church (UPC) in Dundee. Although a reluctant and often embarrassingly shy public speaker, her upbringing in the slums of Dundee helped her to bring a Christian message to the poor of the city in a way they could relate to. On a number of occasions Mary had to show real courage when faced with hostile groups of young men. Livingstone says that when she and some others in the Cowgate Mission attempted to launch open-air services their efforts were continually disrupted by a gang of youths. One night they surrounded her and the leader swung a lead weight so close to her that it nearly shaved her head, but in spite of the intensity of the provocation, Mary never wavered and stood her ground. 'She's game,' he exclaimed, and the gang trooped into her meeting.[10]

The early evidence of religious commitment raises questions regarding one of the myths surrounding Mary's childhood. In her writings she liked to present herself as a 'wild lassie' that was brought to Christ by an old neighbour who told her if she did not mend her ways she would suffer eternal damnation. The idea of burning in hell allegedly worked on her imagination and she thus repented and accepted Christ. This story has been repeated in all biographies of Slessor, including the most recent.[11] The story, however, can be deconstructed on both an empirical and theological basis. All the evidence points to the fact that Mary was in regular attendance at Sunday School and Wishart UPC in Dundee's Cowgate, where she was sent by her deeply religious mother on Sundays with a 'scented handkerchief'.[12] The scented handkerchief not only contradicts the tomboy image, but is also a symbolic token of her mother's commitment to respectability, despite difficult economic circumstance. From a theological point of view, her alleged wild behaviour fits extremely well with the whole process of conversion in Presbyterian doctrine. To be saved involves the repentance of one's sins, thus, there has to be a past to repent, hence the image of the 'wild lassie' persists. Furthermore, what did being 'wild' constitute? Was it merely childish boisterousness or something more serious? There is no evidence that her behaviour ever bordered on the criminal or that she was ever involved with the police, although she did a have a fiery temperament and was actually known as 'fire' by her brothers and sisters. The nickname, however, might also have been given to her because of her shock of red hair; indeed, she was known too as 'carrots'.[13]

Once 'converted', Mary's deeper connection with the church led to self-improvement and to greater social interaction with Dundee's middle class. Mary's education had taken place mainly in factory schools, and the poor quality of the schooling she received left her with only a very rudimentary knowledge of arithmetic and reading. However, she was later introduced to the 'beauties of literature' by an unnamed older, but 'intimate friend', who worked as a bank manager in the city. They discussed papers written by Mary for the UPC Fellowship society and enjoyed reading and discussing the works of Dante and Milton, as well as other literary figures.[14] The church also helped polish her in social terms and that speeded the process of acceptance by the middle class. When the Foreign Missions Board (FMB) of the UPC accepted her as a trainee missionary it was on the basis that in the interim she smoothed out her accent and improved her English. The local minister's wife was on hand to 'introduce her to the manners of the drawing room'.[15] By her mid-twenties Mary, in spite of her working-class origins, was an articulate and well-read young woman who had been to a large extent accepted into middle-class Victorian society and its values. As Buchan says, 'she was only saved from becoming prim and proper . . . by her earthy commonsense'.[16]

Although it might seem as if the answer to why Mary was so receptive to the overtures of middle-class society and enthusiastic towards self-improvement lay in the social connections of religious affiliation, a clue might also be found in the status hierarchies of Dundee's mill culture. As a weaver Mary was viewed as a 'cut above' spinners and ancillary workers. As one spinner put it, 'The weavers thought themselves somethin', aye and winders tae . . . they never looked at us . . . they thought they were somethin' special . . . They used to walk past you as if you were something low and they were "it".' Weavers also wore hats and gloves to work and laboured in cleaner conditions and, unlike the spinners, who finished the day covered in mill dust, they were never dirty. 'Books and magazines' were also circulating throughout the factory, which suggested a literary culture of some sort.[17] Eleanor Gordon summed up the significance of 'pride in one's appearance' in her study of the jute industry, when she stated that it was tied up with 'the notion of femininity and gentility'. She also pointed out that weavers had aspirations of finding a man with a trade behind him and becoming non-working wives, 'that other symbol of working-class respectability'.[18] This does not mean that the weavers had in some way become embourgeoisified, on the contrary, there was a strong oppositional mill culture in operation, but it did point to the importance of respectability as a key component of this lifestyle and one that was shared with the middle classes. In Mary's case a commitment to the values of respectability may have made the transition from one cultural milieu to another less difficult once her superiors had added the social polish.

Her growing interest in literature and theology was matched by a strong attraction to the missionary work of the UPC. This impulse was largely the result of her mother's influence. She was enthralled by the stories of visiting missionaries and took a particular interest in the UPC mission at Calabar. As a result of her mother's influence, when Mary as a child played at keeping school the 'imaginary scholars she taught . . . were always black'.[19] Mary's mother had fantasised that one day her eldest son might become a missionary, but Robert's premature death saw her hopes thrust on Mary. Thus, to a large extent her motivation derived from a sense of duty to the church, to contribute to its work, and to her mother, to fulfil her wishes. Stimulation also came from reading exotic accounts of the 'Dark Continent' in the *Missionary Record* and by listening as her mother did to the blood-curdling tales of visiting missionaries. The immediate trigger, however, was the death of David Livingstone in 1874. Inspired by an appeal to carry on the work of the great Scottish missionary, Mary decided to apply to the Foreign Missions Board (FMB) of the UPC the following year. She was accepted and left Dundee in March 1876 to begin her training for missionary work at Moray House in Edinburgh. The training was academic and intellectual rather than 'practical',[20] which she reflected at a later date ill-equipped her for the realities of missionary work. It would have been better, Mary thought, if students had spent their time learning to mix cement than in analysing biblical texts! She claimed that what missionary work needed was:

> affectionate women who are not afraid of work or of filth of any kind, moral or material. Women who can nurse a baby or teach a child to wash and comb as well as to read . . . If they can play Beethoven and paint . . . and speak French and German so much the better, but we can want all these latter accomplishments if they have only a loving heart, willing hands and common sense.[21]

Nonetheless, equipped or not for what lay ahead, after four months at Moray House she set sail for Calabar – 'the white man's grave' – on 5 August on the SS *Ethiopia*.

In volunteering for missionary work as a single woman she was at this time doing something extraordinary and quite revolutionary. Women in

missionary life were normally married and seen as helpmates to their husbands and as such they were restricted to work considered the province
of the feminine, that is, the education of girls.[22] Shortage of male volunteers forced the missionary societies across Britain to accept females and
Slessor benefited from changing recruitment strategies. As Jane Haggis
points out in her study of Anglo-Indian relations, many of the women
volunteers were drawn to the life of a missionary from a misguided sense
of compassion. They portrayed native women as 'innocent and passive
victims' of a cruel and heartless system of oppression, while portraying
themselves as 'having the virtues and responsibilities of free-born and
independent' women.[23] Not only did this constitute a form of political
delusion by unenfranchised British women, it also created a stereotype
of a victim whose only protection from their abusive menfolk was to be
found in British rule and imperial laws. Arriving in Calabar on
11 September, there is little evidence at this point to suggest that Slessor
was any different to her English middle-class counterparts in her perceptions of Africa and its peoples, particularly the women. An emotional
dualism existed within her: she experienced both revulsion and compassion for the people she was to evangelise. In her first letter home, Slessor
wrote despairingly: 'It is impossible to love these people for their own
sakes, one can only do it for Christ's sake.'[24] Mary encountered a world
fundamentally distinct from her own, but given her experiences of
alcohol-fuelled abuse and poverty there were parallels.

    Christian biographers have strongly emphasised the pioneering role of
Slessor in Calabar and the extent of barbarism found there. Her obituary in *The Scotsman* set the tone for succeeding publications, stating that

> With dauntless courage, she set her self single-handed to the hard task of
> putting down the cruel and barbarous superstitions and customs that were
> everywhere rampant, acquiring by her wise administration and intrepid spirit
> an extraordinary influence over even the most bloodthirsty of the natives.[25]

W. P. Livingstone did his best to underline this imagery of bravery in the
face of barbarism. Words such as 'savages', 'heathens', 'drunkards' and
'murderers' are used freely by him to stress the dangers faced by Mary and,
of course, her ultimate triumph in civilising the barbaric. This image has
also been reinforced in more recent biographies. James Buchan, writing
in the early 1980s, claims that the Calabar chiefs 'killed and tortured . . .
with impunity'.[26] Such emotive assertions, however, create a distorted
picture of the nature of Calabar, or indeed African, society. These societies
had managed to survive in very hostile circumstances for many centuries.
This was achieved by adhering to a common value system which was

Plate 1 *Jane Welsh Carlyle in the year of her marriage (1826): 'Jane Baillie Welsh, Mrs Thomas Carlyle' by Kenneth Macleay.*

Plate 2 *Thomas Carlyle in his early 50s.*

Plate 3 *Jane Welsh Carlyle in her early 50s.*

Plate 4   *The Carlyle home in London: 'A Chelsea Interior' by Robert Tait.*

Plate 5   *Eliza Wigham and her sister, Mrs Edmunds. Note distinctive Quaker dress.*

Plate 6   Madeleine Smith aged about 16; from a family portrait.

Plate 7   Sophia Jex-Blake at age 25.

Plate 8 *Lady Frances Balfour in Canada, 1882.*

Plate 9 *Eustace Balfour in Canada, 1882.*

Plate 10 *Mary Slessor and the children of the Okoyong mission, c.1890.*

Plate 11 *Mary Slessor in her 40s. Note engagement ring.*

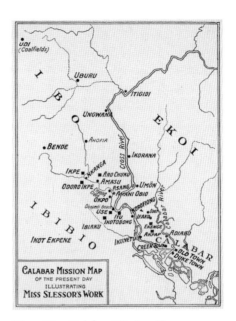

Plate 12 *Calabar Mission Map.*

Plate 13 *Mary Slessor with her adopted family.*

Plate 14   *Elsie Maud Inglis in uniform.*

Plate 15   *Katherine, Duchess of Atholl in 1899.*

Plate 16 *Katherine, Duchess of Atholl electioneering in her constituency in the 1930s.*

Plate 17 *Willa Anderson, University of St Andrews, 1910.*

Plate 18 *Edwin Muir, Glasgow, 1917.*

Plate 19   Willa Muir, Prague, 1945.

Plate 20   Mary Brooksbank, 19 June 1969.

based on a complex mixture of duties, rights and taboos, some of which, for example, trial by ordeal and twin murder, were offensive to Christian eyes. Even Livingstone was forced to concede that the peoples of Calabar were not 'destitute of religious beliefs . . . Nor were their lives unregulated by principles and laws; they were ruled by canons and connections as powerful as those of Europe.'[27] Moreover, these writers fail to appreciate the extent to which Calabar had been influenced by western culture. As Michael Fry, in his recent study of imperialism,[28] points out, the mission there had been an established enterprise for some forty years and the port of Duke Town was relatively 'sophisticated and respectable'. After thirty years of missionary work, there were 174 members in all congregations, although church attendance was put at around 1,000. There were four ordained missionaries, of whom the Reverend William Anderson was the leader, four male teachers and four female, a native ordained missionary and eighteen agents.[29] Mary herself was placed under the supervision of the redoubtable Euphemia Sutherland, a veteran of some twenty-seven years missionary service in Calabar and a 'human dynamo'.[30]

The founding of the mission was due to the work of an Irish clergyman, Hope Masterton Waddell, who became convinced after reading a book on the slave trade while serving in Jamaica that Christianised West Indians should return to Africa to preach the gospel. To that end, and with the permission of the FMB of the UPC in Edinburgh, a mission was established in Calabar in 1846. From its foundation, Hope Waddell adopted a strategy that combined 'bringing social and cultural reform through calls for spiritual transformation'.[31] Thus the Bible was an integral element of a programme designed to elevate the native population both materially and spiritually. It was this strategy that was bequeathed to and adopted by Mary, a fact that questions the pioneering image. But if the conversion strategy was second-hand, the same cannot be said regarding her missionary work and the way she redefined her femininity. In both instances she was pioneering. Mary used idiosyncratic methods in spreading the gospel, and was generally in a state of disorganisation. This meant that although colleagues 'declared that they loved Miss Slessor, they could not work with her'.[32] Mary didn't need them. Regardless of the dangers, or the approval of the FMB, she pushed into the interior of the region carrying with her an unshakeable faith and a manifest desire to improve social conditions. She literally went where no white man would go, penetrating far into the uncharted interior of south-east Nigeria: from Duke Town to Ekenge in Okoyong and, finally, to Itu in Igboland.

In doing so she went native and by adopting this lifestyle, even though described as 'that coarse woman' by a wife of one of the missionaries,[33] she redefined the possibilities for white women: what they could do, and what they could not. She cut her hair short, thus challenging one of the main symbols of Victorian ideals of femininity, long hair. So oblivious was she of contemporary notions of femininity that Mr Gardner, of Arochuku, said that he always walked in front of her so as he would be spared 'the sight of Mary in her single cotton garment, often damp from heat or rains, clinging to her skin'.[34] She refused to wear shoes or socks, or use a mosquito net; she ate native food and drank unfiltered water; she lived in overcrowded mud huts, with animals and humans; and learnt the language. By going native Slessor undoubtedly challenged conventional notions of femininity, although it could be argued that it was not as daring as it would have been for a single woman from a comfortable middle-class background. She was determined to live on her small salary and to send part of it home to help support her mother and sisters. With a history of working for a pittance, she was used to poverty. Thus going without was something that was to prove unproblematic; indeed, the only 'luxury' she could not do without was tea. Moreover, her ability to live native brought her closer to those she was trying to convert, something that was aided by her knowledge of the local language – Efik – which she picked up by ear.

Engagement with the local communities was as empowering as it was exhausting for Mary. She was on call it seems twenty-four hours a day, settling disputes, saving twins from murder, finding a home for abused and unwanted women, educating, evangelising, nursing and administering justice when made a magistrate. The following account is rather typical of the hours she invested in her calling:

> I sat [in court] 8 hours on Thursday, from 6 o/c till night I was occupied on Friday & all night I was out at Ikot Obon with a woman in trouble, got home at dawn & and was at it yesterday till late, was up at midnight with a twin mother who died overnight after a week of severe suffering leaving her babies with us. I've had a hard mornings work getting the body buried & Jeans room cleaned, where she lay.[35]

A fellow female missionary, Miss Ames, also commented on her punishing daily schedule:

> There was no routine with 'Ma'. One hour she might be having a political discussion with a District Commissioner, the next supervising the building of a house, and later on judging native palavers. Late one evening I heard a good deal of talking and also the sound of working. I went to see what was doing and there was 'Ma' making cement and the bairns spreading it on the floor with their hands in candle light.[36]

The cost of these exhausting routines was immense in terms of her health. Africa was a dangerous place for westerners, indeed, in the first forty years of the Calabar mission thirty Scottish missionaries had died and many more had their health ruined. Mary's punishing schedule weakened her and made her more vulnerable to disease and illness. At times, especially in the later years, she could only keep up her punishing schedule by overdosing on laudanum. She was frequently malnourished, living from 'hand to mouth', her hair occasionally fell out, her face was covered in boils at times, and she suffered temporary blindness. An extract from a letter to her friend and confidant DC Charles Partridge gives us some indication of her suffering:

> I went to the 'Commission' & went very ill with at least 100 boils over my head! . . . I lay down . . . & for a whole month I was in one prolonged agony of pain. Then the boils came in shoals, over my face . . . all over my neck & ears . . . I cried like a child. When I was not shrieking all the long weeks, no sleeping draught could keep out the pain, & I am a very shaky bundle of nerves . . . I could not see to read . . . Poor hair! Poor head! It is as bald as a sixpence . . . for the few hairs left on the front are like those of a dolls head put on with bad glue.[37]

But not only was Mary a pioneer, she was also, like other missionaries, a revolutionary. As the Nigerian historian, E. A. Ayandele, points out: 'No society could be Christianized without it being upset to a remarkable extent . . . In a "pagan" society it was the missionary's task to overturn.'[38] Mary endorsed Ayandele's perceptive comment much earlier when she stated: 'They are afraid lest this [Christianity] upset the very roots of their life, by allowing the old groundwork of all their existence to be taken away.'[39] But as a young and inexperienced missionary Mary at this stage was less reflective and as such she saw much to overturn. Moreover, her upbringing and her experience of drink-fuelled male violence also directed her to aspects of African life that she fought most to reform – the condition of women and children, particularly twins and their outcast mothers.

The peoples of Calabar believed that twins were the product of some kind of sorcery or evil spirit and as such they were killed at birth and their mothers forcibly excluded from tribal society. Children of slave mothers were abandoned and left to die. Mary's mission stations became sanctuaries for twin children and she exhorted the chiefs in palavers to allow her to assume responsibility for their welfare. Saving them, however, never meant acceptance: twins were still pariahs. The last twin to be saved by her, Madge, recalled that her rescue branded her as an object of special derision, explaining, 'I go to the market and they know I am a twin, raise two fingers to my face and run away laughing.'[40] However, through her interventions in such cases Mary built up a family of six girls and two boys – her 'bairns'. Some of them, including her favourite daughter, Janie, accompanied her on her return trips home.

Mary's adopted family became increasingly important: indeed, it grew in size as her own family decreased dramatically. The health of her mother and siblings was never robust and despite relocating the family further south to Topsham in Devonshire following the death of her sister, Susan, in April 1883, all her remaining family were dead within four years. Her mother died at the turn of the year 1886–7 and three months later her only surviving sister, Janie, was dead too.[41] Perhaps her relatively indifferent attitude to her health and to the dangers posed by her pioneering activities was the realisation that she had nothing to lose, and the knowledge that in spite of her mother's death she could still live out her wishes – the ultimate form of filial piety. These feelings were likely to have been compounded by the failure of her one, and seemingly only, relationship.

Through a shared love of literature and poetry, Mary became attached to a teacher on the mission staff, Charles W. Morrison from Kirkintilloch, who was eighteen years her junior. He was described as 'delicate, sensitive . . . a loner like Mary'.[42] They became engaged sometime in 1890–1, although no one is certain of the date. The engagement was agreed on the basis that they would work together as man and wife at Ekenge, where she had gone in 1888, in spite of the opposition of the FMB and William Anderson's decision to temporarily withdraw her salary. On this 'she was adamant'.[43] However, the marriage never took place as the Board refused permission for Morrison to leave Duke Town and join Mary at Ekenge. She reacted to the cancellation of the engagement with typical stoicism, saying: 'If God does not send him up here then he must do his work and I must mine where we have been placed.'[44] In spite of her rationalisation, it's clear that Mary was profoundly affected by the termination of her engagement. Among her papers when she died were several of her favourite books with the initials 'C.W.M.' and 'M.M.S.' close together.[45] The collapse of the relationship saw Morrison's health begin to fail and he returned to Scotland before moving to North Carolina, where he lived in a wooden hut. He died some time later when a fire destroyed his literary papers: he simply lost the will to live.

Africa became home for Mary. In any case, she was gradually becoming disenchanted with life in Britain, not simply because she associated it with personal loss, but also due to the general hurly-burly of urban life and the dull conventionalism of social relationships. Scotland was a much-changed place from the one she knew as a young woman: a country in which 'I'm hardly myself'.[46] Although she loved the shops, displaying an uncharacteristic 'revelling for frocks & furbelows',[47] after getting into an 'electric car . . . I nearly shrieked . . . just from the fear . . . It is an awful country for bustle & movement'.[48] In spite of her friends' attempts to persuade her to take a two-year term of leave in October 1907, Mary was eager to return to Africa, saying:

> though it was good to be at home, & to enjoy many things, it is far too tame, & far too exacting, to be borne willingly. Life is so full of conventional duties, which are as hard . . . as the real things of life, but much less satisfactory.[49]

Her experiences and the hardships and premature deaths of her mother and sisters made Mary acutely aware of the need for women to achieve economic independence. The subservient position of African women further intensified her belief. As she explained:

> There is no place for them outside the harem system . . . they have no proper status . . . being simply the creatures of man to be exploited and degraded . . . A girl-child, if not betrothed by her guardian, lacks the protection of law. She can, if not attached to some man, be insulted or injured with impunity.[50]

The solution was economic and involved providing girls and women with farm and industrial work and educational opportunity. From her arrival in 1876 she fought against the practice of fattening pubescent girls to increase their attractiveness as bride fodder, arguing that girls ought to be provided with the same educational opportunities as boys. Five years later Mary began training local females to staff and run orphanages, but it was at Use, in the Itu district, in 1907 that her ideas took a practical form. A settlement was established there for abused women. Fruit trees gifted by the imperial government were planted, and livestock was purchased. All of the women had their own plots to farm and primitive manufacturing using local resources, such as bamboo and coconut, was initiated.[51] In 1908 a Home for Women and Girls was established in Ikot Obong, specialising in teaching females dressmaking skills and basket-making. She also bought land to be worked as a farm.[52] On such farms women were taught basic agricultural skills, including hoeing, sowing and harvesting. Another centre was opened in 1913 in Odoro Ikpe, but by this time Mary's health had seriously deteriorated and little progress was made.

Slessor placed emphasis on practical rather than academic training. In many ways she had no choice, as there were practically no books or writing materials available to her. Rote learning of spelling and arithmetic and the study of biblical texts formed the basis of the curriculum, although creative arts and play were also a part of the school day. A cooked meal was also provided in the middle of the day, something that took until the mid-1900s to be introduced in Scottish schools. Mary's schools were free and open to all ages and social strata. No one was refused, unlike in other establishments where missionaries 'withheld schooling from those who would not agree to be baptised or take the church's sacraments'.[53] Mary was able to keep the preaching and teaching separate and until 1891 classes were delivered in the local language. The main intention was to provide a basis for the industrial training that was to follow. However, with the establishment of formal British rule in that year all instruction in state-funded schools was to be in English; she characteristically defied the ruling. Her schools were contemptuously dismissed as 'hedge schools' by the Governor General and were in time increasingly shunned by the more ambitious pupils looking for work in government service. For this she has been criticised by some Nigerian historians.[54] In spite of this, it has been estimated that she 'personally opened more than fifty elementary schools (some of which closed soon after being opened) and that, by the time of her death, over 2,000 pupils were attending small bush schools that she had started'.[55] These schools were established at no cost to either the FMB or the British administration, with most of the money and materials coming from Mary's own pocket and her friends and admirers back in Britain. Moreover, it could be reasonably argued that it was Slessor's campaigning on the issue of vocational education that led to the opening of the Hope Waddell Training Institute in 1895 in Calabar, which soon became and remained the largest institute of its kind in West Africa.[56]

The promise of education was strategically used by Slessor as a tool in shifting traditional attitudes and bringing about social reform. She realised that the chiefs were hungry for schooling 'for their boys',[57] claiming that they want their 'boys educated and they want someone to guide them safely through the new world in which they are being enclosed by the white man of whom they know so little and whom they fear'.[58] However, in exchange for schools she demanded reforms in the important areas of child marriage, sale of alcohol, Sunday markets and the acceptance of twin mothers.[59] She also used her position as magistrate to improve the position of outcast women. On one occasion she fined a town £3 for not providing water for twin mothers.[60] All this had a salutary affect on the habits and customs of the native population. Slessor could report with pride to DC Partridge's father that her work at Itu had borne fruit, saying:

We have boys educated as far as the ordinary artisans child at home, a reverent assembly worshipping regularly, & intelligently every Sabbath, paying its own expenses, and living Xtian [Christian] lives. The old drinking habits are gone & men are married, & men are buried, & are as sober, & well behaved as they are in your own neighbourhood. They do not shirk the Govts. Work nor need to be asked to do mine, & we now have a cemetery & our first Baptized Christian woman is laid in it with a Xtian burial . . . Surely a change from old times.[61]

But Mary was not simply active in advocating equal opportunities for native females and social reform, she also opposed any hint of male condescension and argued for a more prominent role for women in missionary service. In one of her bibles she wrote in the margins opposite St Paul's rules for the subjection of wives to husbands: 'Na! Na! Paul, laddie. This will no do.'[62] She wrote to DC Partridge criticising him for suggesting that men should not bring their wives to Calabar, saying: 'Women are as eager to share in all the work and sacrifice of the world as men.'[63] Women, she felt, made better missionaries and were more suited to the pioneering role than men. They were less associated with imperial government in the minds of the natives and as a result less likely to suffer opposition. Only when confidence had been achieved would men enter and build up the congregation in the usual missionary manner.[64] She also thought that women would be more sensitive to the customs and practices of tribal society and thus less judgemental or prudish than men. Mary occasionally shocked the colonial bourgeoisie with her relaxed attitude to marriage and dress. She condoned 'friend' marriages for women whose husbands were in gaol or temporarily estranged because she appreciated that women could live only precariously without the protection of a male.[65] When a black male clerk wrote to her asking that her female church members cover their 'nakedness' when they passed by his place of work, Mary answered: 'Rather a tall order, seeing Govt. has planted its shed at the ford where the women cross the Creek to their farms, & which takes a woman up to her armpits.'[66]

Although she promoted women's rights and demanded equal opportunities for both sexes, it would be difficult to describe Slessor as a proto-feminist. As Cheryl McEwan points out, she 'did not perceive the missionary life as one of liberation, rather as one of service, and despite devoting a great deal of energy to the cause of West African women, she remained remote from the debates over the rights of British women'.[67] She opposed the illegal activities of the militant suffragettes, although she was not against votes for women in principle. In a letter to a friend,

Slessor declared that she had little time for the concept of the so-called 'new woman', saying: 'I have enjoyed the old world gentlewomen, who after all are more to my taste than the new women. I'm too old for the new clever independent hand I fear.'[68] For Slessor it was the intimate domain of the home and the church that constituted the proper place for women: 'God – like motherhood is the finest sphere for women, and the way to the redemption of the world.'[69] She also found it difficult outside of Africa to assert her femininity. While serving as a magistrate in Okoyong, she was quite capable of 'administering a blow on the side of the head', in spite of the obvious difference in size and strength, as punishment to an errant husband. However, when Slessor was back in Britain on fund-raising tours, she became embarrassingly withdrawn and unable to speak in the presence of males. If males were allowed in the audience they were to be screened off. On a visit in 1898 she took fright and ran off stage in Edinburgh; in Glasgow at a reception she became so distressed after shaking hands for an hour that 'she could not speak'.[70]

Although open to qualification, the portrait of Slessor thus far is one that might be easily recognised by her legion of admirers. She is caring, particularly in regard to children and abused women, pioneering and motivated by an overwhelming desire to serve her church. But that would be a one-dimensional view. Her activities to have any meaning for a modern audience need to be placed in the context of race and Empire: two of the dominant themes of nineteenth century history.

Race became the dominant scientific discourse in late-nineteenth-century Europe. Charles Darwin's theories on evolution, particularly regarding the survival of the fittest, laid the basis for a division of the world based on higher and lower racial types. As the imperial powers were in this discourse undoubtedly the highest, the native populations of the undeveloped world were the lowest. Slessor, arriving in Calabar in 1876, was in a mindset no different from other missionaries, in spite of her working-class background. Her superiority lay in her colour: to be exact, in her whiteness. Initially, she was shocked at the indigenous culture and lifestyle, but as her knowledge of it grew and her relationship with the people developed, she moved away from this overtly racist discourse. Mary came to view European superiority as based only on knowledge of God and Christian virtues. She argued that once the West Africans accepted God and the codes of behaviour and morality associated with Christianity then any sense of superiority would dissolve. She was strongly opposed to natives turning themselves into Europeans.[71]

Admittedly, there are odd references in her letters that are racist, as well as morally superior and patronising, in tone. As late as 1905 she described the Ibibios as 'ignorant, besotted, [and] cowardly'.[72] Earlier she described Okoyong people as 'addicted to witchcraft . . . lawless . . . oppression and outrage were of common occurrence',[73] and, as Cheryl McEwan points out, on occasions she referred to West Africans as 'simple and affectionate',[74] and patronisingly referred to native men as 'boys'. All her adopted children were given western Christian names. Janie saw Britain as 'home', and English was her first language, although spoken with a strong Dundee accent![75] Thus, undoubtedly, Slessor saw British culture as superior to that of West Africa and 'British rule . . . [as by] far & away the best thing for Africa & for all subject races, that the World Powers know'.[76] She was able to demonstrate her strong sense of allegiance and patriotism during the First World War, saying: 'Oh, I wish I were twenty years younger, and if I were a man! We must not have peace until Germany licks the dirt and is undeceived and stricken once for all.'[77] The question is, how far did her innate belief in superiority of British culture and Christian virtues involve her in the imperial project?

There is an old saying among the Africans that 'When the whites came here they had the Bible and we had the land. Now they have the land and we have the Bible.'[78] The link between religion and imperial expansion could not be more explicit in native eyes. Some modern writers, echoing the sentiments of the imperial authorities, have argued that Slessor had a large part to play in relieving the natives of their land in West Africa. Michael Fry, for instance, has argued that since 'oversight of public affairs took up most of her time, her main achievement was indeed finally imperial . . . she contributed largely to extension inland of British control'.[79] The Governor General of Nigeria, Sir Frederick Lugard, claimed that she had become 'a great political factor of much value to the administration'.[80] This view is somewhat underscored by the lack of progress in bringing Christianity to the native populations. As Mary herself noted: 'They went into rapture over the Gospel, prayed aloud, clasped their hands, shed tears, and then went back to their drinking, sacrificing, and quarrelling . . . "Yes Ma . . . that is right for you: but you and we are different."'[81]

Livingstone gloomily concluded that despite seventy years of missionary work in the Calabar region only 10,800 Christians had been converted and the communion roll only stood at 3,412. As he says, 'No real impression has been made . . . she [Slessor] did what she could do in vain.'[82] Part of the problem was the insistence as central to the conversion process in Presbyterianism that repentance of one's sins is made. The peoples of Calabar had no concept of sin and thus had nothing to repent. What progress was made in converting south-east Nigeria to Christianity after 1900 was made by Efik missionaries when 'Scottish missionaries preachers were least responsible for the transmission of the Christian message in the area'.[83]

Perhaps taking a lead from the popular Victorian travel writer, Mary Kingsley – an acerbic critic of missionaries and their work in Africa, but who nevertheless felt that Slessor's 'great abilities, both physical and intellectual, have given her among the savage tribe a unique position, and won her, from white and black who know her, a profound esteem . . . and the amount of good she has done, no man can fully comprehend'[84] – some historians have placed a more positive spin on Mary's imperial involvement. Proctor argues that it was her humanitarian desire to address injustice, cruelty and suffering among the most vulnerable in south-east Nigeria that 'prompted her to serve both God and Empire'.[85] Taylor argues that through her educational and political activities, Slessor was sowing the seeds of later African nationalism. Her politics were those of 'liberation and amelioration, not of imposition and blatant imperialism'.[86] Underscoring this view, Joseph Anene and Godfrey Brown claim that she fostered an independent, nationalistic spirit that ultimately terminated colonial rule.[87]

Thus, there are some compelling and convincing arguments on both sides. The problem with such highly partisan judgements is that they fail to adequately recognise that the relationship of Slessor in particular and missionaries in general to the imperial project was more ambiguous and complex than they allow for. While not wishing to fundamentally disagree with either of these conflicting perceptions, some modifications are essential if we are to arrive at a fairer assessment of Mary's imperial role.

In confronting that 'awful thing heathenism' and, from a Christian point of view, unacceptable forms of social behaviour, Slessor, like other missionaries, was drawn into a symbiotic relationship with the imperial authorities in a number of important ways. Firstly, in terms of the representation of the African male as drunken, bloodthirsty and promiscuous she along with others provided further justification for the extension of British rule and values. Jane Haggis has observed that female reformers in Britain, by depicting Indian women as abused victims of Hinduism and themselves as free born and independent, were privileging one stereotype over another, and in doing so they were making an important 'contribution to the public perceptions of India as an appropriate subject for British imperial rule'.[88] The appropriation of landscape is also important in this respect. The depiction of Africa as the 'Dark Continent' not only fuelled the imagination of those back home, but also created further pressure for an extension of civilisation. Slessor once wrote: 'I feel drawn on and on by the magnetism of this land of dense darkness and mystery.'[89] As Cheryl McEwan argues, her writings in the *Missionary Record* were part of a literature 'of the imperial frontier, a colonising discourse that titillated Western imagination with glimpses of radical otherness'.[90]

Secondly, the imposition of law and order, the introduction of education and the extension of trade, could only be achieved with assistance from the imperial authorities. In order to implement the 1878 treaty with the kings of Calabar, which outlawed twin killing, human sacrifice and fatal poisoning, the threat if not the actuality of armed forced was necessary. As Buchan states the treaty was the result of 'pressure from [John] Beecroft [British Consul] and the Royal Navy'.[91] The White Queen of Okoyong, as the younger colonial authorities christened Slessor over a gin one night in Calabar, could never have left Ekenge to establish a mission at Itu but for the punitive British military expedition against the Aro people in 1901.[92] Mary herself justified the relationship by declaring: 'God has had to employ the British Government to do what we could not do.'[93] Missionaries were also dependent on the imperial powers for funding, particular in the areas of education and economic development.

Mary herself was a key link between the imperial project and the native populations. Without her presence in Calabar many successful negotiations between British colonial officials and native West Africans would never have been achieved. Her knowledge of the region and her grasp of Efik was recognised and appreciated by officials. Coupled to this was the fact that she was also successful with the Okoyong and Efik peoples in establishing good relations among traditionally warring enemies and allowing British traders to penetrate further into the interior of West Africa. As Livingstone states, the adoption of unrestricted trade 'helped open up the country'.[94] Building the infrastructure of the region and the establishment of manufacturing also created employment for natives and inculcated in them the steady discipline and work ethic associated with capitalist enterprise. When '600 or so of the boys' were taken off a road-building project Mary told the High Commissioner that she was:

> sorry for he would not get a cheaper or safer way of steadying & pacifying & civilizing the country. These Ekit & Aro men, Anan & etc have been utterly transformed by the steady discipline of hours & etc, & are my best friends, & they will go to their distant homes, exponents of the White Man, and thus open his way.[95]

The military and colonial officials followed close on the heels of the traders and the establishment of the Niger Coast Protectorate in 1891

placed the land under formal imperial rule. Once established, the 'benefits' of British rule were bestowed on native populations. British laws
were substituted for local laws and customs that had governed personal
and tribal relationships for centuries. In those parts of West Africa in
which British rule was less tangible, Mary acted as consular agent and
through this office helped to advance imperial interests by establishing
'native courts'. These courts were not simply judicial institutions; they
were designed to assist in the process of bringing considerable areas of
land under colonial control and became in time 'the basis upon which a
British legal system was imposed upon Nigeria' in the twentieth
century.[96] The courts were in session twice a week and sometimes lasted
all day. Mary had responsibility for preparing warrants and summaries,
writing reports on her decisions, supervising punishment, and conduct-
ing correspondence with the District Commissioner.[97] She also had to
meet with chiefs and discuss grievances. One Sunday Slessor stated that
'twenty three chiefs . . . from Ibiaku Itam' attended on her, and this was
a fairly common occurence.[98] In recognition of her work in native affairs,
in May 1905 Mary was appointed a member of the Itu Native Court with
the status of permanent Vice-President, giving her the powers of a magistrate, although she refused payment. This was the first time in the
history of the British Empire that a woman had been appointed a magistrate, an honour that reflected the high esteem the imperial authorities
held her work in. A further honour was bestowed in 1913 when she was
awarded an Honorary Associate of the Order of Saint John of Jerusalem,
of which King George V was the sovereign head, for services to philanthropy.

Thus, although the roles of the missionaries and the colonisers were
symbiotic, they were also in some ways fundamentally antagonistic. As
Fiona Bowie and others point out, 'the colonial authorities were often
unimpressed with the efficiency of the missionaries as agents of colonialism'.[99] This is because the projects were not entirely the same. The
Christian missionaries were intent on saving souls. It was only the realisation that this could not be achieved without interfering with local cul-
tures and by introducing superior values that they were pushed into a
close relationship with the colonialists: something that Mary was
acutely aware of. The interdependence was, thus, one of accident rather
than design; however, the tensions in the relationship were ongoing as
an examination of Slessor's dealings with the colonial authorities shows.

Mary did play a part in the extension of British rule in West Africa,
but at no time did she embrace the grander imperial design. In an important statement she says that

this land belongs to the native and worked by the native, tho' our officers do not believe it . . . I am not only writing rank treason, but I am doing so unrepentantly as we live in the bush under bush conditions, and I owe nothing to the government.[100]

This was further emphasised when she stated to DC Partridge: 'The very men you are educating with gun & motor & Telegraph will turn you all out & keep Africa for the Africans.'[101] Moreover, although she held positions of authority within the Empire, Mary often found herself at odds with the colonial judicial system. As a magistrate she frequently opposed policies that conflicted with local customs and laws. Indeed, she was forced to resign her position in 1909 over a clash with the authorities regarding the rights of native labourers. British companies, engaged in road-building projects, complained to the authorities of Mary's interference in industrial matters and the imperial authorities, who in any case were eager to privilege British law over tribal customs and laws, upheld their complaints. Slessor bitterly remarked, 'I'm dismissed & that by utter strangers . . . I'm too old to be trusted with the affairs of a people.'[102] This attitude is also evident in a letter to the district commissioner when the Akpap tribe complained in 1910 that they were being forced to build a road through a sacred grove of yams. In it she expressed her opposition to such insensitivity, ending the letter with 'I am NOT your obedient servant'. She believed in peaceful conquest through the demonstration of superior values and lifestyles, rather than force of arms, saying, 'I can't bear those dreadful expeditions.'

In spite of her championship of native rights, the relationship between Mary and the people of Calabar was not one of equality. Because of her pivotal role as mediator between colonialists and natives she exercised a degree of power unthinkable for a woman of any social class in Britain. She was a Vice Consul of the British Empire and this guaranteed respect in a highly patriarchal society. One missionary noted that she never allowed 'a native to sit in her presence . . . and she never shakes hands with them'.[103] The mother–child relationship she had with the native peoples also 'involved elements of inequality: she was British, her children were African'.[104] Indeed, in an evaluation of her imperial role, McEwan argues that perhaps Mary's later anti-imperial statements were the result of her marginalisation within colonial affairs as the government took a more active role in administering the Protectorate.[105]

Thus, an analysis of Slessor's work in West Africa raises some of the complexities and ambiguities in the relationship between native people and missionaries, missionaries and colonialists, Empire and the Scots. Her presence in West Africa was undoubtedly of significance to the colonial administration in a numbers of ways. Firstly, her forays into the interior allowed British rule to expand into previously inaccessible territories; secondly, her skills in mediation brought closer links between the imperial powers and the indigenous peoples, particularly with the kings; and, thirdly, the native courts she presided over allowed British law to usurp native customs and traditions. Her importance to the Empire was recognised in the honours bestowed on her when alive, but also in death. When Mary died on 11 January 1915 a state funeral was held in Duke Town. The coffin was draped in a Union Jack and attended by government officials, merchants and missionaries. Great crowds watched the procession, which moved along in silence. The mourners at the graveside sang two hymns – 'When the day of toil is done' and 'Asleep in Jesus'[106] – and she was laid to rest beside William and Louisa Anderson. But Slessor never saw herself as a tool of Empire; in fact, as we have seen she spent a great deal of her time in fighting colonial expansion. She set out to spread the Christian faith and remove the more barbaric customs, without adversely affecting native culture, believing West Africans to be inferior only because they had not accepted the word of God. In this she may have been naive, but as a missionary in West Africa she is still remembered as *Eka Kpukpro Owo* – 'the mother of all the peoples'. She is still revered in Calabar to this day. In 1987 a statue of Slessor holding a pair of twins was erected in her memory and a street was named after her, and the University of Calabar recently launched a medical journal bearing her name.[107]

In her native Dundee there are also memorials to Mary Mitchell Slessor's work and memory, such as the stained glass window in the McManus Gallery and the Mary Slessor Centre. Municipal veneration is not only bestowed for her missionary activity, but because she stands as potent symbol of self-improvement to the working class of Dundee. Mary's life remains testimony to a powerful narrative enshrined in the kailyard school of Scottish literature in which individuals overcome social adversity through the adoption of appropriate values, rather than engage in collective action. In her case it was the values of Presbyterianism: devotion to God, hard work, uncomplaining suffering and service to others. A humble weaver from an impoverished background had become an imperial icon, a role model for those in her social position to emulate. Thus, Mary's legacy is not simply to be located in the mud huts of Calabar, but can also be found reverberating in the slums of Dundee.

NOTES

1. W. P. Livingstone, *Mary Slessor of Calabar: Pioneer Missionary* (1916), p. 323.
2. Livingstone, *Mary Slessor*, p. 344.
3. J. Buchan, *The Expendable Mary Slessor* (Edinburgh, 1980), p. xi.
4. See J. Haggis, 'White women and colonisation: towards a non-recuperative history', in C. Midgley (ed.) *Gender and Imperialism* (Manchester, 1998), pp. 45–78; C. McEwan, *Gender, Geography and Empire: Victorian Women Travellers in West Africa* (Aldershot, 2000); F. Bowie et al. (eds), *Women and Missions: Past and Present* (Oxford, 1993).
5. Letter to C. Partridge, 16 October 1913 (Dundee City Archives)
6. Livingstone, *Mary Slessor*, p. 1.
7. Livingstone, *Mary Slessor*, p. 2.
8. For an extended discussion of the importance of respectability in working-class culture see W. W. Knox, *Industrial Nation: Work, Culture and Society in Scotland, 1800–Present* (Edinburgh, 1999), pp. 94–103.
9. Livingstone, *Mary Slessor*, p. 6.
10. Livingstone, *Mary Slessor*, pp. 8–9.
11. E. Robertson, *Mary Slessor* (Edinburgh, 2001), p. 6.
12. J. Stein, 'Mary Slessor', in J. Harrison Hudson et al., *Let the Fire Burn* (Dundee, 1978), p. 47.
13. Letter to C. Partridge, 15 April 1908.
14. Letter to C. Partridge, 10 January 1911.
15. Robertson, *Mary Slessor*, p. 9.
16. Buchan, *Mary Slessor*, pp. 17–18.
17. E. Gordon, *Women and the Labour Movement in Scotland, 1850–1914* (Oxford, 1991), p. 156.
18. Gordon, *Women*, p. 160.
19. Livingstone, *Mary Slessor*, p. 2.
20. J. Hardage, 'The legacy of Mary Slessor', *International Bulletin of Missionary Research*, 26 (2000), p. 178; C. Christian and G. Plummer, *God and One Redhead* (London, 1970), p. 24.
21. Quoted in Livingstone, *Mary Slessor*, p. 135.
22. Haggis, 'White women', p. 56.
23. Haggis, 'White women', p. 59.
24. Quoted in Stein, 'Mary Slessor', p. 57.
25. *The Scotsman*, 18 January 1915.
26. Buchan, *Mary Slessor*, p. xi.
27. Livingstone, *Mary Slessor*, p. 27.
28. M. Fry, *Scotland and Empire* (2001), pp. 180–1.
29. Livingstone, *Mary Slessor*, p. 25.
30. Livingstone, *Mary Slessor*, p. 32.
31. W. Harrison Daniel, 'Patterns of mission preaching in the UPC of Scotland

Mission to Calabar, 1846–1895', *Bulletin of the Scottish Institute of Missionary Studies*, 8–9 (1992–3), p. 30.

32. Christian and Plummer, *Redhead*, p. 110.
33. Buchan, *Mary Slessor*, pp. 169–70.
34. Christian and Plummer, *Redhead*, p. 176.
35. Letter to C. Partridge, 29 March 1908.
36. Quoted in Livingstone, *Mary Slessor*, p. 236.
37. Letter to C. Partridge, 7 July 1909.
38. E. A. Ayandele, *The Missionary Impact on Modern Nigeria, 1842–1914* (London, 1966), p. 330.
39. *The Women's Missionary Magazine*, July 1912, p. 149.
40. Christian and Plummer, *Redhead*, p. 119.
41. Livingstone, *Mary Slessor*, p. 51.
42. Buchan, *Mary Slessor*, p. 121.
43. Christian and Plummer, *Redhead*, p. 86.
44. Quoted in Christian and Plummer, *Redhead*, p. 89.
45. Livingstone, *Mary Slessor*, p. 115.
46. Livingstone, *Mary Slessor*, p. 244.
47. Letter to C. Partridge, 11 July 1907.
48. Letter to C. Partridge, 27 June 1907.
49. Letter to C. Partridge, 25 October 1907.
50. Livingstone, *Mary Slessor*, p. 221.
51. D. M. MacFarlan, *Calabar: the Church of Scotland Missions, 1846–1946* (London, 1946), pp. 118–9.
52. W. H. Taylor, *Mission to Educate: a History of the Educational Work of the Scottish Presbyterian Mission in East Nigeria, 1846–1900* (Leiden, 1996), pp. 130–1.
53. Taylor, *Mission*, p. 121.
54. Taylor, *Mission*, p. 134.
55. Taylor, *Mission*, p. 126.
56. Taylor, *Mission*, p. 128.
57. Letter to Mr Stevenson, 20 February 1914.
58. Quoted in Taylor, *Mission*, p. 126.
59. Taylor, *Mission*, p. 125.
60. Livingstone, *Mary Slessor*, p. 233.
61. Letter to C. Partridge (senior), 10 January 1911.
62. Quoted in Buchan, p. 195.
63. Quoted in Christian and Plummer, *Redhead*, p. 165.
64. Livingstone, *Mary Slessor*, pp. 320–1.
65. Buchan, *Mary Slessor*, p. 195.
66. Letter to Partridge, 27 April 1910.
67. McEwan, *Gender, Geography and Empire*, p. 58.
68. Quoted in McEwan, 'Mother of all the peoples', p. 147.
69. Livingstone, *Mary Slessor*, p. 322.
70. Buchan, *Mary Slessor*, p. 159.

71. Livingstone, *Mary Slessor*, p. 321.
72. Letter to C. Partridge, 6 January 1905.
73. Quoted in Livingstone, *Mary Slessor*, p. 58.
74. McEwan, *Gender, Geography and Empire*, p. 103.
75. Christian and Plummer, *Redhead*, p. 85.
76. Letter to Mr and Mrs Partridge, 10 March 1910.
77. Quoted in Livingstone, *Mary Slessor*, p. 333.
78. F. Bowie, 'Introduction: reclaiming women's presence', in Bowie, et al., *Women and Missions*, p. 16.
79. Fry, *Scottish Empire*, p. 183.
80. Quoted in J. H. Proctor, 'Serving God and the Empire: Mary Slessor in South-East Nigeria, 1876–1915', *Journal of Religion in Africa*, XXX (2000), p. 45.
81. Quoted in Livingstone, *Mary Slessor*, p. 154.
82. Livingstone, *Mary Slessor*, p. 346.
83. Daniel, 'Patterns of mission preaching', p. 38.
84. M. Kingsley, *Travels in West Africa* (1897), p. 74.
85. Proctor, 'God and the Empire', p. 59.
86. Taylor, *Mission*, p. 133.
87. J. Anene and G. Brown, *Africa in the Nineteenth and Twentieth Centuries* (London, 1966).
88. Haggis, 'White women and colonialism', p. 67.
89. Quoted in Livingstone, *Mary Slessor*, p. 189.
90. J. Comaroff and J. Comaroff, 'Through the looking-glass: colonial encounters of the first kind', *Journal of Historical Sociology*, 1 (1988), p. 9, cited by McEwan, 'Mother of all the peoples', p. 129.
91. Buchan, *Mary Slessor*, p. 47.
92. Livingstone, *Mary Slessor*, pp. 192–3.
93. *Missionary Record*, November 1906, p. 279.
94. Livingstone, *Mary Slessor*, p. 38.
95. Letter to C. Partridge, 30 April 1906.
96. McEwan, 'Mother of all the peoples', p. 147.
97. Proctor, 'Serving God', p. 55.
98. Letter to C. Partridge, 17 January 1905.
99. Bowie, 'Introduction', *Women and Missions*, p. 19.
100. Letter to Mrs Findlay, 24 August 1912 quoted in McEwan, *Gender, Geography and Empire*, p. 39.
101. Letter to C. Partridge, 7 July 1909.
102. Letter to C. Partridge, 9 December 1909.
103. M. Kearny, Great Scotswomen (1933), p. 253.
104. McEwan, *Gender, Geography and Empire*, p. 103.
105. McEwan, *Gender, Geography and Empire*, p. 54.
106. Livingstone, *Mary Slessor*, pp. 339–40.
107. C. Di Domenico and S. McDermott, 'Mary Slessor's letters: images and reflections', *The Nigerian Field*, 65 (2000), p. 126.

7

Elsie Maud Inglis: Scotland's Joan of Arc?

◦

Small in stature and somewhat frail looking, Elsie Maud Inglis appeared to be as far from popular fiction's ideal of the heroine as one could get, yet she had a reservoir of courage and a disdain for danger that would have been considered even a little preposterous in a character in a girl's comic of the time. She possessed a clear and unwavering sense of purpose and a resolute determination to improve the social and political condition of women. These qualities were, of course, seen in others, but what distinguished Elsie from her contemporaries in the pursuit of equality between the sexes was that she stretched the boundaries of femininity that bit further. She campaigned for the right of women to serve at the military front as ambulance drivers, nurses and surgeons. Although rejected by the military authorities in Britain, her Scottish Women's Hospitals (SWH) served with distinction in terrible conditions in France and Serbia throughout the First World War. Heroism was rewarded with eulogies, honours and medals from political leaders and even Queen Mary, who wrote, after Elsie's death in 1917, that her 'splendid service . . . to Serbia can never be forgotten'.[1] But what exactly drove Elsie to put her life and that of others in such great danger in Serbia? How did she balance private and public motivations in this struggle? There is also the impact that Elsie's actions had on the short- and long-term position of women in Britain to consider. Her decision to place country before gender at the start of the First World War posed a major dilemma for the women's suffrage movement, in which she had played a distinguished part. Women were now expected to defend a state that had persistently refused them full citizenship. Moreover, by placing women in uniform, even as non-combatants, she was actively militarising them and at the same time shattering existing standards of femininity. The presence of women at the front gradually changed social perceptions that war was an exclusively male sphere, and that it could be used as a way to define what was essentially feminine and what was masculine. The inclusion of women in the armed forces in recent years as combatants means that they take as well as give life; something that places a question mark over long held beliefs in woman as carer and nurturer.

The issues of women and their militarisation were, however, hardly at the forefront of feminist discourse when Elsie was born in India on 16 August 1864 to John Inglis, of the East India Company (EIC), and Harriet Lowis Thompson, daughter of George Thompson, also of the EIC. The family connection with India could be traced back to Elsie's great grandfather who was secretary to Warren Hastings. John Inglis had absorbed from his father the idea of the British Empire as a great civilising force in the world and when the Crown took over the running of India from the EIC in 1858 he became a member of the newly formed Indian Civil Service. He encouraged native economic development, spoke out against infanticide and promoted female education. By 1875 he had become Chief Commissioner of Oudh and was being touted for even greater things. However, the appointment of Lord Lytton as Governor General put paid to his ambition. John Inglis was opposed to the more aggressive imperialist strategies of the Raj and as such fell out of favour and was passed over for promotion as Lieutenant Governor of the United Provinces. He retired at the age of fifty-six after thirty years of service. It was this idea of Christian service that he instilled in the mind of Elsie from childhood and this continued into adulthood; indeed, she was in almost daily contact with her father until his death in March 1894.[2] Harriet Inglis was equally remarkable, although not as influential on Elsie as her father was. She was a deeply religious woman with a strong and determined character. When she was forced along with her six children in the late 1850s to stay in England for reasons of safety as a result of the Indian Mutiny, Harriet established a successful working-man's club in Southampton. On Sunday evenings she would lecture on religious topics to 'the crowded hall of men'.[3]

Parental influences were underpinned by her formative educational experience. Although John Inglis had decided to retire to Edinburgh to settle his wayward sons to some kind of living, a brief stay in Tasmania was necessary. The Inglis' lived in some comfort in the little town of Hobart, but this was far removed from their previously opulent lifestyle in India. While there a teacher trained by Dorathea Beale, founder of female education at Cheltenham Ladies College, taught Elsie. Miss Knott articulated Beale's vision that 'education would form women into a vast army to serve and uplift society' and this fitted with the Inglis' liberal philosophy.[4] The family left Tasmania in 1878 for Edinburgh and at the age of fourteen Elsie was enrolled in the Edinburgh Institution for the Education of Young Ladies. Although her mother had described her as a 'plodder', she thrived and displayed from an early stage the kind of organisational and leadership qualities that characterised her later life.

Elsie organised a campaign for outdoor recreation for her fellow pupils, edited the school magazine – *Edina* – returning a profit on it, and presided over the Literary and Debating societies. In spite of her studies and extra curricular activities, she always found time for long walks with her father.[5] When she left for Paris in 1882 to finish her education, John Inglis wrote to her expressing his sadness at her departure saying: 'If by any exertion of our will we could know what anyone we loved, and who was absent from us, was doing, I think I should see you, my darling, every minute of the day.'[6] He remained the seminal influence on her intellectual and social development. When a student Elsie organised a small discussion group – the Six Sincere Students' Society – to study the writings of the American philosopher, Ralph Waldo Emerson, particularly his essays on 'Self reliance and heroism', her father naturally was a member. Such was the bond between father and daughter that a friend wrote, 'No biography of her will be true which does not emphasise the beautiful and deep love and sympathy between Elsie and Mr Inglis.'[7]

That bond was strengthened further by the death of her mother in January1885 from scarlet fever. From that day on as her sister Eva explained, 'Elsie shouldered all father's burdens, and they went on together until his death'.[8] Harriet's death was also a turning point in Elsie's psychological development. Until then she had looked upon herself as a 'dreamer' unconnected to and untroubled by the practical aspects of life. She wrote: 'The bottom of the whole evil is the habit of dreaming, which must be given up. So help me God.'[9] The concept of service was to be underscored by this devotion to the practical and the eradication of emotionalism. This mindset was captured in a series of resolutions:

> I must give up dreaming – making stories
> I must give up getting cross
> I must devote my mind to more housekeeping
> I must be more thorough in everything
> I must be more truthful.[10]

Elsie's 'thorough' attitude to life also was reflected in her choice of career – medicine. Sophia Jex-Blake established the Edinburgh School of Medicine for Women (ESMW) in 1886 with tuition fees of £40 per annum. It was affordable and it allowed Elsie the luxury of studying while living at home and caring for her father. However, she soon became embroiled in a series of challenges to the leadership style of Jex-Blake. Her high-handed and authoritarian manner irritated the young women in the School and brought out the combative side of Elsie's character.

Matters came to a head when in July 1888 one student who had missed work through illness failed an examination. On appeal the examiners awarded her a pass; in spite of this Jex-Blake charged her with 'dishonourable conduct'. Another incident involved the Caddell sisters, Grace and Georgina, who were refused entry to the School due to their 'insubordination'. They brought an action for £500 in damages against the ESMW and won the support of Elsie, who argued that the real issue was whether 'female students were to be recognised as serious individuals with a right to run their own lives and protest about unfair treatment as men did'.[11]

Confronting an iconic figure such as Jex-Blake won Elsie a number of enemies, especially since she was utterly ruthless in her dealings with her. With the help of John Inglis and sympathisers, Elsie founded the Scottish Association for the Medical Education of Women (SAMED), which opened a rival school for medicine – the Medical College for Women – in Chambers Street. The new school did not lack money or influence and, in spite of charging lower fees than the ESMW, within two years of its foundation SAMED was able, at a cost of £700, to endow two wards at the Royal Edinburgh Infirmary to be set aside for women students, as well as enlist the services of eighteen distinguished lecturers.[12] After eighteen months at SAMED Elsie moved to the Glasgow Infirmary to study under one of Scotland's leading surgeons, William McEwen, who was not only an innovator in bone surgery, but was one of the first to operate for brain disorders. Moreover, he was free from the kind of prejudices against women doctors that his more misogynist colleagues held.[13] Writing to her father from her lodgings at the YWCA she declared: 'I am going to work like *anything* . . . I mean to be very successful.'[14] At the age of twenty-seven Elsie became a Licentiate of the Royal College of Physicians and Surgeons, Edinburgh, and a Licentiate of the Faculty of Physicians and Surgeons, Glasgow.

To further her knowledge she moved to London to take up a post as Resident Medical Officer to the New Hospital for Women and then to the Rotunda in Dublin to gain experience in midwifery. On the suggestion of Jessie MacGregor, a fellow student at the ESMW, to establish a joint practice Elsie returned once more to Edinburgh and began her work among the poor. She was no stranger to poverty as while a student at Glasgow Infirmary Elsie had worked in the slums. Slum life impacted most heavily on women and this made a deep and lasting impression on her, particularly regarding the powerlessness of women in a strongly misogynist culture. Elsie was shocked when she witnessed a drunken husband kicking his ill wife out of their home and she declared:

He ought to have been horsewhipped, and when I have the vote I shall vote that all men who turn their wives and families out of doors . . . shall be horse-whipped. And if they make the excuse they were tipsy, I should give them double.[15]

The problem was nationwide as she recognised while working at the New Hospital in London. She wrote to her father in despair, saying:

You don't know the trouble we have here with the husbands . . . Any idea that anybody is to be thought of but themselves never enters their lordly minds, and the worst of it is, these stupid idiots of women don't seem to think so either.[16]

Just as she had confronted the authoritarianism of Jex-Blake, Elsie went on a social and political crusade to improve the position of women, particularly in the poorer areas of Edinburgh. With her father's death in March 1894 there was nothing to hold her back. She opened a small hospital staffed solely by women in George Square but when the lease was up on the premises she relocated to the Old Town and The Hospice was opened in January 1904 at 219 High Street. The Hospice was innovatory in its treatment of women and was one of the first hospitals to make anaesthetics in childbirth available to the poorest of women. It also became a centre for district midwifery. Shortly after this, in July 1905, Elsie was offered an appointment as a consultant at Sophia Jex-Blake's Bruntsfield Hospital. From her retirement home in Sussex Blake opposed the appointment and in a show of strength was offered the option of resigning or becoming vice-president of the hospital by the governing body. She chose the first option and Elsie was duly appointed.[17] In February 1911, the Hospice and Bruntsfield Hospital amalgamated, with the latter dealing with medical and surgical cases and the former with maternity and child welfare. Queen Mary visited the new premises in July, which as Lawrence notes 'must have been a bitter pill for Sophia Jex-Blake, who still had three years to live'.[18]

In 1908, as part of her concern for the welfare of children, Elsie opened the first infant milk depot in Edinburgh and began the systematic inspection of babies, an action that foreshadowed the introduction of children's welfare reforms by the Liberal government of 1906–10. Complementing the public dispensation of health care were the acts of private charity by Elsie to her poorer patients. According to Lawrence, 'She paid for treatment out of her own pocket, arranged holidays for them at her own expense, and equipped them with clothes for such occasions.' For this she was 'adored' by them.[19] One grateful father said of her: 'that woman has done more for the folk living between Morrison Street and the High Street than all the ministers of Edinburgh and Scotland itself ever did for anyone'.[20] Elsie could afford to do so. By this time she was the leading female practitioner in Edinburgh reputedly earning somewhere between two- and three-thousand pounds a year, much of this coming from richer patients, and had a substantial residence and a staff of four servants in fashionable Walker Street in the west end of the city.[21]

In spite of her devotion to her poorer patients, Elsie's actions were consistent with her belief in Christian paternalism, of the rich helping the less fortunate. At no time did she question the economic system that created a situation in which people, as one Labour politician later put it, were 'starving in the midst of plenty'.[22] The paucity of her thinking on the subject was demonstrated when she led a research project into poverty and nutrition funded by Edinburgh Town Council in the early 1900s. The findings were published in a report – *Study of the Diet of the Labouring Classes in Edinburgh* – that questioned why prisoners and the inmates of poorhouses had a better diet than those of the 'free labouring classes'. However, all that was recommended were the issuing of food tables and instructions on the rules of diet to the 'steady thrifty poor'.[23] Elsie concentrated on the effects of poverty and avoided questioning the causes. The former held out the possibility of practical relief while the latter led into the more difficult areas of social philosophy, and Elsie was a doer rather than a thinker. As a fellow student once remarked she had a 'masterly grasp of what was practical', but failed to develop any sustained interest in 'the purely scientific side' of medicine.[24]

This was also apparent in her political activity. Elsie was a member of the Women's Liberal Federation and was vice president of the Central Edinburgh Women's Liberal Association for sixteen years. However, she gradually became disenchanted with the Liberal Party. She joined a breakaway group – the Women's Liberal League – in protest over the Boer War, which later became an educational body campaigning for social and factory reform.[25] The Boers deserved their freedom, but in granting them independence Elsie did not envisage the break-up of Empire, indeed, as Frances Balfour states, 'she was an Imperialist in the best sense, and had high ideals for her country and people'.[26] That idealism was also implicit in her support for Irish Home Rule. In a letter to her father, Elsie outlined her vision of future imperial relations:

> I should not wonder if the whole thing makes us devise some plan for one Imperial Parliament and local government for Ireland, Scotland and the colonies, ending in making the integrity of the Empire and the unity of the English-speaking race, more apparent than it is now, and with the Irish contented and managing their own affairs in their own mad way.[27]

Dissatisfaction with the imperial policies of the Liberal leadership was compounded by its insistence in placing party interests before the franchise.[28] Experience in medicine had visibly manifested the subordination of women and Elsie instinctively felt the only way of correcting this was political. Women were to be mobilised as only with the vote could the needs of their sex and that of children be addressed: men were patently uninterested. As she put it, 'Educated women must seize the vote, because only so could they effectively help their downtrodden sisters in the slums.'[29] Elsie felt this could best be done by acting above party and thus she 'severed her connection with the Liberal Party'.[30]

It was while working at the New Hospital in London that she got actively drawn into the women's suffrage campaign. Elsie's first public speaking engagement was on the suffrage question. When she returned to Edinburgh she was determined to build up membership and support among Scottish women for the Scottish Federation of Women's Suffrage Societies (SFWSS), of which she was secretary. Her devotion to the cause was nothing short of heroic. The schedule was punishing, speaking on average at four meetings a week, and travelling as far as Orkney and Shetland to explain the need for franchise reform. She was a confirmed constitutionalist and as such opposed the militant methods of the Women's Social and Political Union (WSPU). After the so-called 'outrages' in 1912, in which militant suffragettes burnt railway stations, post boxes, and other buildings in Scotland, Elsie signed her name to a letter condemning militancy, along with Millicent Fawcett, Eleanor Rathbone, Robert Cecil and Lord Haldane, among others, stating:

> We reprobate in the strongest way lawlessness and outrage on every ground. Conduct involving such methods is, in this country, not only a crime but a blunder . . . If . . . the WSPU proceed to further violence, we can only regard them as more attached to their own methods than to the good of the cause, and as being in effect its worst enemies.[31]

Elsie also rejected the idea that in some way the constitutionalists benefited from the activities of their more militant sisters. In a letter to *The Scotsman*, she argued that it was 'exactly the opposite' and Societies had written to her claiming that after each episode of militancy they experienced real difficulty in attracting people to meetings and that it was virtually impossible to carry on the work of the SFWSS in such an antagonistic atmosphere.[32] Thus, it was only legal protest that won her support. A favoured method was using the courts to exploit legal loopholes in franchise legislation. In 1906 the first contested university seat occurred and a group of women centred round Elsie applied for voting papers and formed themselves into a committee. They argued that the university had no legal right to withhold ballot papers from female graduates since the 1868 University Act specified 'person' rather than 'man'. The case went all the way to the House of Lords, but the law lords found in favour of Lord Ordinary's judgement that 'person' meant 'man'.[33]

It was the very failure of such legalistic approaches and the frustrations that they created among activists that had galvanised the militant suffragettes in the first place. The pace of reform was too slow, but it was the only way forward as far as Elsie was concerned. The suffrage movement was thus deeply divided and by the approach of the First World War was haemorrhaging membership at an alarming rate. The war itself posed further dilemmas for the cause. Women were being called upon to recognise the superior claims of nationhood over sisterhood, and to defend and support a state that had consistently denied them the full rights of citizenship. This dilemma split the Suffragists as well as the Suffragettes. Those who opposed the war did so on the basis that pacifism and feminism were essentially linked, and 'because women knew the price of life they could never consent to the random and wanton slaughter of war. Pacifism was only the natural expression of their womanhood'.[34] The majority, however, took the opposite view. Mrs Fawcett of the NUWSS supported the war as one for freedom and justice. Just as the Suffragists were struggling to promote the rights of women, so Britain was actively defending the rights of small nations and international justice. Thus the two struggles were inextricably linked in her mind. The WSPU took the view that without victory over Germany there would be nothing left of democracy and any hope of women receiving the vote would disappear.[35] These women, who had tried to bring about political change through acts of violence and lawlessness, were now pressing white feathers into the hands of conscientious objectors and non-service young men.

Elsie sided with the pro-war element in the suffrage movement. She was of the opinion that the war offered an opportunity for women to provide invaluable service to the nation state, which in time would be recognised and prove them worthy of the vote.[36] It also allowed women to refute the well-worn argument that since they played no part in the defence of their country they were not entitled to have a say in the way it was run. Elsie argued that women could prove their worth by serving as doctors, nurses and auxiliaries. Although fifty when war broke out in August 1914, she volunteered her services to the Royal Army Medical Corps (RAMC) as a surgeon, but was told to 'go home and sit still' by an officer.[37] As commandant of the Sixth Edinburgh Voluntary Aid

Detachment, which trained women in how to set up hospitals, first aid and stretcher drill, she also offered its services to the War Office but they were rejected too.[38]

Frustrated by the authorities' opposition, Elsie formed the SWH and offered her services to France and Serbia. She recognised the huge propaganda value of such an organisation for the women's cause. Writing to Mrs Fawcett in October 1914, Elsie said,

> I cannot think of anything more calculated to bring home to men the fact that women can help intelligently in any kind of work. So much of our work is done where they cannot see it. They'll see every bit of this.[39]

However, an inspired idea was one thing, putting into operation was something quite different. Properly equipped field hospitals needed money and lots of it. To raise the necessary funds Elsie opened a subscription putting up £100 of her own money to kick-start the campaign. She had estimated that the SWH would need somewhere in the region of £50,000 as it would cost around £1,000 to equip and run a hospital of a hundred beds and employ a staff of four doctors, two senior and two junior, and ten nurses for six months. NUWSS' newspaper – *The Common Cause* – published an appeal and 10,000 leaflets were distributed around Scotland. This did much to improve the cash flow, but what turned a trickle into a flood was the mass meeting held at Kingsway Hall, London, on 20 October 1914. Speaking on the subject of 'What women can do to help the war', Elsie won over the rank and file of the suffrage movement and the money poured in reaching a staggering total of £450,000 by 1918.[40] The Glasgow Suffrage Society alone sent never less than £1,000 a month to the SWH.[41]

Although it was known as the SWH it was never purely a Scottish initiative, in fact, only thirteen members of the original units were Scottish; of the rest five were Irish, three were Welsh, and fifty came from England.[42] Two units were established: the first at a disused Cistercian abbey at Royaumont, around twenty-five miles from Paris, and a second at Kragujevatz, Serbia; later, the number of units increased in proportion to the spread of hostilities. After organising the affairs of the SWH at home and spearheading the funding drive, Elsie herself arrived in Serbia and was able to file her first report on 11 May 1915. As war is not unrelenting and the intensity of the fighting is conditioned by various factors, including weather, supplies and the physical and mental condition of the soldiers, when Elsie arrived in Kragujevatz there were no wounded men to deal with as Serbia had successfully repelled an earlier Austrian assault and was enjoying a breathing space from war. Thus, the first few months were spent coping with a typhoid epidemic and preparing for the eventual onset of hostilities. There was time for leisure activities and life could be described as almost idyllic, until the combined German and Austrian assault in the October of that year. From that point on life for Elsie and her women was one of blood, of suffering and, for some, death. However, this is not the place to discuss in detail the horrendous conditions the women faced, or the various personality clashes among the leadership, or the infighting, indeed, that has been well told elsewhere by Leah Leneman and Margot Lawrence, but a number of select quotations may convey the dangers and the privations they were exposed to.

During December 1916 the Serbian and Russian units served by the SWH were being forced out of occupied Rumanian territory by a ferocious enemy assault. Elsie and her women were evacuated from Bralia to another town on the border – Galatz. Although the distance between the towns was only fifteen miles, the journey took fifty-six hours. The sheer number of wounded and dying men in the hospital at Galatz overwhelmed Elsie and her staff, in spite of working a twenty-four hour stretch. The head cook, Mary Milne, described the scenes as 'terrible' and unbearable and that the 'cries and groans of the poor fellows [still] haunt one'. Elsie herself spoke of being plunged into a 'nightmare'.[43] Saving lives was a dangerous occupation and on a number of occasions the women were close to death themselves. Mary Milne recorded in her diary the bombing of Medjidia, Rumania, where a unit of the SWH was stationed: 'Suddenly it seemed as if the end of the world had come – 60 bombs were dropped on the town . . . the place was in darkness with the earth and debris that shot into the air . . . shells were whistling through the air – machine guns rattling.' Another time she remarked somewhat nonchalantly that it was 'rather disconcerting cooking with shells flying through the air & shrapnel raining around us'.[44] Privation was also never far away. On the retreat to the Russian border in December the women were reduced to eating 'slices of sour, black, "green fluffy" mouldy . . . bread'.[45]

Elsie was exposed to two tours of duty. The first came to an end when the all-conquering German and Austrian armies swept the Serbian forces back to the Russian border towards the end of 1915 and the SWH units there were grudgingly repatriated, arriving back in Britain in February 1916. Before returning to duty in September that year, Elsie did much to raise public awareness of the plight of the Serbians among the British public. A flag day was held and hundreds of lectures were successfully delivered throughout the country.[46] She was guest of honour at a reception on 3 April at which Crown Prince Alexander and the Serbian Prime

Minister, Pashitch, were present and where she was awarded the Order of the White Eagle, the country's highest honour.[47] Although feted by the Serbian authorities, her relationship with the SWH Edinburgh and London committees was strained to breaking point as her leadership of the organisation was being undermined, and her contribution undervalued, by those she criticised as creating unacceptable delays in despatching volunteers and equipment to the field, and of having a restrictive vision of the possibilities for extending the work of the Hospitals. A move to resign was halted by the recognition that the SWH needed Elsie and her name more than she need it, although this did not prevent her from resigning from her role as commissioner and honorary secretary of the Edinburgh committee.[48] Her second tour of duty was thus under the auspices of the London committee, who paid for the equipping and the maintaining of the units. It came to an end in October 1917, shortly after the Russian Revolution. The situation had becoming highly dangerous and the new Bolshevik authorities were eyeing the SWH suspiciously. However, Elsie refused to leave the battle zone unless what remained of the Serbian division went with her and the SWH to safety. When the revolutionary authorities agreed this, they made the long journey to the port of Archangel and home. In any case, it is doubtful that she could have gone on for any greater length of time, as she was desperately ill, and had been since late September. Mary Milne said of her:

> She was unable to leave her tent; and from then on she was more or less ill all the time. Some days she was well enough to sit outside her tent in the sunshine; but whether in her tent or outside, she directed all.[49]

The cause of her illness is unknown, although Leah Leneman claims that it was some form of cancer and that Elsie had known she had the disease before she left Britain.[50] Unfortunately, there is no way of proving this since the death certificate failed to record cancer as the cause of death and her biographers, Frances Balfour and Margot Lawrence, never mentioned it. It may simply have been that her body was worn out with overwork and under-nourishment. The punishing schedule of medical and political activity would have obviously impacted on Elsie's health even before she arrived in Serbia. Before the war her only release from continuous activity was her annual holiday and her health regime. Each September she would depart for a fortnight to some out-of-the-way place, 'where not even her letters were sent after her'. All that was required was hot water for bathing and 'her paintbox'.[51] In Edinburgh, Elsie stuck to a health regime that included cold baths, long walks and open windows.[52]

Whatever the cause of her decline, Elsie in typical fashion soldiered on. During the four-week train journey from Hadji Abdul, Rumania, to the port of Archangel in Russia, she insisted on dressing every day, in spite of being in considerable pain. After some delay, the SWH, Serbian officers and soldiers left Archangel on 15 November for Britain arriving in Tyneside seven days later. Elsie was determined to say farewell to the Serbian officers, and as Miss Arbuthnot, grand-daughter of Sir William Muir, wrote, she stood on deck of the SS *Porto*,

> her face ashy pale and drawn, her worn uniform and faded medals, and none who saw her could forget, as she stood there extending her hand to each officer to kiss and flashed at each of them the smile that spoke of an unquestionable spirit.[53]

She died shortly after this in Newcastle on 26 November. The body lay in state in St Giles' Cathedral, Edinburgh. Members of the royal families of Britain and Serbia, the Scottish Military Command, and others, including twenty-five Serb boys who had made the 'Great Retreat' and who were now attending school in Edinburgh, attended the funeral. Mourners, of whom *The Times* noted a large number were women, 'the great majority wearing black', lined the streets in their thousands.[54] The coffin was covered with the Union Jack and the flag of Serbia, and mounted on a gun carriage drawn by six black horses. She was buried in the Dean Cemetery. The press issued eulogies. The *Scots Pictorial* considered her 'a supreme heroine in a time that has produced many heroines and she laid down her life for her fellow beings as truly as . . . she had she given it on the battlefield'.[55]

However, some members of the SWH, who were critical of her leadership, her moralising, as well as her puritanical attitudes, painted a very different picture of Elsie to that found in the adoring, almost sycophantic, media representations. What irritated them the most were her high-handedness and her vicious temper. She requested that the nurses, ambulance drivers, cooks and junior staff address the officers of the unit as 'Ma'am' since 'Sir' was out of the question, which reduced the transport unit and the others to 'hysterical' laughter.[56] She also disapproved of women swearing, which in her eyes was a habit 'far more disgusting and disagreeable' than spitting.[57] Serious beyond words and without a sense of humour, Elsie could never see the funny side of situations. As such she held herself aloof from those below her and her manner was stiff and formal. As Mary Milne noted in a letter, 'the dear lady forgot how to play *many* years ago'.[58] Moreover, she used herself as a standard with which to judge the merit and work of others and when they failed to meet her criteria Elsie lost her temper, which made some of the women in the unit question her leadership style. Ellie Rendell, a medical student with her SWH unit, said of Elsie:

> She is not a good leader. She gets very much fussed and loses her temper easily, rapidly and often unjustly because she is in too great a hurry. Also she is very shy and can't make conversation. She takes no personal interest in anyone and is therefore not at all popular.[59]

However, some of the other women with the unit saw Elsie 'as a remarkable leader' and 'most awfully kind',[60] and nurse Edith Collins was not alone when she spoke of the profound loss she felt at her passing, saying: 'She was mother to us and the Serbs loved her also. I am proud I had the honour of working under her until the last.'[61]

Elsie's character and leadership style obviously inspired highly partisan memories among the women of the SWH, which suggests a much more complex personality than the simple, heroic figure of the media. However, both critics and supporters alike failed to understand her as a personality or her motivations. The military representations and images attached to her funeral, that is, the coffin on the gun carriage, the cavalry horses, the flags, provide insights not only into the way her memory and life were mobilised by the British authorities behind the war, they also tell us something regarding the way Elsie saw herself. In opposing the internationalist wing of the NUWSS she had put country before gender and her patriotic feelings intensified as the war progressed to the extent that when offered the responsibility for a hospital for women suffering from venereal disease she refused as she felt that Serbian wounded soldiers had prior claim to any available medical care. Elsie justified her decision in a way that exposed her middle-class morality and bias, and questioned her feminism, by saying:

> It was very difficult to refuse with our modern vision of the solidarity of womanhood, but the Hospital was not open for the safety of the women, but for the protection of the German army. To have taken over that work would have been to encourage vice, and that we could not do.[62]

One might have expected a greater sensitivity to the plight of these women by someone who had campaigned for women's rights and who had worked among the poor of Edinburgh and Glasgow, but it would appear that as far as Elsie was concerned the international sisterhood did not include 'loose' women or prostitutes, who were left to suffer for their immorality and sinfulness. In any case, to treat these women would have placed in jeopardy her strategy of treating soldiers to gain recognition of the importance of women's contribution to the war effort and, hence, advance the case for women's inclusion in the constitution. If restricted only to caring for women, and fallen ones at that, then male stereotypes of femininity in general, and female doctors in particular, would have remained unchallenged. It would have also placed a barrier between Elsie and her perception of her destiny.

Her death was one of martyrdom to the service of the nation and in many ways she convinced herself that the role of martyr was her fate. An incident that offers some support for this interpretation occurred in Notre Dame cathedral, Paris, which Elsie had entered on her way back from Royaumont in late December 1914 for prayer and reflection. She felt she was not alone, and that someone was trying to communicate with her. After initially resisting the impulse to turn round, she eventually did and behind her was a statue of Joan of Arc. Lawrence says that 'to the end of her life, Elsie held that Joan of Arc had had some message' for her and that she drew strength from it.[63] The question arises: did Elsie deliberately evoke the spirit of Joan of Arc? Did she feel some kind of affinity with her, that somehow she was being called to perform a higher more noble sacrifice for her country as Joan had done for hers at Orleans in 1429? Elsie must have been aware of the iconic status of Joan in feminist circles throughout the world. Indeed, at the Seneca Falls convention in 1848 when the first call had been made for women's suffrage in America, Elizabeth Candy Stanton exhorted her audience to show the 'same religious enthusiasm that served Joan of Arc to her work'.[64] She might also have been aware of the narrative of Joan's calling to serve her country and her subsequent trial in 1431. Joan spoke of being in communication with saints, in particular Catherine of Alexandria and Margot of Antioch. The parallels with her life and those of the virgin saints are extremely powerful. Although from humble backgrounds, they were able, through their obedience to a Christian God, to overcome their social disadvantages and go on to play an important role in public life. They resembled Joan 'not only in their wisdom and their nature, but also in their capacity to endure great suffering as a result of their fidelity to the Christian God'.[65] Elsie clearly saw similarities with her life and character and that of the Maid of Orleans. In the first instance, it was Joan's very ordinariness that made these parallels possible. Marina Warner said of her that 'she is a universal figure who is female, but is neither a queen, nor a courtesan, nor a beauty, nor a mother, nor an artist of one kind or another, nor until . . . 1920 . . . a saint'.[66] There was also her faith and that she, like Elsie, was a virgin.

From her earliest years her father had taken care to instil in Elsie a strong set of Christian beliefs. Even during her student days she went to church twice on Sundays with her father, in the morning to St George's Free Church and in the evening to the Episcopal Cathedral in Edinburgh. Her sister, Eva, remarked of her that 'she had a vision, for her life was based on profound trust in God'.[67] Among the very few papers found in her desk after her death were the words to a hymn by the nineteenth-century poet and hymnist Frances Ridley Havergal, and as they lay beside a few letters of her parents, the sentiments must have been very personal and important to her. The final verse contained the words:

> O Saviour I have proved
> That Thou to help and save art really near
> . . . The cross is not removed
> I must go forth to bear it as before
> But leaning on Thine arm I dread its weight no more.[68]

Perhaps her beliefs and her work compensated for her single status. Although her sisters all married Elsie never did, indeed, there is no evidence that she ever had a suitor. However, equally there is also no evidence that she was a lesbian. She seemed to enjoy men's company and revelled in the attention paid to her by Serbian officers, in particular their practice of kissing her hand. But she failed to attract any sustained interest from the opposite sex. Her biographer rightly dismisses the idea that it was something to do with her profession, as of the fifty female registered medical practitioners in Britain in 1885, eighteen were married. Instead, Lawrence suggests that it was more to do with the fact that men were put off by her 'advanced' views and those who might have shown an interest failed to measure up to Elsie's idea of masculinity, which was based on her idolised father. Her attraction to men was as a mother rather than as a lover.[69]

Outwardly her life was busy with her practice and her suffrage work, but inside there was an acute sense of loneliness. In her unpublished semi-autobiographical novel *The Story of a Modern Woman*, written in 1910, the main protagonist, Hildeguard, is a teacher, spinster, 'facing middle age, outwardly cheerful . . . [but] oppressed by loneliness, depression [and] doubt'.[70] To combat these feelings of aloneness and lack of fulfilment Hildeguard throws herself unequivocally into causes whose realisation lies somewhere in the future. She also surrounds herself with children who need her support and love. For Hildeguard solace is to be found only in the continued selfless devotion to work and family, but for Elsie war provided what peace could not: the opportunity for fulfilment. Everything else seemed only to offer disappointment and disillusionment. The suffrage movement, which was Elsie's 'cause', was reeling from the public backlash against militancy and the withdrawal of the Manhood Suffrage Bill by the Liberal Prime Minister, Herbert Asquith, in January 1913, and votes for women seemed as far off as ever. All that lay ahead was her work among her patients in Edinburgh. Demoralised Elsie left for America but her stay there failed to reinvigorate her or improve her health, which had deteriorated due to overwork. Then war broke out in August 1914 and Elsie at last found the moment in history when public and private motivation synchronised and the SWH was born.

Elsie formed the SWH fully knowing the dangers in which she was placing herself and her volunteers. She was without fear, but as her sister Eva remarked, she was childless and 'without children there was no link to the future'.[71] The women members of the Scottish Hospitals were in the main also single, but there was a significant and profound difference between them and other women that had served in a wartime capacity before them: they were not under the control of men and they were socially heterogeneous. Throughout history women have always been involved in war in some way or another. Wives and/or camp followers saw to the cooking and washing, as well as providing more intimate services for marching armies. Women also from the Crimean War onwards served as nurses, although not in field hospitals. During the Anglo-Boer War (1899–1902) unexpectedly high British casualties and the documented uselessness of male orderlies saw the demand for women nursing staff increase dramatically. In recruiting women nurses the military were aware that such a move would pose major problems in defending current perceptions of femininity. Therefore, women were only accepted by the RAMC for nursing if they were from respectable backgrounds, and could be vouched for by at least one 'lady'. The authorities hoped that social class would impose restraints on the degree of fraternisation by nurses with wounded infantrymen from the working class.[72] It was also clear that their co-option for war service would not be allowed to threaten existing gender roles and hierarchies. Women had to be portrayed as helpmates to men, getting them fit to return to the front, but not assuming anything resembling a male role.[73]

The question was how was that definition of femininity to be maintained and made transparent? In this context the style of uniform became a highly vexatious issue for the military. Were women to be dressed in such a way as to emphasise their femininity and thus their sexual attractiveness, or were they to wear uniforms that disguised their sexuality and allow them to blend in more easily with the men? The former option was out of the question even for the women. Grace Ashley-Smith, leader of the First Aid Nursing Yeomanry during the Anglo-Boer War, dismissed a nurse 'who insisted on wearing white drawers with frills under her khaki skirt', saying that 'no women's movement could have survived those frilly drawers on parade'.[74] The latter option, as Enloe points out, sacrificed 'whatever privilege males get from being soldiers and whatever protection women are supposed to get from their vulnerability'.[75] Elsie was untroubled by such concerns and her SWH unit, although with no formal military association, dressed themselves up in uniforms of Scots 'grey' with tartan fringes, with a skirt and a military tunic: the feminine militarised. The ambulance drivers, however, were more sexually ambiguous in dress, preferring trousers to skirts, and wore their hair short like men. Reflecting its adoption of the structures and procedures of the military, the SWH also issued its own medals to women who had served for two years or more. The design pictured a kneeling woman drawing towards her a wounded man and shielding him from the 'grim figure of death intent on dealing a fatal blow'.[76]

The British public were now being accustomed to seeing women in uniforms and in a period of total war aware of their involvement in munitions and public service work. The placing of women in military uniforms and imposing military discipline on them created the possibility that one day women would be actively involved in combat situations. However, by allowing women to fight standard ideals of 'feminine, masculine, family and country' are profoundly challenged. The whole idea of a woman, and what it means to be a woman, becomes in such circumstances subject to redefinition to allow for the construction of a new form of femininity: one that confronts any notion of essentialism in men and women. If women are innately peace-loving and life-affirming, since their primary role is one of nurture, and men war-like, how could they even contemplate enlisting, far less fighting?[77] Finally, is equality of sacrifice in pursuit of a patriotic cause to be celebrated or condemned by women, since 'militaries are institutions predicated upon violence'?[78]

Elsie never lived long enough to have to wrestle with such issues and how they divide women. In spite of her work for the women's suffrage movement in Britain, in some ways she was the antithesis of a feminist; indeed, her life was a series of contradictions. She was an upholder of the traditions and ideals that underpinned the British Empire, which under the influence of her father, she saw as a force for good and a bulwark of civilisation. But she also supported the claim of the Irish for Home Rule, a concession by the British which might have presaged the end of Empire and given encouragement to aspiring nationalist movements in the colonies. She toiled among the poor women of Edinburgh's Old Town, but her Liberal beliefs in the sanctity of private property prevented her from attacking the root causes of their poverty. She worked tirelessly on behalf of the suffrage cause, but accepted in 1914 that her country had a superior claim on her services than had her sex. Although to be fair, she did believe that by entering the war and proving that women could make as valuable a contribution as men this would deliver the long awaited franchise. However, it could be argued, as Ann Summers does, that the 'ambition and energy which might have been channelled into demands for political and economic equality was drawn off into a range of subordinate activities within a rigidly hierarchical male organisation'.[79] Elsie after all was forced to form the SWH solely through the short-sighted rejection of the RAMC, but it is clear that if the circumstances were different she was willing to accept incorporation into what was clearly a misogynist institution. Was her desire to serve, which seemed instinctive rather than philosophical, a public or a private motivation? Perhaps it was a combination of both, but it is well to remember the mental state that Elsie was in prior to war breaking out. She was tortured by feelings of loneliness and was personally deeply unfulfilled. All that kept her going at this time was her commitment to the Christian ideal of service. The war allowed for the transformation of this commitment into a heroic sacrifice for King and Country. She saw herself as part of a continuum of women, such as Joan of Arc, who had made the ultimate sacrifice for their country and her fellow human beings. Unlike Joan, Elsie was not burned as a witch, but feted as a hero both in Serbia and in her country of birth. The Serbs had decorated her with their highest honour, the Order of the White Eagle, and nearer home in commemoration of her life the Elsie Inglis Memorial Maternity Hospital was opened in Edinburgh in 1925, and served women in the city until it closed down in 1988.

Sir William McEwen, in the foreword to Frances Balfour's short biography of Elsie, remarked that 'the record of work [of] she and her Hospital Units . . . forms a story of women's pluck and heroism which will last forever'.[80] Lady Frances Balfour also claimed: 'They are worthy to stand beside the older pioneer, Florence Nightingale.'[81] Leah Leneman has questioned this optimism, asking why, in spite of her heroic work, is she not as well remembered as Florence Nightingale? Her answer is that she was too conformist and thus 'failed to break the mould', and that women doctors, although profusely thanked and praised for their services in the war, after it was over were as 'marginalized as they had been before'.[82] This is to take a one-dimensional view of Elsie and the impact she had on women's lives, and also ignores the Anglo-centric bias in national histories, something that is gradually being reversed. Elsie was

Scottish and her story was dramatic and eventful, but underlying the thrilling narrative were deeper questions concerning the conflict women face over the priorities of gender and the pull of the wider allegiances of state and nation, and how our idea of a woman is socially constructed. These conflicts and issues remain ongoing.

NOTES

1. *The Times*, 30 November 1917.
2. M. Lawrence, *Shadow of Swords: a Biography of Elsie Inglis* (London, 1971), p. 34.
3. F. Balfour, *Dr Elsie Inglis* (1920), pp. 10–11.
4. Lawrence, *Shadow*, p. 39.
5. Balfour, *Elsie Inglis*, p. 33.
6. Quoted in Lawrence, *Shadow*, p. 48.
7. Quoted in Balfour, *Elsie Inglis*, p. 47.
8. Lawrence, *Shadow*, p. 49.
9. Balfour, *Elsie Inglis*, p. 39.
10. Balfour, *Elsie Inglis*, p. 39.
11. Lawrence, *Shadow*, p. 55.
12. Lawrence, *Shadow*, pp. 55–6.
13. L. Leneman, *Elsie Inglis: Founder of Battlefield Hospitals Run Entirely by Women* (Edinburgh, 1998), p. 18.
14. Quoted in Lawrence, *Shadow*, p. 57.
15. Quoted in Lawrence, *Shadow*, pp. 57–8.
16. Quoted in Lawrence, *Shadow*, p. 62.
17. Lawrence, *Shadow*, p. 79.
18. Lawrence, *Shadow*, p. 87.
19. Lawrence, *Shadow*, p. 71.
20. Quoted in Balfour, *Elsie Inglis*, p. 136.
21. Lawrence, *Shadow*, p. 84.
22. J. Wheatley, *Starving in the Midst of Plenty* (Glasgow, 1923).
23. Lawrence, *Shadow*, p. 78.
24. E. Shaw McLaren, *Elsie Inglis: the Woman with the Torch* (London, 1920), p. 14.
25. Balfour, *Elsie Inglis*, p. 117.
26. Balfour, *Elsie Inglis*, p. 123.
27. Balfour, *Elsie Inglis*, p. 94.
28. Balfour, *Elsie Inglis*, pp. 92–3, 117.
29. Lawrence, *Shadow*, p. 81.
30. Balfour, *Elsie Inglis*, p. 129.
31. *The Times*, 23 July 1912.
32. *The Scotsman*, 14 February 1914.

33. L. Leneman, *A Guid Cause: the Women's Suffrage Movement in Scotland* (Aberdeen, 1991), p. 69.
34. S. A. van Wingerden, *The Woman's Suffrage Movement in Britain, 1866–1928* (Basingstoke, 1999), p. 159.
35. van Wingerden, *Suffrage Movement*, pp. 159–62.
36. Lawrence, *Shadow*, p. 19.
37. Lawrence, *Shadow*, p. 98.
38. Balfour, *Elsie Inglis*, p. 154.
39. Quoted in Balfour, *Elsie Inglis*, p. 161.
40. Lawrence, *Shadow*, p. 102.
41. Lawrence, *Shadow*, p. 111.
42. A. F. Cahill, *Between the Lines: Letters and Diaries from Elsie Inglis's Russian Unit* (Durham, 1999), p. 13.
43. L. Leneman, *In the Service of Life: the Story of Eslie Inglis and the Scottish Women's Hospitals* (Edinburgh, 1994), pp. 95–6.
44. Quoted in Leneman, *Service of Life*, p. 78.
45. Quoted in Leneman, *Service of Life*, p. 80.
46. Balfour, *Elsie Inglis*, pp. 192–3.
47. Lawrence, *Shadow*, p. 174.
48. See Leneman, *Service of Life*, pp. 59–62, for a fuller discussion of the issues.
49. Diary entry for 26 September 1917, quoted in Cahill, *Between the Lines*, p. 302.
50. Leneman, *Service of Life*, p. 137.
51. Balfour, *Elsie Inglis*, p. 130.
52. Lawrence, *Shadow*, p. 66.
53. Quoted in Balfour, *Elsie Inglis*, p. 253.
54. *The Times*, 30 November 1917.
55. Quoted in Lawrence, *Shadow*, p. 281.
56. Leneman, *Service of Life*, p. 73.
57. Leneman, *Service of Life*, pp. 95–6.
58. Cahill, *Between the Lines*, p. 188.
59. Quoted in Leneman, *Service of Life*, p. 76.
60. Quoted in Cahill, *Between the Lines*, p. 188, and Leneman, *Service of Life*, p. 76.
61. Quoted in Leneman, *Service of Life*, p. 140.
62. Quoted in M. Krippner, *The Quality of Mercy: Women at War. Serbia 1915–1918* (Newton Abbot, 1980), p. 161; E. S. McLaren (ed.), *A History of the Scottish Women's Hospitals* (1919), p. 168.
63. Lawrence, *Shadow*, p. 110.
64. A. L. Burstow, *Joan of Arc: Heretic, Mystic, Shaman* (New York, 1986), p. 130.
65. K. Sullivan, 'I do not name to you the voice of St Michael': the identification of Joan of Arc's voices', in B. Wheeler and C. T. Wood (eds) *Fresh Verdicts on Joan of Arc* (London, 1996), p. 103.

66. M. Warner, *Joan of Arc: the Image of Female Heroism* (London, 1991 edn), p. 6.
67. McLaren, *Elsie Inglis*, p. 16.
68. Quoted in Lawrence, *Shadow*, p. 90.
69. Lawrence, *Shadow*, pp. 93–4.
70. Lawrence, *Shadow*, p. 91.
71. McLaren, *Elsie Inglis*, p. 21.
72. C. Schmitz, '"We too were soldiers": the experience of British nurses in the Anglo-Boer War, 1899–1902', in G. De Groot and C. Penniston-Bird (eds) *A Soldier and a Woman: Sexual Integration in the Military* (Harlow, 2000), p. 62; C. Enloe, *Maneuvers: the International Politics of Militarizing Women's Lives* (London, 2000), p. 214.
73. A. Summers, *Angels and Citizens: British Women as Military Nurses* (London, 2000 edn), pp. 239, 243.
74. Summers, *Angels*, p. 237.
75. C. Enloe, *Does Khaki Become You: the Militarization of Women's Lives* (London, 1983), p. 119.
76. Leneman, *Service of Life*, p. 214.
77. For a stimulating discussion of these questions see N. A. Dombrowski, 'Soldiers, saints or sacrificial lambs? Women's relationship to combat and the fortification of the Home Front in the twentieth century', in N. A. Dombrowski (ed.) *Women and War in the Twentieth Century: Enlisted With or Without Consent* (London, 1999), pp. 2–37.
78. Dombrowski, 'Soldiers', p. 4.
79. Summers, *Angels*, p. 249.
80. Sir William McEwen, 'Foreword', in Balfour, *Elsie*, p. 6.
81. *The Scotsman*, 19 October 1923.
82. Leneman, *Elsie Inglis*, p. 86.

8

Katherine, Duchess of Atholl: The Red Duchess?

⌒

To some writers Katherine Marjory Ramsay, wife of the seventh Duke of Atholl, is a contradiction. Although raised in privilege and married into one of the country's premier aristocratic families, during the 1930s she appeared to reject her class and party by espousing the cause of Republican Spain, earning notoriety in the press as the 'Red Duchess'. For her actions she was cast into the political wilderness, disowned by fellow Conservatives and her own constituency party, losing her seat in parliament in a by-election in 1938, in spite of the fact that she was Scotland's first elected female MP and the first woman to hold a ministerial position in a Tory government. This transition from 'a leading Conservative diehard', a defender of Empire, to an outspoken supporter of the leftist Spanish government has been described as 'little less than incredible' by one historian of the Tory party in this period.[1] A. S. Williams, in a recent book on influential women of the 1930s, also expressed incredulity that a 'dark blue Conservative' could emerge as a supporter of the Republican side in the Spanish Civil War.[2] Katherine's political inconsistency has, thus, been the subject of much comment and speculation. Some historians, like Williams, have argued that her concerns were humanitarian rather than political; a view shared by Katherine's biographer, Shelia Hetherington.[3] The 'righting of wrongs', therefore, became the key to understanding the contradictions in the political position of the Duchess in the 1930s. Her interventions in Spain are interpreted as entirely consistent with her past record of improving social provision for women and children and helping to alleviate suffering wherever it occurred in the world. Indeed, Brian Harrison, in his book on British feminism between the wars, has argued that, although on the surface she was an anti-feminist, she extended 'a feminist influence despite herself'.[4]

What this essay will do is argue that far from being inconsistent, the Duchess' politics in this period, and before and after, were entirely consistent with her elitist and imperialist views, and that this can be demonstrated not simply in the arena of foreign affairs, but in domestic politics and on social issues as well. As Ellen Wilkinson, MP for Jarrow, once remarked, Katherine may have been for an aristocrat unusually hard-working and socially concerned, but at heart she was still the 'oh-so Conservative Duchess'.[5]

Katherine, or Kitty, as she was known, was born on 6 November 1874 in Edinburgh to Sir James Ramsay, the tenth baronet of Banff, East Perthshire, a historian and mountaineer, and his second wife, Charlotte Stewart. Her childhood was not a happy one. Both her parents were rather aloof and cold. Displays of emotion were frowned upon, an atti-tude reinforced by her mother's adherence to Christian Science. Their detachment forced Katherine to withdraw into a world of books and music. The fact that as a child her health was never robust only served to make her lonelier as it reduced contact with her siblings. The emo-tional deprivation of her childhood created in the adult Atholl the same kind of disdain for affection, spontaneity and sympathy that her parents displayed. Shelia Hetherington says that, although as an adult she loved children, Katherine could never 'pick up a niece to hug or embrace her'.[6] There was also enormous academic pressure placed on her shoulders and she was enrolled in the Wimbledon High School for Girls. At the age of seventeen she took the examination for Associate-ship of the Royal College of Music (RCM), passed and became a full-time student in 1892. From that date until 1895 she immersed herself in music, winning a piano scholarship in 1893, which she gave to a less well-off student. While there Katherine walked in the footprints of some illustrious figures in the history of music; her near contemporaries included Ralph Vaughan Williams and Gustav Holst. However, she never completed her studies and returned at the request of her parents to Banff.

If Katherine was not by now fully aware of the class system and her position within it then her decision to abandon her studies must have driven it home in a very personal and powerful manner. While studying at the RCM, Kitty formed an attachment to her tutor's son, Ted Butler. The humble circumstances of the Butler family were not in keeping with the social aspirations of the Ramsay family and she was ordered home and soon engaged to the Marquis of Tullibardine, five years her senior. They were married in St Margaret's, Westminster, in July 1899 after some delay while Bardie, as he was known, took part in General Kitchener's Nile Expedition. After this she followed him in his various military adventures: firstly, in South Africa, during the Boer War, where she com-posed a pipe tune for his regiment, the Scottish Horse, and produced a book – *Muster Roll of Perthshire* – listing the biographical details of each man from the shire who had served in the conflict, which evolved into a larger volume – *A Military History of Perthshire*; and, secondly, in Egypt, during the First World War, where she did voluntary hospital work and organised entertainment for the troops. For her services to the war effort Katherine was made a Dame of the British Empire in 1918.

To all appearances they seemed a devoted and loving couple, but the marriage soon faced difficulties. Katherine was unable to have children and thus she failed the first requirement of a wife of an aristocrat – to provide an heir. For someone who believed that the capacity for motherhood was for women 'the basic fact of our physical existence',[7] childlessness created within her a deep sense of failure and this remained with her always.[8] Whether failure in this area drove her husband elsewhere is a matter of speculation, but Bardie it seems had little respect for the vow of fidelity in marriage. He was a serial adulterer whose numerous liaisons resulted in the births of at least two illegitimate children. As she had done as a child, Katherine escaped from this unsatisfactory aspect of her marriage by absorbing herself in intellectual matters and political and social affairs.

However, it was as her husband's helpmate that she was introduced to the rough and tumble of parliamentary politics. In the 1906 general election Bardie stood as Conservative candidate for East Perthshire; although he lost, he was immediately adopted as prospective parliamentary candidate for West Perthshire, with Katherine invited to become president of the West Perthshire Women's Unionist Association. During the 'People's Budget' election in 1910, she campaigned strongly for Bardie, going out canvassing and speaking at numerous public meetings on his behalf. He won the seat and they relocated to Eaton Place, London. While the MP for West Perthshire, at King George's request, Bardie successfully interceded in the dockers' strike of 1912. The strike was part of a wave of industrial discontent that was sweeping the country. There were also troubles in Ireland and with militant suffragettes. Women suffrage campaigners went militant under the leadership of the Pankhursts and this added to the general social turmoil in British society at this time. Both Bardie and Katherine opposed all women's suffrage organisations, whether constitutional or militant. They firmly believed that a woman's place was in the home and patronisingly stated that women did not want the vote and that those with large families had no time for politics.[9] Their views earned them the contempt of Lady Frances Balfour, especially Bardie for his attempt to link the issue of venereal disease with the suffrage cause in a debate in the Commons. Balfour stated that her disgust for Bardie was undying, saying: 'I heard the debate, and never shall I "forget" or forgive it.'[10]

It is clear that Katherine saw only better-off women, those with time on their hands, as suitable candidates for enfranchisement as before a woman could enter the field of parliamentary politics she had to have gained experience in local government. Katherine herself was a member of twenty-five different committees by 1920, including the Perthshire Education Authority.[11] To demand a similar level of participation from other women highlighted not only her privileged lifestyle, but also her remoteness from the everyday working lives of her social inferiors. To most married women, even those who were middle class, domesticity was a full-time occupation. Her failure to comprehend the lives of less-privileged women was also demonstrated during the highpoint of the interwar economic depression, when she argued that the rich were suffering as much as the poor and the unemployed. The Atholls did have to sell some of the better pieces of family jewellery and their home in Eaton Place, London, and move to a smaller, less luxurious house, and it seems to forgo entertaining at home in favour of eating out at hotels and restaurants. As she remarked in her book – *Women and Politics* (1931) – in all seriousness: 'Where English people make more use than formerly of London hotels and restaurants, it is often, because owing to small domestic staffs, they do not find it easy to entertain guests at home.'[12] The Atholls' 'straitened' circumstances, however, had less to do with the depression and more to do with her husband's lack of business acumen. He put money into the most hair-brained business schemes, such as the Atholl Steel Houses in 1925: a venture that flopped in spite of support from the Prime Minister as, in spite of housing shortages, there were few people willing to live in a house made of metal that was cold in the winter and too hot in the summer.[13] But sentiments such as the Duchess' concerning her poverty in a period of mass unemployment, hunger marches and the dole only served to underline her continuing ignorance of the lives of the mass of the British people and her insensitivity towards them.

Her opposition to franchise reform also rested on the defence of the realm argument. As men were the defenders of the nation state, she argued, they were more entitled to the vote than women as they were prepared to risk their lives for its preservation. Speaking alongside Lord Curzon at a meeting of the National League for Opposing Women's Suffrage in Glasgow on 12 November 1912, she argued: 'I do not think that we, who are incapable of taking upon ourselves the burden of national defence, should have the decisive voice in questions of peace and war.' Two years later in Edinburgh she claimed that the 'business of government rested on forces in which it is impossible that we should serve'.[14] Katherine's opposition to the extension of the suffrage to women on the same basis as men continued into the interwar period, in spite of the passing of the Representation of the People Act of 1918 that gave the vote to women over the age of thirty. A private member's bill introduced by Labour MP William Adamson, in 1924, to place women on the same electoral footing as men was strenuously opposed by her on the grounds that an all party conference was needed to discuss the constitutional implications of such a move. On this occasion Katherine overplayed her hand and her opposition to the bill only served to arouse the indignation of fellow MPs and women's groups. The main thrust of her argument against the equalisation of electoral qualifications for women and men was that it would put women in a majority, but only because of the sacrifice of 740,000 men in the Great War.[15] If such morally offensive sentiments were not enough, she also added that by widening the franchise 'even women tinkers would be entitled to vote',[16] a jibe that led Frances Balfour to point out: 'To be illiterate has never excluded men from the franchise.'[17] In spite of her increasingly preposterous resistance, the franchise was reformed in 1928, lowering the voting age for women from thirty to twenty-one years, the same as men.

Such prejudice poses fundamental questions for Brian Harrison's view that the Duchess was a feminist in spite of herself. Generally speaking, feminism is a movement that seeks to empower women by abolishing the impediments that exist to prevent them exercising the full rights of citizenship. It seeks to place women on the same basis as men both legally and politically, and to correct abuses in the workings of the labour market. Equality of the sexes is, therefore, the principle on which the movement was and is based. Although the Duchess sought to improve the social position of women and children, it was not intended to empower them or bring about a greater level of equality in society. Indeed, the Labour MP for Cumberland, Wilfred Roberts, recalled her arguing in parliament that children were needed in factories because their little hands could get under the machines and Elizabeth Mulhouse, who later campaigned with the Duchess in Perthshire for the Spanish cause, opposed her on the local Education Authority when she supported farmers who wished to employ children to pick potatoes at half pay.[18] As far as women's rights were concerned, Nancy Astor remarked, 'she never sees straight'.[19] However, Katherine's views did not totally favour subordination of women to men. She realised that the franchise had altered the political position of women in Britain, as had her own entry to parliament, and that this had implications for the family and household relationships, although 'the supreme sphere of women must remain the home'.[20] Marriage came to be viewed by her as a partnership rather than an institution of subordination. In a speech to the Joint Committee of Edinburgh Women's Organisations in December 1923, the Duchess declared:

> Fifty years ago, the ideal wife was one who said 'Amen' to her husband whenever he opened his mouth. Today that idea has been abandoned and we have instead an ideal of comradeship, of partnership in life, happiness and difficulties alike.[21]

Indeed, the title of her autobiography – *Working Partnership* (1958) – provides an insight into the way that the Duchess had gradually altered her views on marriage. However, her activity on behalf of women and children during her time in parliament might be best interpreted as in the tradition of Tory paternalism rather than in any latent feminist sense.

Her first intervention in social affairs came in 1912 when she was invited to become a member of a Scottish Office committee investigating the medical and nursing services in crofting areas. Katherine was appalled at the conditions crofters were living under, but although medical services were improved, nothing was done to alter the balance of ownership of land in the Highlands and Islands, or address the widespread incidence of poverty, something that was at the root of the causes of ill health in that part of Scotland. The Atholl family after all was among the largest landowners in Britain. As a member of a committee set up by the Secretary of State for Scotland to investigate the problems and conditions of travelling people north of the border, the Duchess and the other members recommended offers of housing to tinker families in areas of continuous employment, but only if those who accepted resettlement agreed to sign the pledge to eschew alcohol, showing that her brand of reform had an authoritarian and moralistic side to it. While serving as Parliamentary Secretary to the Board of Education she also supported raising the school leaving age and sponsored an inquiry into educational provision for canal-boat children, as well as addressing the stigma attached to illegitimate children. However, balancing these social concerns was Katherine's strong opposition to the introduction of equal pay for men and women in civil service in the 1930s on the grounds that men had families to support. In her analysis women were divided into married and single, men were regarded generically. Single men were thus paid more than single women for doing similar work. As a result, many single women were condemned to poverty through arguments such as these.

To Katherine the most important role for women was motherhood and to that end she applauded all state legislation that restricted the hours of work for them and promoted their health.[22] As far as she was concerned the traditional Christian family with clearly demarcated gender roles was the ideal: an endorsement of the ideology of separate spheres. As she put it:

> Is there a woman who is both wife and mother, who does not feel that, even if she may be contributing to the family income, the sense of primary responsibility for the maintenance of wife and children is one of the finest elements in a man's character, something that calls out, as little else can, his best and most continuous efforts?[23]

Any attempts to interfere with 'the need for maintaining marriage as we know it' would only bring despair and unhappiness. In *Women and Politics* she criticised alternatives to Christian marriage, such as polygamy, companion marriages, and pre-marital sex, which were being advocated by philosophers and writers, such as Bertrand Russell in his book *Marriage and Morals* (1929), claiming that a woman's position could only be safeguarded through traditional marriage forms.[24] Thus, Katherine could at this point see no alternative for women but domesticity, which she saw as consistent with their biological purpose. However, this posed the question: what special characteristics did she possess to allow her a role outside the home?

Katherine had, as we have seen, a long record of service in local government and was childless. She also did not enter the Commons as MP for West Perthshire until she was forty-nine, well beyond child-bearing age. Thus, she was the ideal female candidate in her view. However, she had to be persuaded by Lloyd-George when on a visit to Blair Castle to stand for parliament. Although King George advised her against standing, as he felt it was impossible to combine her social role with a political one, Katherine with the support of her husband decided to stand for parliament. She was proposed as Unionist candidate for South Edinburgh to take the place of the ex-Lord Advocate, C. D. Murray, but was passed over in favour of Sir Samuel Chapman. In the 1923 general election, however, success was achieved after a gruelling campaign in which she spoke to 'overflowing audiences' in Crieff and Kinross.[25] However, the outcome had less to do with Katherine's electioneering skills and more to do with her social position. She literally inherited the seat from her husband, as did other female MPs in the 1920s, for example, the flamboyant Nancy Astor. In spite of this, she only won by 150 votes from the Liberal candidate but in doing so Katherine gained membership of the most exclusive male club in the country – the House of Commons. Her maiden speech was a long rambling one, but it

clearly spelled out her political beliefs and priorities: Empire, protectionism, welfare of women and children, and anti-socialism. The speech was
well received within the Tory party and was reprinted in full in the right-
wing periodical *National Review.*

To Katherine Conservatism stood for freedom and individualism and
the absence of state control or interference in industry: 'The essence of
the teaching of Christianity translated into politics.'[26] As she put it in a
speech at the opening of the Empire Unionist Carnival in Birmingham in
November 1924:

> They [Unionists] stood for a great cause, the particular essence of which
> rested on freedom and good will – freedom for the fullest possible develop-
> ment of private initiative and industry, as opposed to a system that would give
> the State control; freedom of career for the development of the individual as
> opposed to a system which would make for a rigid uniformity in all persons.[27]

The immediate party approval of her sound views on Conservative policy
disguised the fact that the Commons was not so female-friendly; indeed,
women MPs were as scarce as gold dust as political parties refused to
select them as parliamentary candidates, all they wanted was the female
vote. Only thirty-three women were selected as prospective parliamentary candidates by all parties between 1918 and 1945 in Scotland, and
over the period 1918–92 only twenty-four have been returned as MPs.[28]
Having performed the amazing feat of actually being elected to parliament, they faced further barriers as there were few facilities specially
reserved for women. The Labour MP Edith Summerskill recalled that in
the 1930s there was only one room for female members, with a small
washroom off it containing a Victorian washstand with a tin basin. The
Duchess of Atholl had to dress half in the room and half in the corridor.
As Summerskill put it:

> on changing her frock, [the Duchess] present[ed] her back to the half-open
> door to enable her maid, standing in the corridor, to fasten the numerous
> small buttons which only the maid's practised hand could manipulate.[29]

In spite of the primitive changing conditions and the prevailing dominant male culture of Commons life, Katherine soon won recognition
from the Tory leadership as a conscientious, hard-working MP who performed consistently in debates with the opposition. When the Tories
were returned to power following the 'Red Scare' general election of
1924, the Prime Minister, Stanley Baldwin, invited her to become
Parliamentary Secretary to the Board of Education. Although some in the
party felt that Nancy Astor, as the longest serving female MP, should

have been appointed to the position, as far as Baldwin was concerned Katherine was the more able and steady of the two.[30] Her elevation, however, demonstrated the truly misogynist attitude of senior Tories towards women.

The President of the Board of Education Lord Eustace Percy was the younger son of the Duke of Northumberland, a bully and woman hater, who viewed Katherine's appointment as a kind of slur on his manhood. Percy systematically undermined his Parliamentary Secretary at every turn, allowing her very little discretion in decision making and denying her encouragement. He also marginalized her role at the Board by keeping her out of the way as much as possible. She was sent on weekly prize-giving visits to schools and despatched to international education conferences abroad. In spite of this, Katherine was successful in opposing Percy's attempts to make economies in educational provision by reintroducing fees for elementary education and delaying entry to school until children were seven years old. Her social status and connections allowed her to make a successful appeal over Percy's head direct to Stanley Baldwin. This earned her the enduring hatred of Percy and other senior Tories.

In spite of her stand on delayed entry and school fees, Katherine's position on education, and its purpose, was far from liberal. She argued quite forcefully that education should be based on utilitarian values and that practical training was of more value than intellectual study to working-class children, since very few of them had the ability to take advantage of the latter. As far as she was concerned working-class children were in school to learn to labour, to accept discipline and to execute the commands of their superiors. Speaking to teachers at Southwell Diocesan College in Derby in 1926, Katherine argued:

> They should not be . . . surprised if men who best realized the acuteness of foreign competition looked to the schools to add to the efficiency of industries. It was part of their task to turn out boys and girls trained to concentrate on whatever might be their work and to persevere with their task until it was finished.[31]

Her elitist attitude to education was exposed when she opposed plans by the Labour government in 1930 to raise the school leaving age from fourteen to fifteen declaring that it was 'a gross waste of public money'.[32]

Shelia Hetherington claims that Percy's negative attitude towards Katherine made her 'nervous' and as a result her performances at the Despatch Box in the Commons began to suffer. She became long-winded and lacked self-confidence;[33] indeed, her fellow Conservatives dubbed her the 'Begum of Blair', as her interventions in the Commons and at party conferences induced a kind of torpor in her listeners.[34] Perhaps, it was her political marginalisation and sense of isolation that drove Katherine at the age of fifty-one into the arms of her long-standing admirer, Ted Butler, who by this time was married and a grandfather. They remained close until his death in 1952. Hetherington claims that the relationship was 'platonic',[35] but Butler's letter suggested something a little more intimate: 'My birthday was the happiest one I have had for years. Exactly ten months have passed since a certain luncheon . . . Bless you for it – Always your affectionate EMB.'[36] However, Katherine's emotional torture at the Board of Education did not last beyond 1929 as the Tories lost the general election and a minority Labour government, with Ramsay MacDonald as prime minister, replaced them. Relegated to backbench status she revelled in the parliamentary freedom afforded to her. She became attached to some unpopular political causes which created difficulties with her own party whips, but, at the same time, allowed her to engage with women's issues abroad.

Katherine's involvement in improving the conditions of women and young girls in Africa and India has been much praised;[37] however, it has to be placed in the context of her strong imperialist sympathies; indeed, attachment to Empire is perhaps the key to understanding her politics. Love of Empire was embedded in her psyche at an early age through the personal experiences of her parents and remained with her until her death in 1960. Her mother's parents were murdered in the Indian Mutiny of 1857, and Charlotte experienced recurring nightmares throughout her life as a result; something that Katherine must have been aware of as a child. Her father, along with Joseph Chamberlain and other MPs, left the Liberal Party after Gladstone's conversion to Irish Home Rule in 1884. She also experienced the tragedy of colonial warfare when her brother, Nigel, was killed fighting in the Boer War; a war in which, as we have seen, she was deeply involved. Thus, from childhood through to adulthood Katherine was steeped by personal and political experience in the righteousness of the imperial cause. She grew up convinced of the civilising mission of the imperial project and the need to preserve the unity of the Empire at all cost. As she made clear in her book – *Women and Politics* – it was a responsibility of British citizens, particularly women, to help the peoples of the 'Colonial Empire' and 'keep them on a straight course'.[38] For these reasons she opposed nationalist and independence movements both at home and abroad. She spoke against Home Rule for Scotland in the 1930s, arguing that it would weaken Britain's defences and deprive the Westminster parliament of some of the best minds in the country.[39] Thus, her approach to the position of women in the British colonies has to be interpreted within the imperial context.

After attending a meeting in London in 1929 under the auspices of the Church of Scotland Mission to the Kikuyu peoples of Kenya, Katherine was shocked to hear of the practice of circumcising young females, and almost immediately, along with the MPs Josiah Wedgwood, Eleanor Rathbone, R. A. Butler, and Edith Picton-Turberville, she organised the all-party Committee for the Protection of Coloured Women (CPCW). The CPCW campaigned for colonial governments to provide legal protection to girls wishing to avoid circumcision. The Duchess raised the matter in the Commons and forced the Colonial Secretary, Lord Passfield (Sydney Webb), to take up the issue. She also represented the CPCW in Geneva at the International Conference on African Children in 1931, where she called on colonial powers to put an end to the practice of circumcision. Although the Committee's impact was negligible and the practice of circumcision continued unabated in Kenya,[40] the Duchess refused to drop the issue and was active in pursuing it throughout the 1930s. However, her crusade against circumcision, laudable as it may seem, can be interpreted in a number of ways. While she was genuinely appalled at the practice, the Duchess was also emphasising the importance of the civilising mission of Empire and, at the same time, making a case for its extension. As historians of gender and Empire have shown in the case of missionaries, in spite of their convictions and desire to improve the position of the native peoples, their depiction of tribal customs and traditions as barbaric and the African male as depraved, was unconsciously a justification of the need for British law and rule.[41]

The coupling of defence of Empire and women's position was also used to significant effect in her campaign against the India Bill in 1933, which intended to grant self-government to the Indian people. Katherine argued that the tradition of child marriages in India was barbaric and a sign of the moral depravity of Indian males and thus an indication of their unfitness to have control over their own affairs. In her pamphlet – *The Main Facts of the India Problem* (1933) – and speeches she also reprised the arguments used in opposition to the women's suffrage campaign in Britain, only this time it was non-gender specific. She argued that the 'political classes in India' only constituted a small minority of the country's vast and religiously diverse population, the rest were illiterate and inexperienced in running the affairs of state and maintaining public services. As far as she was concerned British personnel were essential to ensure that India was efficiently governed.[42] She pounced on the findings of the Simon Commission's 1928 report, which stated that in those areas of India granted some measure of autonomy under the Chelmsford-Montagu reforms of the post-war years there had been a marked deterioration in the provision of public services. Katherine claimed that Indian medical officers were incapable of performing administrative tasks and unable to control their staff.[43] The final grievance against the proposed legislation was trade, and it was her fear that Britain's economic interests would be harmed in India following home rule that convinced Katherine, along with five other MPs, to resign the government whip in May 1935.[44]

In doing so she aligned herself clearly with the pro-imperial right-wing of the Conservative Party. To make this public Katherine spoke on behalf of Randolph Churchill in the Wavertree by-election in Liverpool in January 1935. He stood as an independent Conservative against the official candidate of the party and his intervention split the vote and allowed Labour unexpectedly to win the seat. Party members roundly condemned Churchill's actions and those who had supported him, including Katherine. She also drew closer to Winston Churchill over India and, although not a member of his India Defence League, Katherine corresponded with him and supplied him with information for inclusion in his speeches. However, as a result of the Italian invasion of Abyssinia, she reapplied for the party whip and, following Baldwin's intercession, it was restored to her on application in September 1935. Katherine's local constituency party, however, was more understanding of her position and they agreed to allow her in future to take an independent line if she found herself in opposition to the government and/or its policies. Little did they realise that they were providing a political noose from which the Duchess would voluntarily hang herself.

Her growing reputation as a political maverick was confirmed over her stance on the Spanish Civil War: a position that conferred on her the title of the 'Red Duchess', although never was a designation more undeserved than in this case. Katherine became embroiled in Spain through her support for the victims of the war: women and children. She had been suspicious of the intentions of the fascist powers in Europe, indeed, Katherine felt that Hitler posed a greater threat to the peace of Europe and the integrity of the British Empire than did Stalin. This conviction emerged after reading the unexpurgated version of Hitler's *Mein Kampf* in German in 1935. Aware that the edition published in English two years previous was a watered-down version of the original, along with the Friends of Europe group she had the full text published in English and passed a copy to the Prime Minister and Winston Churchill. The remilitarisation of the Rhineland by Hitler in 1936 and the outbreak of the Spanish Civil War the same year reinforced Katherine's view that Britain had to resist with force if necessary Fascist expansion in Europe. As she put it in the Commons in November 1936:

> If you can keep the peace in Europe, you will keep the peace over a great part of the world . . . and if you can keep this country safe, it will mean the safety of the British Empire as a whole, because we are the nerve-centre of the Empire.[45]

Her refusal to appease the fascist powers brought some stinging criticism from members of her constituency party and Lord Londonderry.[46] This reached a crescendo as she became increasingly involved in the civil war in Spain.

The Spanish situation had been sparked by the attempt of rebel elements in the army led by General Franco to overthrow the democratically elected left-of-centre Republican Government. From his base in Morocco Franco launched an assault on mainland Spain in July 1936 with the backing of Germany and Italy. The fighting was fierce and like any civil war there were atrocities on both sides. The war soon assumed the status of a *cause célèbre* among the European Left as it was seen as a fight for democracy against fascism. Britain's hands were tied by signing a non-intervention pact with twenty-seven other countries, including Germany and Italy, agreeing not to intervene in the fighting or supply weapons and other materials to either side in the conflict. The treaty was blatantly disregarded by the fascist powers and they liberally supplied the rebels with guns and other equipment. Italy sent some 100,000 men and American companies, such as Ford and General Motors, and the British firm, Rio Tinto Zinc, supplied the rebels with foreign exchange at ridiculously low rates. While Franco and his troops enjoyed the illegal aid, the Spanish government was refused the right to buy food and arms on world markets. As the situation deteriorated the Soviet Union sent aid to the beleaguered Spanish authorities and in Britain volunteers, along with those in other countries, raised the International Brigade to fight on the Republican side. Although the Soviet Union never provided assistance on the same scale as that given to the rebels by fascist powers and big business, its intervention paved the way for the formation of a Communist-led government in 1937.[47] Spain was now divided both ideologically and militarily and one had to decide which side one was on.

The Duchess, and a few others in her party, criticised the non-interventionist position of the British government. Along with Eleanor Rathbone MP, Ellen Wilkinson MP, Wilfred Roberts MP and Isabel

Brown, Communist activist, she formed the National Joint Committee for Spanish Relief (NJCSR) towards the end of 1936. Her actions were condemned by powerful Catholic interests in West Perthshire and Conservative Central Office was also disapproving.[48] In January 1937, along with Ellen Wilkinson and Eleanor Rathbone MPs, and Dame Rachel Crowdie, of the nursing profession, Katherine visited Spain as part of an all-woman delegation inquiring into the conditions in schools, hospitals and prisons and was appalled at the 'plight of the refugee children'.[49] As a result, the Basque Children's Committee, with Katherine as chairman, arranged for the evacuation of 4,000 Basque children to Southampton where they were placed in camps until it was safe to return to Bilbao. Another venture under the patronage of the Duchess was the British Youth Foodship Club that collected money and made garments to support a children's home in Madrid.[50]

The intensity of the Duchess' commitment to the Spanish cause brought a public denouncement by a Catholic member of the executive council of her West Perthshire constituency party, Colonel Rupert Dawson, the laird of Orchil. Dawson put a (unsuccessful) motion forward stating that her actions were contrary to 'the principles and interests of the Conservative Party', and went on to publish his allegations in *The Patriot* and this, according to Hetherington, led to the belief 'in the minds of the party that . . . Kitty had gone communist'.[51] The 'Red Duchess' was created and that image was further embedded in the psyche of the party when Katherine resigned the government whip in April 1937 in protest over the repeated violations of the Non-Intervention Pact by the Fascist powers. Serious damage was done to her standing in the Conservative Party after a newspaper report stating that she had spoken at a meeting in Glasgow of the International Peace Campaign at which 'The Red Flag' was sung while she was still on the platform. The Dunblane branch of the party refused to allow her to address any further meetings under its auspices,[52] and there were several high profile resignations from the West Perthshire constituency party, and even Oswald Mosley's Blackshirts held opposition meetings in Crieff, Aberfeldy and Auchterarder.[53]

In spite of mounting difficulties within the party over her position on Spain, Katherine continued her work of educating the British people regarding the folly of non-intervention. In 1938, *Searchlight on Spain* was published by Penguin Books and was an instant bestseller, shifting 100,000 copies in a matter of weeks, and translated into French, German and Spanish. The total sales amounted to 300,000. The book provided a detailed history of the events leading up to the civil war, a graphic account of the desperate plight of the Spanish people, and called for the lifting of the arms embargo on the Republican government. It was dedicated: 'To all those Spaniards who are fighting or toiling for national independence and democratic government against horrendous odds.' This was not the first time Katherine had ventured into print in support of the Republican cause; earlier she had written the 'Introduction' to Arthur Koestler's personal, but pro-Republican, account of the civil war – *Spanish Testament* (1937). For her championship of the Republican cause she was affectionately known in Spain as the 'La Duquesa Inglesa'.

At home she was seen in a different and more hostile light as matters within the constituency party came to a climax following Anthony Eden's resignation as foreign secretary in February 1938, when the Duchess abstained in a vote of confidence motion in the government. On 28 April she wrote to Chamberlain threatening to resign the party whip because of the continuing arrival of Italian troops in Spain in contravention of the Non-Intervention agreement. Chamberlain pre-empted Katherine by withdrawing the whip from her and letters exchanged between them were published in *The Times* the next day.[54] The local executive by a vote of nineteen to six votes passed a motion of confidence in Neville Chamberlain's government and called for a propaganda campaign to bolster support for its foreign policy in the constituency. At a meeting in May 1938 it was decided by twenty-one votes to six not to reselect Katherine as their candidate in the next general election and to begin the search for one who would support the government's foreign policy.[55] She was not present at the crucial meeting as she was attending the high society Caledonian Ball in London.[56] Unknowingly, Katherine made her last appearance in the Commons in July 1938 to refute a suggestion by the MP for Bury St Edmonds that she was a recruiting agent for the International Brigade.[57]

The final and decisive meeting of the West Perthshire Conservative Association took place in November 1938 at the behest of the Atholls. The timing of the meeting was not fortuitous for Katherine as it took place shortly after the Munich Agreement between Germany and Britain that led to the ill-fated 'Peace in our time' declaration by Chamberlain. She was in America at the time on a fund raising tour in support of Spanish refugee children, and while there she met with President Roosevelt in spite of the opposition of the British Embassy. However, on hearing the news of the Munich treaty she returned to Britain and circulated her constituents with a letter condemning Chamberlain's actions. This antagonised and further alienated support within the constituency party. The meeting proved one thing: the Duchess was out of touch with her party members and the only votes cast in her favour came from those who lived under the shadow of Blair Atholl. The original motion of the May executive meeting in support of the government was carried by 273 to 167 votes.

However, before the executive could act on the vote, Katherine, in spite of Churchill and others advising her not to do so,[58] surprised everyone by applying for the Chiltern Hundreds and forcing a by-election in December 1938. She was no doubt encouraged by Vernon Bartlett, who had taken the same course of action, and as an Independent had given the government a bloody nose in winning in stunning fashion the Bridgewater by-election earlier that year. The Duchess stood as an Independent, disregarding the advice of both Churchill and Bob Boothby to stand as an Independent Conservative.[59] The election itself was widely reported in the press as a referendum on Chamberlain's policy of appeasement. She was not, however, completely alone and was able to count on the support of her allies, Churchill and Boothby. Even the Spanish Communist leader, Dolores Ibarruri, *La Pasionaria*, sent her a telegram of support.[60] Churchill wrote to *The Times* declaring his admiration and backing for her stance against appeasement, saying:

> You stand for the effective rearmament of our country, and for an end to the procrastination, half-measures and mismanagement, which have led us from a safe position into a state of woeful, unpreparedness and danger . . . You are no doubt opposed by many Conservatives as loyal and patriotic as yourself, but the fact remains that outside our island your defeat at this moment would be relished by the enemies of Britain and of Freedom in every part of the world.[61]

This, however, was as far as Churchill was prepared to go in supporting the Duchess and the same was true of Boothby. The Tory chief whip, James Stuart, assured both men that if they spoke on behalf of Katherine during the election campaign he would withdraw the party whip from them. The feeling that to ignore Stuart's threat and speak for her would lose both MPs the support of their constituents was enough for them to limit themselves to messages of support and little else, although during the campaign Churchill was on the phone to Katherine every evening. Thus she was left to fight what one historian claimed was 'one of the dirtiest by-election campaigns of modern times'[62] without the physical support of the Tory party's most influential anti-appeasers.

In contrast, the Conservatives inundated the constituency with senior ministers and MPs and there was a veritable deluge of pro-Chamberlain propaganda; one pamphlet had the names of seventy Conservative MPs urging electors to vote for the government's candidate, local farmer

William McNair Snadden.[63] Her landed opponents used their money to influence the outcome of the election in subtle, but dubiously legal, ways. Estate workers had their wages increased in return for returning the 'right' vote, and on the Muir and Ancaster estates farmers and tenants had their rents abated for the duration of the election campaign. Local businesses refused to display handbills of the Duchess.[64] The only thing Katherine had in her favour was that she was spared further opposition by the withdrawal of the Liberal candidate and promises of support from the Labour party. However, her campaign was a disaster from start to finish. She toured West Perthshire with a map of Europe failing to realise that few of the voters were interested in foreign affairs. A Mass Observation poll had shown that 65 per cent of the voters were interested in home affairs, while only 15 per cent claimed to be concerned with political events in Europe. On top of this her meetings were poorly advertised and she tended to concentrate on the faithful rather than take her anti-appeasement message into the towns. Indeed, she refused to speak at all in Dunblane, the second largest town in the shire.[65] On polling day there was a blizzard that deterred voters from travelling to the polls – those that did were assisted by the fleet of cars at the disposal of her rival. In spite of all this, Katherine only lost the seat by a narrow margin of 1,313 votes, on a turnout of only 66.6 per cent, a figure that was 7.3 per cent lower than in the 1935 general election.[66] If she had waited, as Martin Pugh suggests, until the euphoria over Munich had died down she probably would have held on to her seat.[67] However, the result was hardly a ringing endorsement of Chamberlain and his government's foreign policy. Hearing of her defeat, Ivor Cobbald, the brother-in-law of James Stuart, sent her a telegram that underlined the dirtiness of the election, saying: 'Am delighted you are out. Hope my Rannoch people voted against you. Now you might find the time to remove your Basque children from Suffolk.'[68] The Duchess consoled herself by playing Beethoven's *Waldstein* and *Appassionata* sonatas, hoping, she said, 'that she would now have more time for her husband and for music'.[69] Spain itself surrendered to the Nationalist rebels in March 1939 shortly before the outbreak of the Second World War.

Did she deserve the opprobrium that was hurled at her by her fellow Tories? Was she in fact a 'Red'? Katherine's love of Empire and the way in which welfare concerns were intimately connected with more overt strategic interests should warn against such an interpretation. As Tom Buchanan points out, the Duchess saw the war in Spain in strategic terms, that is, victory for Franco would make Spain a client state of the fascist powers, which would threaten France and 'above all Gibraltar and British imperial interests in the Mediterranean'.[70] In addition, there is her much-publicised criticism of the Soviet Union. From the late 1920s to the early 1930s she was on friendly terms with exiled Russian leaders, such as Kerensky,[71] and, partly as a result of their influence and her own research, she began to draw attention to the question of forced labour in Russia, claiming in 1928 that there were around 260,000 forced labourers. In a letter to *The Times* she commented on the number of labour camps that existed in the Soviet Union and detailed the terrible conditions that existed within them.[72] She also joined the Christian Protest Movement to spread the facts about the persecution of religion in the Soviet Union.[73] Presiding over the annual breakfast of the Religious Tract Society, the first woman to do so, Katherine claimed that Soviet-inspired anti-religious propaganda had spread to Britain and had taken practical shape in the form of a League of Militant Atheists. To counteract these sinister tendencies she stressed the importance of 'clean literature' for young people and preserving 'at all costs Christian foundations of home'.[74]

In her capacity as chairman of the Conservative Sub-Committee on Russian Trade, she was an enthusiastic opponent of 'dumping' by the Russians of cheap timber and other agricultural products in Western Europe and the potential harm this might do to the British economy. Her fears were articulated in a speech to the women's branch of the City of London Conservative and Unionist Association. Katherine stated: 'When we look at Russia we are faced with the greatest menace to trade that the modern world has ever known and with the greatest tragedy from the humane point of view the world has ever known.'[75] She also called on the British people to boycott buying Soviet produce as long as 'the Russians were conscripted and kept on short rations'.[76] Her views on the Soviet menace were formalised in 1932 in a book on forced labour and social conditions in the Soviet Union – *The Conscription of the People* – in which she claimed that the Five Year Plan 'is a plan tending to undermine capitalist stabilisation . . . a plan of world revolution'. Indeed, such was the ferocity of her attacks on the Soviet Union that Isabel Brown refused to appear on NJCSR platforms with the Duchess until she toned down her anti-communist views.[77] It is ironic that after the Second World War Katherine was referred to as the 'Fascist Beast' for her support of various anti-communist organisations such as the British League for European Freedom.[78]

The Duchess of Atholl died in 1960 after breaking her femur while climbing over a wall; Bardie had died eighteen years before her. Her life had been a remarkable testimony to principle. No one can doubt her courage in pursuit of her beliefs, although one might question her political judgement at times, particularly during the Spanish Civil War. As Bob Boothby said of her: 'She had moral courage which seemed at moments to amount to recklessness.'[79] Katherine appeared not as a grande dame, but as 'an inspired, but humourless headmistress, slight, uptight and uncompromising'.[80] Much of her life was devoted to public service, and although she took up women's issues in and out of parliament, it took her until nearly the end of her life before she recognised that there was a place outside the home and a role in society for women that amounted to more than just wife and mother. Her time in parliament and her spectacular career did little to improve the political prospects of women, even those fortunate enough to be elected as an MP.

Fortunately, women pursued their own agenda, finding work in increasing numbers, balancing the demands of family and occupation, and participating more actively in the political sphere. After nearly a century of campaigning they have decisively broken through the political 'glass ceiling' in Britain. In 1997, 120 women, constituting 18.2 per cent of the total number of elected MPs, were returned to the Westminster parliament and, in Scotland in 1999, forty-eight women, or 37.2 per cent of the total, were returned as MSPs, the highest proportion of female representatives in national government anywhere in the world, outside of Denmark, Sweden and Wales. Thanks to these efforts politics is no longer the pastime of the male or the privileged minority.

NOTES

1. N. Thompson, *The Anti-Appeasers: Conservative Opposition to Appeasement in the 1930s* (Oxford, 1971), p. 120.
2. A. S. Williams, *Ladies of Influence: Women of the Elite in Interwar Britain* (London, 2000), p. 108.
3. Williams, *Ladies*, p. 128; S. Hetherington, *Katherine Atholl 1874–1960: Against the Tide* (Aberdeen, 1991), p. xiii.
4. B. Harrison, *Prudent Revolutionaries: Portraits of British Feminists Between the Wars* (Oxford, 1987), p. 315.
5. E. Wilkinson, *Peeps at Politicians* (London, 1930), p. 37.
6. Hetherington, *Katherine Atholl*, p. 53.
7. Quoted in Williams, *Ladies*, p. 119.
8. Hetherington, *Katherine Atholl*, p. 53.
9. Williams, *Ladies*, p. 116.
10. F. Balfour, *Ne Obliviscaris. Dinna Forget*, vol. II (London, 1930), p. 158.
11. Hetherington, *Katherine Atholl*, p. 86.
12. The Duchess of Atholl, *Women and Politics* (London, 1931), pp. 42–3.

13. Williams, *Ladies of Influence*, p. 121.
14. Quoted in A. Summers, *Angels and Citizens: British Women as Military Nurses 1854–1914* (London, 2000 edn), pp. 235–6.
15. C. Burness, 'The long slow march: Scottish women MPs, 1918–1945', in E. Brietenbach and E. Gordon (eds) *Out of Bounds: Women in Scottish Society 1800–1945*, (Edinburgh, 1992), pp. 162–3.
16. C. Law, *Suffrage and Power: the Women's Movement 1918–1928* (1997), p. 196.
17. *The Times*, 6 March 1924.
18. J. Fyrth, *The Signal was Spain: The Aid Spain Movement in Britain, 1936–39* (London, 1986), p. 202.
19. Harrison, *Prudent Revolutionaries*, p. 76.
20. *The Times*, 22 November 1924.
21. The Duchess of Atholl, *Working Partnership* (London, 1958), pp. 135–6; *The Times*, 28 December 1923.
22. Atholl, *Women and Politics*, pp. 104–12.
23. Atholl, *Women and Politics*, p. 123.
24. Atholl, *Women and Politics*, pp. 113–24.
25. *The Times*, 26 November 1923.
26. *The Times*, 29 July 1924.
27. *The Times*, 29 November 1924.
28. A. Brown et al., *Politics and Society in Scotland* (Basingstoke, 1996), p. 173.
29. E. Summerskill, *A Woman's World*, p. 60, quoted in Williams, *Ladies of Influence*, pp. 116–17.
30. C. Sykes, *Nancy: a Life of Lady Astor* (London, 1972), pp. 281–2.
31. *The Times*, 28 November 1926.
32. *The Times*, 2 December 1930.
33. Hetherington, *Katherine Atholl*, p. 110.
34. Williams, *Ladies of Influence*, p. 115.
35. Hetherington, *Katherine Atholl*, p. 123.
36. Quoted in Hetherington, *Katherine Atholl*, p. 122.
37. See Williams, *Ladies of Influence*, p. 117.
38. Atholl, *Women and Politics*, p. 169.
39. Hetherington, *Katherine Atholl*, p. 152.
40. Hetherington, *Katherine Atholl*, pp. 136–7.
41. See J. Haggis, 'White women and colonisation: towards a non-recuperative history', in C. Midgley (ed.) *Gender and Imperialism* (Manchester, 1998), pp. 45–78.
42. *Glasgow Herald*, 5 December 1933.
43. *Hansard*, 280, col. 1606.
44. Atholl, *Working Partnership*, p. 199.
45. *Hansard*, 317, col. 339.
46. Hetherington, *Katherine Atholl*, p. 171.
47. Williams, *Ladies of Influence*, p. 110.

48. Hetherington, *Katherine Atholl*, p. 176.
49. Hetherington, *Katherine Atholl*, p. 184.
50. Fyrth, *Spain*, pp. 247–8.
51. Hetherington, *Katherine Atholl*, p. 189.
52. Hetherington, *Katherine Atholl*, p. 191.
53. Wiliams, *Ladies of Influence*, p. 125.
54. Williams, *Ladies of Influence*, p. 125.
55. S. Ball, 'The politics of appeasement: the fall of the Duchess of Atholl and the Kinross and West Perthshire By-election, December 1938', *Scottish Historical Review*, LXIX (1990), pp. 58–66.
56. Hetherington, *Katherine Atholl*, p. 196.
57. Hetherington, *Katherine Atholl*, p. 198.
58. R. R. James, *Bob Boothby: a Portrait* (London, 1991), p. 187.
59. James, *Boothby*, p. 188.
60. Williams, *Ladies of Influence*, p. 126.
61. *The Times*, 13 December 1938.
62. James, *Boothby*, pp. 187–8.
63. James, *Boothby*, p. 187.
64. Ball, 'Appeasement', p. 79.
65. Ball, 'Appeasement', p. 72.
66. Ball, 'Appeasement', p. 77.
67. M. Pugh, *Women and the Women's Movement in Britain, 1914–1959* (Basingstoke, 1992), p. 208.
68. James, *Boothby*, p. 189.
69. M. D. Stocks, 'Katherine, Marjory, Stewart-Murray', *Dictionary of National Biography, 1951–60* (London, 1971), pp. 926–7.
70. T. Buchanan, *Britain and the Spanish Civil War* (Cambridge, 1997), p. 32.
71. Hetherington, *Katherine Atholl*, p. 151.
72. *The Times*, 22 December 1931.
73. Atholl, *Working Partnership*, p. 193.
74. *The Times*, 31 May 1933.
75. *Glasgow Herald*, 11 December 1931, quoted in E. M. Catton, 'How consistent was the Duchess of Atholl in her attitude and actions in the 1930s?' (M. Litt. Thesis, University of St Andrews, 2003), p. 26.
76. *The Times*, 10 December 1931.
77. Fyrth, *Spain*, p. 202.
78. Hetherington, *Katherine Atholl*, p. 225.
79. *The Times*, 27 October 1960.
80. Stocks, 'Katherine', p. 926.

9

Willa Muir: Living with Genius (2)

ᗧ

Willa Muir, like Jane Welsh Carlyle before her, stood in the shadow of her celebrated husband, Edwin, and as a result she suffered a similar form of social invisibility that Jane regularly mentioned in her voluminous correspondence. Although talented in their own right, both women lived their lives in the service of genius. Unlike Jane, however, Willa was not restricted to the domestic sphere; the world she lived in was one in which opportunities were expanding, and it was possible for a woman to see herself as something other than simply a homemaker. The granting of the vote in 1918, the growth in white-collar employment, the opening up of higher education, and entry into the professions, allowed women to penetrate the public sphere in ways that were unthinkable in the middle of the nineteenth century. While Jane was confined to pontificating on and satirising the domestic, Willa, by expressing herself in a much more public way, was able to become the person Jane could have been if she had lived in a different age. Through her novels and political writings, she analysed the place of women in modern Scotland in a compelling and original manner; indeed, it would be difficult to think of any other woman in the last century who has made a greater contribution to feminist theory in Scotland than Willa. But for all this, there existed within her an emotional conflict between a need to belong, to be attached to someone or some place, and the academic analysis of female subordination, which ensured that the message and the messenger were in contradiction. Her desire to satisfy Edwin's emotional, intellectual and physical needs above her own wants, showed Willa in personal life to be little different from other women, such as her mother, whom she came to despise for their deference to masculinity. The title of her autobiography – *Belonging: a Memoir* (1968) – written towards the end of her life is in a word the summation of her philosophical view of the relationship between men and women and society, while at the same time it also provides a strong clue as to her essentialist needs as a woman. Thus, Willa's life is interesting and instructive, not only because of the insights into the emotional and psychological problems of a highly gifted woman living with such a troubled and tortured genius as Edwin undoubtedly was, and having to take second place to that genius, but also because it dramatises the conflict between the private and the public spheres, the tremendous emotional dependency of a woman on a man, and the public proclamation of female independence and denial of subservience.

The need to belong was evident from her early childhood. Willa (Wilhelmina after her maternal grandmother) was born at 14 Chapel Place in Montrose in March 1890, the first child of four, to Peter and Elizabeth Anderson. Her parents were first cousins and at the time of their marriage in February 1889, Peter was the owner of a fairly prosperous draper's business in Montrose, while Elizabeth, a rubber worker's daughter, was working as a dressmaker in Edinburgh. Although clearly part of an urban culture, the Anderson's family origins lay in Unst, Shetland. Their first tongue was a Norse dialect used in Shetland and Willa's earliest memory of talking was in that idiom, although she soon had added a 'broad Montrose', as well as a 'kind of English'.[1] The English was used in a private school in Bridge Street, Montrose, which she attended from the age of three years. Private education was a reflection of the growing prosperity of the Andersons and shortly her other siblings joined her at Bridge Street School. However, family fortunes took a turn for the worse when her father died of phthisis, a respiratory disease, when Willa was only nine years of age, with her baby sister dying the following year. These events were to prove emotionally scarring and drove her, particularly in later life, to seek a father-figure, something she made explicit in an unpublished work – *This Lop-Sided World* – where she argued that women had a 'tendency to be attracted to a father-figure'.[2] It also caused Willa to look on her time in Montrose with a mixture of contempt and hatred. She noted in her journal in 1948 that 'I realised how much I feared and loathed that house [in Montrose] . . . too many dead people . . . my father, my baby sister, grannie, mother and [brother] Willie'.[3]

After the father's death, her mother carried on the business as best she could, while her grandmother looked after Willa and her siblings. Income fell and economies were made through sending the children to Townhead Elementary School, which she described as 'a drab, grey stone building', where the curriculum was based on the 3Rs and the school environment authoritarian. 'What we read and wrote mattered little', she declared, 'but failures in memory, in accuracy, especially in spelling and arithmetic, or misdemeanours, like whispering in class, were punished by blows on the palm of the hand from a hard leather tawse.'[4] Willa remained there for three years until she won a scholarship at the age of twelve to the fee-paying, middle-class Montrose Academy. The Academy placed emphasis on the study of the Classics, in fact, it was the first public school in Scotland to place Greek on its syllabus. Greek and Latin, inspired by the principal teacher, John Yorsten, became her favourite subjects; indeed, she was the school's star pupil. Between 1905 and 1907 Willa won the English Medal, the Angus Medal for Latin, the Duke Medal for Greek and passed her Higher examinations with distinction, coming fourth in the University of St Andrews Bursary Competition.[5] However, in spite of impressive academic progress, she was acutely aware of herself as an outsider, saying: 'Being a bursar . . . instead of a fee-paying pupil, was a social stigma . . . I had to live down my bursary.'[6]

As an undergraduate at St Andrews, Willa immersed herself in the collegial life of the university. She was a member of numerous societies, including (predictably) the Classical Society, the Women's Student Debating Society, the Student Representative Council, and was a member of the editorial board of the student publication – *College Echoes* – to which she contributed some articles. Willa was also deeply involved in politics as vice-president of the Women Student's Suffrage Society and (later) as a founding member of the university's Fabian Society. Her political philosophy encompassed traditional Liberal emphasis on the rights of the individual and the socialist desire to provide opportunity for all through the agency of the state. As she defined it: 'Socialism is individualism in its right mind . . . Everyman must have an equal opportunity.'[7] Academically, Willa was also shining. After two rather ordinary years, she graduated in 1910 with first class honours in Greek and the Humanities, returning the following year to study English Language and Literature and Modern History, and winning the class medal in English Literature. St Andrews recognised her undoubted ability by awarding her the Berry Scholarship, which allowed her to continue with her studies for another year.

Growing a little tired of academia and needing a steady flow of income, Willa found a teaching post at Brancepath Rectory Home School in County Durham in 1912. However, her disintegrating relationship with her fiancé Cecil, a rugby-playing type whom she had met while at St Andrews, and who was seeing a series of other women, saw her return home two years later. Willa ended the relationship in typical fashion by throwing his engagement ring into the sea off St Andrews pier.[8] Another pull factor was the deterioration of her brother Willie's mental state. He suffered from hallucinations and delusions of persecution and was committed to the James Murray Royal Asylum in Perth.[9] Willa managed to find a post as teaching assistant in the Latin Department at the University of St Andrews, and it was during her stay there that she became interested in educational psychology and won a research award from the Carnegie Trust to study a number of linked projects under the heading of 'Mental association in children' at Bedford College, London. Her accent and small-town background made her feel ill at ease with the College and its students, being 'too ladylike'. In September 1917, Willa was drafted into war work at the Board of Agriculture and it was perhaps the burden of combining paid employment with academic study that caused her to fail to complete her thesis, which by this time had been narrowed to an 'Analysis of the problems raised by sex education'.

After the war Willa found herself a lecturer and vice-principal of a small Teachers' Training College in London. While working there she had met a shipping clerk with literary pretensions, Edwin Muir, at a party at an old university friend's mother's house in Glasgow, in September 1918, and almost instantly fell in love with him. Her love for Edwin immediately proved costly. She was dismissed from her lecturing position for proposing to marry a man who did 'not believe in God'.[10] Another post she held for a year, as a headmistress of a day continuation school for drapery employees, before being sacked for tolerating 'late coming', practising 'unconventional' teaching methods, and encouraging singing and dancing.[11] However, by this time she had married Edwin on 7 June 1919 at St Pancras Registry Office on the grounds that 'if we had any children I shouldn't like them to be bastards'.[12] However, while the marriage may have had been agreed for rather conventional reasons, it was to be a partnership of the most 'advanced' kind, as Willa makes clear:

> He [Edwin] refused to . . . [be] a dominant male, and I refused to be pushed down into female subserviency. I was not caught, any more than Edwin was, in the . . . false dilemma, of being top dog or bottom dog, in which so many lovers let themselves be confined. A belief in true love was my brand of non-conformism, and it matched Edwin's in many ways. True love . . . never seeks to exert power . . . Punishment and forgiveness seemed to me equally irrelevant.[13]

In spite of their avant-garde ideas and their involvement in the London literary scene – Edwin had become assistant to A. R. Orage, editor of the *New Age* – the home they set up was never considered by Willa to be unconventional or Bohemian, although 'rooms might be untidy with books and papers', and their circumstances in the beginning poor, 'chairs and beds were comfortable, meals reasonably punctual, the ambience tranquil'.[14] Edwin's reputation was growing and he was appointed drama critic of *The Scotsman*, but success soon turned to disenchantment. As the pace of life in London became frighteningly fast, Willa found herself and Edwin to be 'drowning in a flood of people'.[15] Moreover, they were forced, as Edwin states in a letter to a friend, to 'only write things that kept us from our work . . . So in 1921 . . . we threw up everything and went to Prague.'[16] This was the beginning of a long sojourn that would take them through Czechoslovakia, Germany, Austria, France, Italy, Scotland, England and the USA and would last the best part of thirty years or so. The restlessness, on one level, was part of the search for somewhere to belong to; on another, it was to be part of 'a wide literary culture', to be part of the 'world of books'.[17]

The flight to Prague was only made possible by the $120 a month Edwin earned by contributing articles to the American weekly, *The Freeman*. After a year or so in Prague the Muirs moved to Dresden. While there a chance encounter with the radical educationalist, A. S. Neill, who was an old friend of Willa's from her university days, led to an invitation to join him at Hellerau, where he had founded an international school. While Willa taught, Edwin roamed the forest, read and fired his imagination. The idyll was soon over as the great inflation of 1923 in Germany bankrupted Neill and forced the closure of his school. The Muirs, as Willa recalled, 'feeling like cowards . . . decided to runaway' to Italy to share the expenses of a house occupied by some friends of Edwin's. On the rail journey to Forte dei Marmi, near Florence, Edwin confessed to Willa that a young woman, known only as Gerda, at Neill's school was in love with him and that he intended to return to Hellerau to be with her. Interestingly, just one week before he married Willa, Edwin had confessed his love to another woman, Jane Leitch, comparing them to Dante and Beatrice, and declaring: 'Though I will not see you, except when Fate decides so, I shall love to think you are living and breathing in such and such a human habitation'.[18] Had Willa known this the marriage may not have taken place, but in the case of Gerda, she like many other women in this situation blamed herself for what had happened, saying:

> In Hellerau I had devoted my energies more to Neill's school and the Eurhythmic community than to Edwin . . . I had been too busy, too much occupied with day-to-day school matters and finally too concerned with the troubles coming from the outside world. I had almost been treating Edwin as a brother, like Neill.[19]

Edwin did not return to Hellerau and chose to stay with 'Peerie' Willa, as he affectionately called her, and there is no other evidence that the marriage was endangered by his future behaviour towards other women. If anything Willa became even more fiercely attached to him and overly protective. In a letter written a few years after Edwin's death, she recalled that he was 'a soft-shell crab and I was his carapace', and easily lost her temper by 'unfounded criticism' of him.[20] Her own shell was a cigarette, and she always carried in her bag 'a packet of fags, my cigarette holder, cotton wool and a lighter', at the expense of any cosmetics.[21]

The collapse of the Hellerau establishment did not spell the end of the relationship with A. S. Neill. The American money had dried up with the closure of *The Freeman*, and in desperation Willa wrote to Neill asking if he would let them stay at his Sunday Mountain (Sonntagberg) school until they found an alternative source of income. Their stay on the mountain was again idyllic, with even less demands on Willa, but it was also once more only temporary. Neill's refusal to follow Austrian national curriculum guidelines and the hostility of the locals to what they saw as a 'heretical' and dangerous experiment forced him to cut his losses and return to England, where he established the famous Summerhill school in Lyme Regis.[22] By this time the Muirs were 'Rich, with a capital R'. A New York publisher had asked them to translate a trio of plays of the German writer Gerhart Hauptman into English blank verse at $100 a play.[23] This was the beginning of a long and distinguished career in this field that culminated in the translation of Franz Kafka's novels *America* and *The Castle* into English. Willa also translated work under the pseudonym of Agnes Neill Scott.

After a brief stay in England, the Muirs headed to Montrose to live for a time with Willa's family. Although it was not a happy stay, it was in Montrose that Willa began the outlines of an essay – *Women: An Inquiry* – published by Hogarth Press in 1925, which marked her out as a serious theorist of feminism. The essay itself was completely ignored by the media, with the exception of a review in the *Times Literary Supplement* in November that year, but it still remains an important document in the evolution of feminist thought in Britain, as it was one of the first to articulate a fully developed concept of separate spheres. After detailing examples of male domination throughout history, Willa argued that it was the outcome of an irrational impulse in men 'rooted in fear'. Domination was then the product of a deep psychological insecurity in men. Overcoming this was tied to a recognition of the different roles that men and women played in life and in accepting them as different but equally important. This, she argued, would lead to the achievement of an ideal state between the genders and create the basis for a harmonious balance between men and women.[24] As she put it:

> Unconscious life creates . . . human beings: conscious life creates . . . If men are stronger in conscious life, their creative purpose must express their strength. Men should excel in translating life into conscious forms, women in

fostering the growth of life itself. Men will create systems of philosophy or government, while women are creating individual human beings.[25]

Women dealt with the concrete, while men were more inclined to the abstract; women were concerned with internal dynamics of relationships, while men looked outward; women were at their most creative in the performing arts, such as singing and dancing, because of their closer connection with human life, while men because of their detachment were solely capable of creating that fusion between form and content that distinguished great art.[26] Thus, 'men', as Willa concluded, 'create the ideas, women make use of them; women create human beings, men make use of them',[27] or more succinctly, women feel, men think.

However, far from being a document of female emancipation, the essay in many ways provides a theoretical/philosophical justification for continuing subordination since the roles that men and women play in society seem to be genetically governed or at least pre-ordained. As Allen notes, the essay was an unconscious endorsement of a patriarchal structure of home and society that had served to tie women to the domestic sphere and which all her life Willa had rebelled against.[28] Perhaps, this view owed something to the awe she held Edwin in and her sense of inferiority as regards his intellect. She was always of the opinion that 'my own writing could never have been as important as Edwin's'.[29] Edwin himself did little to alleviate her sense of inadequacy as a writer and in some ways compounded the feeling. Willa claimed that he 'deplored my attempt in Dresden to write a Noah's Ark play in contemporary language. I gave it up. I shouldn't have given it up (someone did it years later successfully)'.[30] Some twenty or so years later he also drove her to suicidal despair by ignoring the draft of her novel – The Usurpers – that dealt with their time in Prague in the 1940s, saying:

> I had a fit of black despair and resentment when I had finished it, just because Edwin let it lie for days before reading it . . . I wanted him to show enthusiasm and interest; he *never said* a *word* . . . It was his apparent indifference that got me down; I could see how little value he attached to the *expectations* he might have of it, how little real importance it would have. Perhaps, he is right, thought I, this book . . . is really a very second-rate production: it won't matter to anyone. It made me suicidal for some hours until I go the better off it.[31]

A. S. Neill pointedly asked Willa some years later if she 'felt that Edwin's work was so important that you took second place . . . [and if] you did sacrifice something of yourself as Edwin's Frau'.[32]

Shortly before the publication of *Women: An Inquiry*, Willa fell pregnant at the age of thirty-five. This resulted in a miscarriage, an event that left her 'feeling forlorn and empty, reduced in spirit and weak'.[33] Two years later she gave birth to a son, Gavin, but only after some sixty-five hours in labour. Edwin in a letter to Violet Schiff spoke of her having 'had a very bad and severe time' being 'twice under chloroform and twice under twilight sleep'.[34] Willa had been 'ambivalent' towards her second pregnancy and this, perhaps, influenced her child rearing practices, as did her psychological training. It was in some ways more of a research project than the close and intimate relationship we associate with a mother and child. Willa kept a journal that detailed Gavin's development during the first six months of his life in which he was only once referred to by name, as Allen says, Gavin was treated as a 'phenomenon rather than as a person'.[35] Moreover, Gavin was never prioritised over Edwin. When her brother, Willie, and her mother died in early 1930, Gavin, aged only thirty months, was left in a local Montessori school, while Willa and Edwin left for Mentone on the French Rivera.

Perhaps as a consequence of the trauma surrounding the deaths in her family and the need to come to terms with it, in the 1930s Willa wrote a few novels and enjoyed her most creative period until the publication of her autobiography in 1968. Her most ambitious piece of writing was *Imagined Corners* (1931), but there were also two other novels – *Mrs Ritchie* (1933) and *Mrs Grundy* (1936). In the first novel, Willa began with a simple proposition: what would her life have been like if she had married Cecil instead of Edwin and settled in Montrose (Calderwick in the novel)? From that premise she undertook an analysis of small-town life in which she saw women as 'cornered' by tradition and religion into passive acceptance of a patriarchal social structure. While the analysis is quite pessimistic, the novel does hold out some hope for women as the title suggests possibility as well as limitation, being 'cornered is only an imaginary constraint'[36] and, thus, the trap can be sprung by a leap in consciousness. The catalyst for this is the heroine's (Elizabeth Shand) sister-in-law's (Lizzie) return from Italy. Lizzie is sophisticated and newly widowed, and through their interaction Elizabeth realises she has to face her life and what it has become with Hector honestly. By reassessing her life she sees through the pettiness and the vanities of Calderwick society and becomes more open to the new possibilities of personal and sexual freedom, which results in her leaving Scotland with Lizzie at the close of the novel for a new life abroad.

Although Willa in a letter to the novelist, Neil Gunn, claimed that she was 'trying to illumine life not reform it',[37] there is a strong feminist motif running through the novel in its attacks on the institution of marriage and its rigid division of labour, and the role of the church in subduing female sexuality and robbing women of their natural confidence. Elizabeth until Lizzie's return had accepted a masculine definition of her social position and her sexuality: 'she was herself-and-Hector'.[38] Thus her whole identity was defined through marriage. She was to cook, clean, sew and, at the same time, provide moral guidance to men and add decoration and refinement to their homes:

> Hector, like all other men of his acquaintance, accepted unthinkingly the suggestion that women were guardians of decorum – good women, that is to say, who could not be referred to as skirts. Good women existed to keep in check men's sexual passions. A man, driven by physical desire . . . is mad and reckless and his sole protection from himself is the decorum of women. They believed that any decent man would afterwards be grateful to a woman who had prevented him from seducing her . . . the 'weaker sex' – a phrase constantly on their lips and in their minds – was an accusation against women for not being entirely exempt from frailty . . . Lizzie Shand used to say to her friends that in Scotland man's chief end was to glorify God and woman's to see that he did it.[39]

Inevitably, in this one-sided relationship there were double standards:

> In Calderwick wives were not so well provided for as husbands. Wives . . . do not forgather in drunkenness so Elizabeth was denied that relief. Nor could she . . . count on any woman she knew . . . The only thing she could have done was to be unfaithful to her husband, but for a Calderwick woman to do that . . . There was no easy drift to which Elizabeth might commit herself except the traditional stream of respectable wifehood. Both as a member of society and an individual she was more buffeted than Hector.[40]

This state of affairs was buttressed by theological teachings. The Reverend William Murray in the novel takes the view that the 'female sex was devised by God for the lower grades of work and knowledge'.[41] This was a consequence of original sin and later in the story, Elizabeth, in a moment of clarity, realises just 'how insulted I was when I was told that woman was made from a rib of man, and that Eve was the first sinner, and the pains of childbirth are a punishment to women'.[42] Consequently, both Elizabeth and Lizzie reject Christianity and its God as male contrivances to subordinate women and in doing so they also reject the land of Calvinism – Scotland.

Willa returned to the theme of religion and to Calderwick in the follow up to her first novel – *Mrs Ritchie* – which sank without trace after being savaged by critics. The novel failed in a number of fundamental ways: the writing was poor, the dialogue stilted, the context barely sketched and psycho-babble is used to make up for the lack of proper character development. However, in spite of this, the theme of religion is powerful and Annie Ritchie's fundamentalism not only turns her into a monster, but also sees her destroy her family and ultimately herself.[43] Willa confessed that the pounding she had taken had shaken her faith in her novel.[44] But she had no more success two years later with *Mrs Grundy*, which, as Allen notes, was greeted with a 'perfunctory indifference . . . and rapidly descended into the realms of literary obscurity'.[45] This was a pity because the novel, although described as 'a slap dash performance'[46] by Willa, has some interesting observations to make on the character of Scotland in the 1930s and the position of women at this time: something that Edwin did in a factual way with his social study – *Scottish Journey* (1936). Mrs Grundy was derived from a caricature in *Punch* of an old woman who represented the traditional values of English conservatism, that is, anti-French, against change, and so on, and in the late nineteenth century she was transformed into a lower middle-class wife who constantly berates the upper classes for their immorality.[47] Willa took the character of Mrs Grundy and created a Scottish version – Mrs MacGrundy – who is of 'the same kind, with a slightly different angle of distortion owing to the character of the Scots, who have usually sought religious rather than social sanctions for respectability'.[48]

Although we are invited to laugh with the author at the hopelessly out-of-date attitudes and values and the pomposity of Mrs MacGrundy, there is also the view expressed that she is 'a negative, thwarted perversion of what might have been or might yet become a national consciousness. Like Mrs Grundy she can create nothing new; she is merely obstructive and deferring, where she is not a passive reflection of the status quo.'[49] Under the influence of Mrs MacGrundy, Scotland has become a nation of 'pompous prigs and facetious sniggerers'. The pomposity of the middle classes is underpinned by a concept of respectability derived from Presbyterianism, which itself has 'alienated the Scots from a true knowledge of themselves and of their community'.[50] The alienation has impacted most on and has been more deeply felt by women, who, in Willa's opinion, have made the greatest sacrifices in terms of their feeling and emotions to the service of the Kirk and masculinity. As she puts it:

> the farm labourer's wife is too often regarded as a mere convenience for her husband and her family even [among] the . . . middle classes in the towns, for all their clothes and houses, the women are still to a great extent the unacknowledged servants of their men.[51]

Confined mainly to the domestic sphere, ambition in women, beyond finding a husband and becoming a respectable wife and mother, was frowned upon as unnatural and unrespectable. Mrs MacGrundy, in a conversation on authority, argues that

> no woman could possibly become the 'Head' of anything. Women . . . needed a man to direct them . . . women should defer to men as a way of 'managing' them. So they agree[d] that in any professional organisation, where there was even 1000 women to one man, the representative of the male sex must be elevated to authority over women.[52]

Willa returned to the subject of women and their subordination in 1936 in a short piece written for the *Left Review*. Here she argued that, in spite of Scotland being 'by and large' a socialist country, the ideology of separate spheres was still dominant. The woman occupied and largely controlled the domestic arena, since husband and children were 'entirely dependent on her services'.[53] In contrast, the public space was still the domain of men, who were ceded by women all 'the say'; in fact, Willa argued that it was, 'politically speaking', more difficult to tempt an 'ordinary Scotswoman' into 'the open as the occupants of a Hindu zenana'.[54] However, unlike the nineteenth century, the sphere occupied by women was becoming more open to intrusion from the state in the form of compulsory schooling, medical inspection, housing and welfare benefits; moreover, the economy was becoming much more competitive and in this new economic order the mother was increasingly at the mercy of external economic agencies and forces. The consequence of all this was to devalue, to lower the prestige of the mother, as the provision of these essential caring services for their families were gradually being appropriated by the state, or as in the case of food and other necessities severely rationed by the decline in standards of living in the 1930s. The mother was no longer an equal partner in marriage as the balance between 'prestige and rights' has been fundamentally altered by these economic and political changes. Fathers were also affected by the difficult economic circumstances of the 1930s, but as they did not exclusively occupy the domestic sphere and had a greater connection to the public world of politics and work, they had the real possibility of having some kind of influence on the direction of policy.[55] The solution, as far as Willa was concerned, lay not in greater state intervention, or in the provision of more welfare, but in the creation of a 'fifty–fifty partnership between men and their wives', and in a retreat from the ideology of separate spheres to an environment where 'a mother . . . [was] a political comrade, with an economic status of her own and a "say" in public affairs'.[56] This belief she carried to the grave, claiming in a final (unpublished) essay in 1960–1 that 'I see coming a harmonious partnership between man and women

. . . a general climate of opinion in which all notions of dominance by either sex have been eliminated'.[57]

However, one might have concluded that Willa's move towards the politicisation of the private sphere was influenced by the events in Europe, but although the rise of Hitler and 'his Nazi gangsters' deeply troubled the Muirs, she claimed that they became 'not more politically-minded but less so', indeed, Edwin spent much of the 1930s analysing his dreams, rather than the international political situation.[58] Ironically, the early to mid-1930s were among the happiest years that Edwin, Willa and Gavin spent together as a family. With her mother's money they rented a house at 7 Downshire Place, Hampstead, London, for £120 a year, close to where the novelist Catherine Carswell and her husband lived. They felt once more at the cutting edge of literary affairs. However, tragedy struck when a petrol tanker knocked down Gavin while out walking with his nanny and the Muirs' dog, Matthew. His leg was broken in two places and he suffered from severe concussion. To overcome his trauma and to get him away from London's 'incessant motor traffic', the family moved back to Edwin's birthplace in Orkney. After three months there they were offered a house by James Whyte, bookseller and owner of the literary journal – *The Modern Scot* – in St Andrews and, believing it would be a more 'satisfying place for Gavin to grow up in', they accepted, although not without a struggle. Edwin had felt socially and spiritually at home in Orkney and Willa had to convince him that St Andrews would prove more conducive both intellectually and financially. Willa was also concerned for her health. She had felt some displacement of her internal organs while playing football with Edwin and Gavin and the only doctor available in Orkney to treat her was 'elderly, ham-fisted and inexpert'.[59]

St Andrews initially proved to be ideal. Edwin and Gavin were happy and Willa found the required medical assistance for her trouble. However, after the excitement of settling in paled, the Muirs found the town and the university to be snobbish, insular and old-fashioned. Edwin, in spite of his literary standing, was refused a temporary lectureship when war broke out in 1939. Professor Blythe Webster, of the department of English, said of him that 'he was a crofter's son who had never been to university and his qualified wife . . . is nothing but a pain in the neck', moreover, he was a man ' who wrote for the papers'.[60] Gavin's schooling also proved to be troublesome. Willa objected to the use of corporal punishment and removed him from Madras College and placed him in the privately run, all-boys preparatory school, New Park. Although short of money most of the time, translation work allowed them some degree of comfort. When war broke out in 1939 military conscription created labour shortages within education and Willa was taken on as a teacher in Classics in New Park at £3 a week and her lunches. Edwin, who had left school at fourteen and had no educational qualifications, was considered illiterate by the authorities and refused English teaching, instead, he was employed stamping papers in the Dundee Food Office, and in his spare time took part in Home Guard activities. Both Edwin and Willa had shifted from a pacifist position to outright opposition to Hitler and the Nazis. As Willa put it: 'One does not carry on a dialogue with a beast of prey . . . it was a relief that Britain was preparing to resist the Nazi evil, although the prospect of war flooded Edwin and me with woe as well as personal grief.'[61]

Although Willa recorded that she 'liked the little boys she taught',[62] one of the school's former pupils, Bill Adams, says that they 'mocked her for her scruffy appearance and unconventional clothing and for the unpleasant odour which she allegedly exuded'.[63] Certainly, Willa was unconcerned with fashion and 'never gave much heed to clothes as long as they were dark blue or black',[64] but she was also far from well during her time at New Park, as Edwin explained in a letter to a friend:

> All winter Willa was teaching in the school that Gavin goes too, and I am working in the Dundee Food Office. We found it a hard strain – we're no longer young – to get up at 7 every morning and go through a settled routine all day, after keeping no times for twenty years. It quite exhausted us, and about three months ago I broke down with a strained heart . . . and Willa, after enduring it longer, followed my example a week ago. So that now we have, almost literally, one heart between the two of us . . . we had no leisure: we worked and went to bed.[65]

Willa never returned to New Park and in 1942 the Muirs left St Andrews for Edinburgh where Edwin had secured a position with the British Council organising 'programmes and entertainment' for allied soldiers – Polish, Norwegian, Free French and Czechs.[66] The close association with the Czech troops led to Edwin requesting the British Council to allow him to contribute something to the rebuilding of the country at the end of the war. His request was accepted and he was installed in Prague as the Director of the British Institute, where Willa joined him, and Gavin went to the University of St Andrews.

Edwin lectured on English Literature at Charles University until the opening of the British Institute and very quickly the Muirs were absorbed into the intellectual and social life of post-war Prague. On his sixtieth birthday he was awarded an honorary Ph.D. by the university and, on the surface, it seemed as if life could not be better, despite continued wartime shortages of food and other essentials. However, as Willa noted, troubles both personal and political were brewing and turned their stay into a 'catastrophe'.[67] The British Council adopted a more hands-on approach to its activities and that led to the appointment of specialist instructors in music, education and medicine and inevitably led to the gradual marginalisation of the British Institute and its activities, and of Edwin as Director. Greater emphasis was placed on the 'British Way of Life' and functions became black tie affairs, which was far removed from the more informal and, at times, anarchic regime under Edwin's director-ship.[68] The deterioration of relationships between Edwin and the British Council in Prague was mirrored in the increasing political tensions inside Czechoslovakia. From 1947 the Communists, who were the largest party in the country, began a campaign of political action and intrigue designed to bring about a Soviet-style regime. This culminated in a putsch in February1948, which led non-Communist ministers to resign and to the suicide and/or murder of Jan Masaryk in protest at the imposition of a Stalinist system of government. Edwin and Willa opposed the Communist take-over and strongly resented the extinction of democracy and the restrictions placed on freedom of expression and speech that fol-lowed. However, Edwin continued for some months after the putsch to lecture and carry on his British Council work, but, as Willa explained, 'the strain was wearing us down, the double strain of life in the Council and under the Communist Government'.[69] Edwin was granted a transfer on the grounds of ill health and they left for Cambridge, England, in August of that year, where almost immediately he suffered a nervous breakdown and Willa a disabling back condition.

From Cambridge they moved to Edinburgh, then London, and with Edwin's health continuing to improve, he accepted a position with the British Council in Rome, a city which they both came 'to love'.[70] The 'good life' (*la dolce vita*), however, was brought to an abrupt end by the decision of the British government to reduce the subsidy to the Council and to re-orient its activities away from Europe towards the Far East and South America. However, by this time Edwin had been asked to accept the post in 1950 as Warden of Newbattle Abbey College, Dalkeith, near Edinburgh, which was newly established as a centre for adult education. Although Edwin was by now sixty-three years old and Willa sixty, they both were enthusiastic about the challenges ahead. But as in all the other episodes in their life what started out as idyllic grad-ually descended into catastrophe and disaster, although not always of their own making.

Part of the problem at Newbattle was Gavin's descent into some kind of madness. Willa fails to mention this in *Belonging*, as does Edwin in his autobiography – *An Autobiography* (1954) – and instead almost exclusively dwells on Edwin's experiences and his victimisation and eventual sacking. But as Allen says, Gavin at Newbattle had become 'an unknown and unknowable figure . . . who communicated with them only in frenzied and angry outbursts'.[71] Willa recognised him as having a split personality, saying that:

> *What* can get deep enough in him to harmonise his conflicts? We do all we can by providing a loving, kind environment, but he is still on the defensive, putting up his armour against a hostile world, being himself hostile in his interpretation of stray words and gestures. In this split, this cutting off, this projection of an invisible line, one side of which is all suspect . . . he asserts himself . . . in the wrong ways, by withdrawal, suspicion, rudeness, deafness. And yet there is inside of him a fountain of affection . . . a warmth and simplicity, that would make him very loveable and charming were he to let it flow spontaneously.[72]

However, rather than deal sympathetically with his condition, he was subject to continued criticism and his mother's 'psychological theorising'. Some of the college residents of the time spoke of Willa and Edwin's resentment of his presence, with Edwin particularly 'splenetic about it'.[73] According to the poet Tom Scott, there was 'a definite and unpleasant tension between Gavin and his mother'.[74] Willa even put her chronic back pains down to 'a nervous condition', which would be resolved 'if [only] Gavin were to be on a more even keel'.[75] There is no doubt that Gavin was a difficult person to deal with, but much of this was the result of his accident when a young child, but it was also connected with his upbringing and the way that Willa never favoured him over Edwin, and his thwarted ambition to become a concert pianist owing to his inexplicable deafness.[76]

The other problem was one connected with the ethos of the College and Edwin's vision of its role and future. He had proved in the past an inspiring teacher, but a less than competent administrator and, when called upon, politician; in this respect, Newbattle was no different to experiences in Prague or Rome. The romantic poet and educational visionary was, in Willa's scenario, crushed by the manoeuvring of 'more contracted minds which distrusted the kingdom of the imagination – the Scottish trade unions to begin with'.[77] Edwin saw students pursuing knowledge, in particular literature, for the benefits it would bring to them without consideration as to cost or to utility. And this approach was successful in attracting twenty or thirty students per annum, with some, such as George Mackay Brown and Tom Scott, going on to find fame as poets and/or novelists, while others gained entry to Ruskin College, Oxford. However, the College's governing body was strongly of the opinion that the institution should be self-financing and that this could be achieved by increasing numbers through the provision of short-term courses, which went against the residential ethos of Newbattle. Although a deal with the National Coal Board saved the College from closure, Edwin made a number of enemies and, as Willa would have it, there was a campaign that 'Muir Must Go'.[78] This was disingenuous on Willa's part since, as the philosopher and friend, John MacMurray, pointed out to her in a letter, it was from the very outset clear that the College 'in a few years would have to become at least nearly self-supporting', and it would have been surprising if Edwin himself was not aware of this.[79]

However, the strain of hanging on became too much for Edwin and he began to complain of chest pains, while Willa herself in 1954 was admitted to hospital for the removal of non-malignant lumps. Her life was in the balance, as Edwin makes clear in a letter to a friend:

> I've been very worried for a long time about Willa's health, and last February . . . the surgeon operated on her, but found . . . an older growth behind the one shown on the x-ray. Two days later the internal bleeding was still going on, and another operation had to be made to stop it. For some days she hovered between life and death, but then gradually began to recover. Then pleurisy set in . . . but at last she came back to life . . . All this is the last phase of a long illness that cast anxiety over her and me. Now that the operation has been successful . . . I feel as if we are beginning to emerge out of a long dark fog of anxiety into the light again.[80]

Shortly after this, the Muirs left Newbattle with bitter feelings, but an invitation to Edwin from Harvard University to be the next Charles Elliot Norton Professor for the academic year 1955–6 sweetened the pill and did much to 'ease . . . the manner of our going'.[81] Willa and Edwin set sail for Cambridge, Massachusetts, in August 1955, and were almost immediately impressed by the less stuffy and less class-conscious lifestyle of Americans, but the materialism was decidedly unappealing. As Willa said: 'we could not agree that the only way to live was to sell and the only way to enjoy living was to buy'.[82] However, the mighty dollar wined and dined them and allowed them a certain amount of travel. They met and became friends with a number of American poets, including Robert Frost and Robert Lowell, as well as some expatriate academics, such as I. A. Richards.

However, the most indelible mark that America made on them was to make them realise 'how European they were'.[83] It was this realisation that led them back to Britain.

Edwin's first choice of a new home was Orkney, and although they spent some time there, he realised that the 'damp dark' winters on the island would only serve to worsen his already failing health. On a suggestion of the academic and poet Kathleen Raine of Girton College, and John Holloway of Queens' College, Cambridge, the Muirs bought a cottage in a small village – Swaffham Prior – near the university. However, Edwin's health continued to deteriorate and on 3 January 1959 he died 'just after answering the doctor's morning greeting'.[84] His death moved Willa to declare:

> That was the end of our story . . . it was not the end of Edwin's poetry or my belief in True Love. But any story about human beings is bound to have an end, like this story about us, a pair of ingenuous people who fell in love and went journeying together through life, blundering by good luck in the right directions so that we came to a lasting wholeness and joy in each other . . . We belonged together.[85]

Thus, under the construction placed on the relationship by Willa, finally belonging became inextricably bound up in the persona of Edwin: the poet, the teacher, the thinker and the visionary. Liberation for her was the act of selfless devotion to his genius, and everything else, country, career, family, friends, and even her son, were secondary to this goal. However, Willa's personal papers qualify the story of selflessness and devotion, as the promotion and protection of genius came at some cost to her own self-esteem and her ambition. In spite of her ideals, her marriage was never completely one of equals, and in many ways it proved little different to the traditional division of labour between the sexes that she despised so much in her writings. As in the case of Jane Welsh Carlyle, household responsibilities, including the supervision of servants, fell mainly on Willa; although no one could argue they were carried out with the same rigour as in the Carlyle home! Even the physical space was unequally shared as Edwin had the study at the top of the house in Hampstead and Willa the kitchen. The main difference between Willa and the 'wee auld mithers' of *Mrs Grundy* was that her work as a teacher and translator allowed her to make a substantial contribution to household income over time and afford her some degree of independence. But her freedom was constrained by the necessity to meet Edwin's needs and this from time not only frustrated her, but also created resentment. By promoting his work above hers any recognition of joint efforts, particularly in translation, went to Edwin. It was simply believed that in any joint venture Edwin had to be the dominant force, as Willa bitterly recorded in her journal:

> I am a better translator than he is . . . most of the translation, especially of Kafka, has been done by ME. Edwin only helped. And every time Edwin was referred to as THE translator . . . I was too proud to say anything; and Edwin himself felt that it would be too undignified to speak up . . . So that now, especially since my breakdown in the middle of the war, I am left without a shred of literary reputation . . . I seem to have nothing to build on, except that I am Edwin's wife and he still loves me. That is much. It is almost all, in a sense that I could need. It is more than I deserve. And I know, too, how destructive ambition is, and how it deforms what one might create. And yet, and yet, I want to be acknowledged.[86]

Willa was also unhappy with the place accorded to her in Edwin's autobiography. Although Edwin says that his marriage was the 'most fortunate event in my life',[87] Willa is only referred to on twelve occasions and his selective recollections of events and feelings 'was profoundly painful to her'.[88] And as Allen points out, 'She found herself unable to control the fire of resentment and hurt caused by Edwin's knowing omission of any of the experiences which had shaped their relationship.'[89]

With Edwin's demise Willa gradually experienced a renewed desire to resume her literary career and in that sense death was artistically liberating. As A. S. Neill perceptively said to her: 'Time you ceased to be known as Edwin's Frau.'[90] In 1965, at the age of seventy-five, she wrote *Living with Ballads*, which one reviewer considered to be an important landmark in the re-evaluation of popular culture in Scotland.[91] Three years later her own memoirs were published to critical acclaim and a year before her death at the age of eighty Willa published some of her poems – *Laconics, Jingles and Other Verses* – of which unsurprisingly the best were 'nearly all to or about Edwin'.[92] Willa Muir contributed a great deal to feminist thought in Scotland at a time when such views were unpopular. However, there was an inconsistency in the relationship between the messenger and the message. Willa attacked existing institutions such as marriage and the church for the role they played in the subordination of women, but in her own life she willingly accepted a part that reduced her to one of service to genius. She advocated women taking control of their lives but, as far as we know, Willa was never a member of any women's organisation, save for a brief association with the suffrage movement as an undergraduate at the University of St Andrews. Essentially her politics were on the left; however, she withdrew from the Labour Party in the 1930s and joined the Scottish National Party, and thereafter remained a passive onlooker of the political scene. Belonging to Edwin, and caring for and nurturing his talent and well-being was, at the end of the day, more important than the political struggles for women's rights. Such inconsistency should not, however, detract from her analysis of the place of women in Scottish society, which was pioneering, and even today remains powerful, in spite of the changed socio-economic conditions women now find themselves in.

NOTES

1. W. Muir, *Belonging: a Memoir* (London, 1968), p. 19.
2. K. A. Allen, 'The life and work of Willa Muir, 1890–1955' (unpublished Ph.D. thesis, University of St Andrews, 1996), p. 13.
3. Quoted in Allen, 'Willa', p. 33.
4. W. Muir, *Living with Ballads* (London, 1965), pp. 13–14.
5. Allen, 'Willa', p. 47.
6. Quoted in Allen, 'Willa', p. 24.
7. *College Echoes*, 23 February 1912, quoted in Allen, 'Willa', p. 71.
8. Muir, *Belonging*, p. 12.
9. Allen, 'Willa', p. 77.
10. Muir, *Belonging*, p. 26.
11. Muir, *Belonging*, pp. 51–2.
12. Muir, *Belonging*, p. 25.
13. Muir, *Belonging*, p. 138.
14. Muir, *Belonging*, p. 170.
15. Muir, *Belonging*, p. 54.
16. Letter to Stephen Hudson, 7 May 1924, in P. H. Butler (ed), *Selected Letters of Edwin Muir* (London, 1974), pp. 34–8.
17. Muir, *Belonging*, p. 170.
18. Quoted in Butler , *Selected Letters*, pp. 19–20.
19. Muir, *Belonging*, pp. 84–5.
20. C. Soukup, 'Willa in wartime', *Chapman*, 71 (1992–3), p. 20.
21. Soukup, 'Willa', p. 22.
22. Muir, *Belonging*, pp. 108–9.
23. Muir, *Belonging*, p. 106.
24. A. Smith, 'And woman created woman: Carswell, Shephers and Muir, and the self-made woman', in C. Whyte (ed.), *Gendering the Nation: Studies in Modern Scottish Literature* (Edinburgh, 1995), pp. 43–4.
25. W. Muir, *Women: an Inquiry* (London, 1925), p. 15.
26. Muir, *Women*, pp. 30–8.
27. Muir, *Women*, p. 40.
28. Allen, 'Willa', pp. 199–200.
29. L. Soukup, 'Belonging', *Chapman*, 71 (1992–3), p. 33.

30. Willa Muir's *Journal*, 20 August 1953 (Willa Muir Collection, University of St Andrews, MS38466/5/5).
31. *Journal*, 22 February 1952.
32. Letter to Willa Muir, 12 August 1959 (Willa Muir Collection, MS38466/g/8/N3).
33. Muir, *Belonging*, pp. 121–2.
34. Letter to Violet Schiff, 8 November 1927, in Butler, *Selected Letters*, pp. 64–5.
35. Allen, 'Willa', p. 224.
36. Smith, 'And woman', p. 41.
37. Letter to Neil Gunn, quoted in J. Pick, 'Introduction', in W. Muir, *Imagined Corners* (Edinburgh, 1987 edn), pp. viii–ix.
38. Muir, *Imagined Corners*, p. 65.
39. Muir, *Imagined Corners*, p. 77.
40. Muir, *Imagined Corners*, p. 118.
41. Muir, *Imagined Corners*, p. 16.
42. Muir, *Imagined Corners*, pp. 216–17.
43. J. Caird, 'Cakes not turned: Willa Muir's published novels', *Chapman*, 71 (1992–3), pp. 14–18.
44. Allen, 'Willa', p. 274.
45. Allen, 'Willa', p. 299.
46. Muir, *Belonging*, p. 194.
47. W. Muir, *Mrs Grundy* (1935), pp. 1–19.
48. Muir, *Mrs Grundy*, p. 95.
49. Muir, *Mrs Grundy*, p. 67.
50. Allen, 'Willa', p. 299.
51. Muir, *Mrs Grundy*, pp. 113–14.
52. Muir, *Mrs Grundy*, p. 125.
53. W. Muir, 'Women in Scotland', *Left Review*, 2 (1936), p. 768.
54. Muir, 'Women', p. 768.
55. Muir, 'Women', p. 769.
56. Muir, 'Women', p. 770.
57. *This Lop-Sided World*, (Willa Muir Collection, MS38466/2/8), p. 82.
58. Muir, *Belonging*, p. 158.
59. Muir, *Belonging*, p. 182.
60. Quoted in Allen, 'Willa', p. 296; Muir, *Belonging*, p. 190.
61. Muir, *Belonging*, p. 204.
62. Muir, *Belonging*, p. 206.
63. Quoted in Allen, 'Willa', p. 327.
64. Soukup, 'Willa in wartime', p. 22.
65. Letter to Alec (?), 12 June 1941, in Butler, *Selected Letters*, pp. 129–30.
66. Muir, *Belonging*, p. 208.
67. Muir, *Belonging*, p. 227.
68. Muir, *Belonging*, pp. 228–9.

69. Muir, *Belonging*, p. 240.
70. Muir, *Belonging*, p. 251.
71. Allen, 'Willa', p. 472.
72. *Journal*, 30 September 1953.
73. Quoted in Allen, 'Willa', p. 472.
74. Quoted in Allen, 'Willa', p. 336.
75. *Journal*, 12 September 1953.
76. Muir, *Belonging*, p. 306.
77. Muir, *Belonging*, p. 276.
78. Muir, *Belonging*, p. 281.
79. Letter to Willa Muir, 18 August 1964 (Willa Muir Collection, MS38466/ M(ii)/5).
80. Letter to Joe (?), 7 June 1954, in Butler, *Selected Letters*, p. 168.
81. Muir, *Belonging*, p. 284.
82. Muir, *Belonging*, p. 293.
83. Muir, *Belonging*, p. 304.
84. Muir, *Belonging*, p. 316.
85. Muir, *Belonging*, p. 316.
86. *Journal*, 22 February 1952.
87. E. Muir, *An Autobiography* (London, 1954), p. 154.
88. Allen, 'Willa', p. 477.
89. Allen, Willa', p. 477.
90. Letter to Willa Muir, 4 September 1964 (Willa Muir Collection, MS38466g/8/N3).
91. *Scottish Studies: The Journal of the School of Scottish Studies, University of Edinburgh*, 9 (1965), p. 224.
92. P. H. Butler, 'Willa Muir: the writer', in C. J. M MacLachlan and D. S. Robb (eds), *Edwin Muir: Centenary Assessments* (Aberdeen, 1990), p. 71.

10

Mary Brooksbank: Work, Poverty and Politics in Twentieth-Century Scotland

୶

Mary (née Soutar) Brooksbank came into this life with very little in terms of material comfort and died being not that much better off. Indeed, her working life was a constant struggle against low wages, poverty and unemployment. There was nothing exceptional in this as many women of her class faced similar battles against hardship. What made her special were her poems and songs, which not only provided glimpses into that world of getting by and making ends meet, but added a great deal to our knowledge of the hidden inner sphere of the work place. The indomitableness of the human spirit in conditions of adversity also shines through, as does her desire to make a difference to the lives of those around her. Mary's questioning of the condition of the poverty stricken among Dundee's working class led her firstly into industrial activity and, as her consciousness grew, to becoming one of the first female members of the Communist Party of Great Britain (CPGB). Although she later resigned from the CPGB, her involvement with the Far Left was quite unique for a woman in Scotland and in Britain at this time, and, one might add, since. In spite of the fact that the Left in general have consistently promoted the rights of women over other political parties, they have failed quite miserably to draw women away from the centre ground of mainstream politics in Britain and in other countries. Women and radical politics it would appear make ill-suited bedfellows. What pushed Mary in the opposite direction is, therefore, of some importance in understanding the larger issue of the political psychology of women. Why did the desire to redress inequalities in the distribution of wealth and power burn much more strongly in her than in other women? Of course, one might argue that the same question could be directed at men, since the membership of the CPGB has always been small compared to other mainstream political parties, but, as we will see, it was a far greater step for a woman to take in becoming an activist than a man.

Perhaps some kind of industrial and/or political role might have been predicted for Mary given her family background. Her father, Alexander, had had a varied working life since his birth in the parish of Cairn Conan, near Arbroath, in 1867. As a young boy of eleven he worked in a boot factory, where he lost three fingers of his right hand in an accident. From there he found casual work as a caddy on a golf course, before going on the tramp, or the 'tober', as it was called in this part of Scotland. According to Mary, he went all over Scotland, even to England, working on farms, in coal mines, and on the Forth Rail Bridge, although at the time of her birth he was working as a shore labourer.[1] She celebrated his itinerate working life in her poem 'Song of the Tramp'. Her mother, Roseann, was the illegitimate daughter of an itinerant farm worker, Paddy Reilly, and worked intermittently as a fisher lassie and as a domestic servant. Having saved thirty shillings, they married in June 1888 in Inverness and after three days of celebration they were left with nothing other than the clothes they wore and had to walk all the way to Aberdeen.[2] It was here in Ship Row, in a single end with no water supply, that Mary was born unfortunately blind on 15 December 1897. After twelve months her sight was restored and she followed a conventional path of educational development for a girl from a poor working-class family. She attended Summer Street elementary school in Aberdeen, before transferring to the Convent of the Sacred Heart. At the age of eight her family moved to Dundee; a step that brought about the first social awakening in Mary.

Her father found a job in the docks and while there continued his fight to improve the horrendous working conditions of the dockers and to win recognition from the employers for trade union representation. Mary remembered in her poem – 'The Docker' – her father: 'Tired and wearied humpin' coal; cauld, sweaty sark, hand a' hackit. Sic a life for a man tae thole.'[3] While engaged in this struggle he became influenced by James Connolly, the socialist and Irish nationalist, and attended meetings of the Marxist Social Democratic Federation in Edinburgh. The family home became a gathering point for activists among Dundee's shore labourers and the conversations that took place, the songs and poems that were recited and sung, made an impression on the young Mary, as did her surroundings.

Housing in Scotland was by any standards appalling with over 50 per cent of the population in 1911 living in one or two rooms, although in Dundee even ten years later it was closer to 60 per cent.[4] At 18 Dempster Street, Mary asked: 'Hoo we a' lived I dinna ken, Wi' nine o' us crammed in yonder';[5] at 110 Blackness Road, she said that 'the overcrowding was atrocious, as were the toilet facilities . . . we had one WC between four tenants';[6] and when she married Ernest Brooksbank, a tailor with one leg and a weak heart, in October 1924, the couple found a house in Foundry Lane that 'could only be described as an outsized dog kennel – the sloping walls, the plaster all broken, the door could not be opened fully for the head of the bed'.[7] Things were not much better in St Andrew's school, which she attended, in Dundee's Overgate: 'The conditions [beggard] all description. The filth from the WCs littered the play-ground.'[8] The unsanitary and overcrowded conditions were breeding grounds for all sorts of disease, indeed, Mary's baby brother, aged two-and-a-half years, died of diphtheria in Blackness Road. The state of the children was also pitiful. Mary remembered running 'barefitted in ragged claes, in summer days and winter'.[9] The toll such conditions took of the lives of children in Dundee was appalling; in fact, infant mortality statistics show that out of the fifteen principal towns in Scotland in 1904 Dundee was by far the worst, with a rate of 174 per 1,000 births.[10]

Mary was a bright pupil but like most girls of her social class educa-tion was seen as secondary to getting a job, finding a husband and start-ing a family. Economic circumstances dictated that work came before ambition. In one of her *Mill Songs* – 'A Dundee Lassie' – Mary recalled that 'I'd liked tae been a teacher, but I never got the chance'.[11] Even before she was able to work, Mary was kept off school to look after her siblings while her mother was working in a jute mill. Jute was the main employer in Dundee with just under 70 per cent of employed females working in the industry in 1911, and outnumbering men by a ratio of three-to-one. Even by contemporary standards the number of working married women was exceptionally high; indeed, in Glasgow women only constituted 30.6 per cent of the total occupied population, while in Dundee it was 43.7 per cent.[12] Of this number, it was estimated that one-third of those women over twenty were married.[13] The high level of married working women in the industry provided the illusion that women's wages were simply supplements to the earnings of their hus-bands, although in many cases these women were the chief breadwinners in their families. The Dundee Social Union's survey into housing and industrial conditions in Dundee in 1904 found that out of a sample of 3,039 families, 1,062 were dependent solely on the earnings of women; and that of a larger sample of 5,888 households over 50 per cent of the wives were either working or temporarily unemployed.[14]

Mary's own entry into mill-work as a bobbin shifter in the Baltic Mill was cut prematurely short when the School Board found she was under-aged, but she finally was taken on as a shifter in the spinning department alongside her mother. The training was on the job through observation and practice and Mary 'quickly learned to spin up ends'.[15] The hours of work were long from 6 a.m. to 6 p.m., but the day did not end there as Mary like other girls of her age and class were expected to take a share of domestic duties, thus, another 'two or three hours at the steam wash-house, cleaning, washing, scrubbing'.[16] Generally, at the turn of the nine-teenth century women earned around 42 per cent of the average male wage, but in Dundee women jute workers' pay in the spinning depart-ments was below the average paid to women in textile trades.[17] Even the highest paid weaver earned at least six shillings a week less that the lowest paid male labourer in the industry.[18] Mary's song – 'Oh, Dear Me' – remains a powerful indictment on the poverty and exploitation that these women faced in Dundee in the early decades of the twentieth century. She wrote:

> Oh, dear me, the mill's gaen fest,
> The puir wee shifters canna get a rest,
> Shiftin' bobbins, coorse and fine,
> The fairly mak' ye work for your ten and nine.
>
> Oh, dear me, I wish the day was done,
> Rinning up and doon the Pass is no nae fun;
> Shiftin', piecing, spinning warp, weft, and twine
> Tae feed and cled ma bairnie affen ten and nine.
>
> Oh, dear me, the warld's ill-divided,
> Them that works the hardest are aye wi' least provided.
> But I maun bide contented, dark days and fine,
> But there's no much pleasure living affen ten and nine.[19]

Although the song contains an element of ennui, indeed, bordering on fatalism, the truth is that the women mill-workers were in constant con-flict with their employers. They flouted the authority of male supervisors whenever they could, as Mary recalled in her song – 'The Spinner's Wedding':

> The shifters they're a' dancing,
> The spinners singing tae,
> The gaffer's standing watching,
> But there's nothing he can dae.

The women also took more formal action. Official statistics show that between 1889 and 1914 there were 103 recorded strikes involving women in the jute industry in Dundee, with most of them concerned with the issue of wages, although there was also a large number of disputes over working conditions and bad materials.[20] The women were organised in the Dundee and District Union of Jute and Flax Workers, which was established in March 1906, and had a membership of 9,264 by 1913.[21] Mary's first experience of industrial action came in 1912 with a strike against the provisions of the National Insurance Act. The legislation required certain groups of workers to pay 6d per week towards insuring themselves against unemployment and sickness. While this was affordable by skilled male workers, those in less well-paid positions found the extra outlay a real burden. Engineering and shipbuilding apprentices struck work, and the women in the jute industry followed suit. The clashes with the authorities gave Mary her 'first lesson in class warfare . . . I felt indignant that the police should follow us around'.[22]

There is no evidence that her brush with the law was a politicising experience, as before the First World War she seems not to have been a member of the youth section of any political party. However, the war changed all this, and like many young people, it radicalised her. Voluntary recruitment was proportionately higher in Scotland than any other part of the United Kingdom, and when conscription was introduced in 1915, there was hardly a family untouched by the war. It was the personal tragedies that profoundly affected Mary and pushed her towards a strongly critical position of the war and the conduct of those who were responsible for running it. She remembered a young teacher who was on her way to join her husband in India, being lost at sea with their child when her ship, the SS *Persia*, was torpedoed by a German submarine. Mary said, 'I was 17 . . . and highly-strung and sensitive. I brooded so much over the tragedy that I would frequently wake in the night screaming.'[23] Nearer home the loss of the cousin of her close friend Annie, 'grieved me'.

The end of the war brought economic prosperity and higher standards of material well-being for many Scots, but the climate of optimism this created soon gave way to despair and hopelessness as the economy crashed in 1920 following the collapse of the short-term restocking boom. In this atmosphere, the jingoism and triumphalism of 1918, Lloyd-George's 'Land Fit for Heroes' slogan, all looked decidedly threadbare in terms of their appeal to the electorate. Employers began an assault on wages and working conditions, which generated a great deal of anger and resentment among workers, particularly demobilised soldiers. The impact on Mary was significant: 'All this time I was reading, thinking, attending meetings [and] . . . at the age of twenty-one I joined the Communist Party . . . I had become, and still am, a militant atheist.'[24] Among the many books she devoured at this time, John Reed's *Ten Days that Shook the World* (1919), Robert Tressell's *The Ragged Trousered Philanthropist* (1914) and the novels of Jack London had the most influence on her political development.[25]

Unemployed, in 1922 Mary accepted a place on a government-sponsored training scheme in domestic skills. In return for receiving unemployment benefit she attended classes from 8 a.m. to 4 p.m. in cookery, sewing, dressmaking, and first aid in the home. After qualifying she found work in the Arms Hotel, Coldstream, in the Scottish borders. The work was socially isolating and the only 'outings' she had were joining the 'busman' to pick up guests or visitors at the railway station in Cornhill. Disillusioned with rural living, Mary moved to Glasgow where she found work firstly in a boarding house, and then later as a lady's maid to an old woman. Gradually, she realised that she was temperamentally unsuited to 'the soul-destroying futility of domestic work, the same tasks day after day got me down completely',[26] and after six months in Glasgow a mixture of depression and homesickness drove her back to Dundee and the jute industry. Mary found work as a spinner in the Eagle Mill, before moving to what was to be her last position in the industry at Laings' mill.

Mary had by now built up something of a reputation as a local working-class activist in the struggle against unemployment. This was highly unusual even in the more militant Scottish labour movement. As Patrick Dollan, leader of the Glasgow Independent Labour Party, said, 'it was not considered good form for women [in the 1920s] to appear on the platform at Co-operative or other working class meetings'.[27] Indeed, working-class activists envisaged very few, if any, changes in the traditional role of women in society. Part of their critique of capitalism was based on the subversion of family values that, as a member of the Social Democratic Federation in Dundee put it, forced the man to sit at 'home and let the wife go out and earn the dollars'.[28] Mary refused to accept such a restricted and stereotypical role and her political activity (allegedly) occasioned three spells in prison.[29] For disrupting the two-minutes' silence on Armistice Day, she was arrested along with another activist, Jock Thomson. He pleaded with the court to find her not guilty, saying that 'she was a young woman [who] . . . had taken no active part in the disturbance'.[30] It had little impact on the court and Thomson was sentenced to three months, while Mary received forty days in Perth prison for her part in the demonstration. For disrupting a religious meeting in the Caird Hall against Bolshevism she was fined three guineas. The next occasion was either during the General Strike in May 1926, or sometime after it. Mary herself is quite unsure on this, but it seems that she was arrested for breaking into a special Town Council meeting on 'the not genuinely seeking work' clause, which forced men and women to make fruit-less daily journeys in search of work that was not there. In this instance, she was not charged but held in a prison cell for 'observation' for three weeks, as the authorities levelled accusations regarding her sanity. They claimed that the recent death of her brother had destabilised her mind and was responsible for her wayward and incomprehensible behaviour. A crude insanity test was performed by the Deputy Chief Constable, who asked her a series of questions, such as the date of the Battle of Waterloo. In Perth Prison, she was kept apart from the other prisoners, while outside Dundee's Council of Action gathered a petition signed by 10,000 people demanding her release. The Railway Women's Guild in Perth, a Communist Party body, organised food parcels containing soup, beef and potatoes, milk, biscuits and oranges, although the oranges were confis-cated because of the impact their smell had on the other prisoners.[31] She was eventually released and fined a token amount of £2.

The final spell of incarceration was the result of a fully documented riot that took place in Dundee on 24 September 1931. The late 1920s and early 30s in Dundee, and elsewhere in Scotland, were marked by unemployment on a mass scale. Nationally, unemployment was running at around 25 per cent in the early 1930s, although in parts of the west of Scotland it was much higher, with Motherwell and Wishaw experiencing unemployment rates of 49 and 53 per cent respectively during late 1932 and early 1933. Dundee was the major black spot in the east of Scotland with 37,000 persons registered as unemployed in 1932, while in the jute industry unemployment was running at 50 per cent.[32] The response to the depression was the hunger march and Mary was deeply involved with the Communist-led National Unemployed Workers Movement (NUWM), organising concerts for those out of work, and with the Working Women's Guild campaigning to improve conditions in the poor-house. Activity came to a head towards the end of September 1931 when the police, using horses and batons, inexplicably broke up a demonstra-tion organised by the NUWM in the city centre, involving thousands of people. The *Dundee Free Press* described the scene:

> Three meetings had begun but for a few minutes when suddenly a posse of police advanced with drawn batons on the crowd. They made their way towards one of the platforms, and arrests were made.
>   . . . Attempts were made to break up the crowd. This was accomplished all the more readily when a squadron of mounted police from Bell Street arrived a few minutes later and charged into the crowd. Old men, women and chil-dren were knocked to the ground in the wild struggle to get away from the horses' feet – an almost impossible task in such a densely packed street.[33]

After the charge a string of running battles between demonstrators and the police, lasting from 7 to 10 p.m., ensued in the streets in and around Albert Square, later spreading to the Hawkhill, Dudhope Crescent Road and Hilltown areas. A number of shops had their windows broken and some looting took place. There were fifteen casualties treated in the Dundee Infirmary and countless others at home. The police arrested twenty-one males, mainly young unskilled workers, and one woman – Mary Brooksbank – on charges of mobbing and rioting. Along with the others, Mary was held in Perth Prison for three months without trial before eventually being sentenced to three months' imprisonment.

Her ordeal failed to curb her enthusiasm for politics, and shortly after she was released Mary began organising women in the Dundee Working Women's Guild (DWWG) in opposition: firstly, to the Anomalies Act of 1931, which prevented women and casual workers claiming unemployment benefit; and, secondly, to the Means Test when it was introduced in 1932 by the National Government in an attempt to slash public expenditure. The DWWG attracted 300 women at its peak and did some stirring campaigning on behalf of the aged and the inhabitants of poorhouses, represented the unemployed at tribunals, and sold the Communist paper the *Daily Worker*. They set up early warning systems using a bell against unannounced visits by Means Test inspectors and generally harried the authorities whenever and wherever they could. 'We got them shifted . . . [and they] had to flee for [their] live[s].'[34] Mary helped school these women in public speaking, in chairing meetings and other administrative tasks, as well as teaching them the 'rudiments' of politics and generally building their confidence.[35]

Mary did not just fight against poverty she actually lived it. Her involvement with the CPGB, the DWWG and the NUWM saw her blacklisted by the employers in the early 1930s. Out of work, with her husband ill and little money coming in, desperation forced Mary to sing for money in the streets of Newport and Tayport on the Fife side of the River Tay. The blow to her husband's sense of masculinity was shattering and when she returned he said: 'For God's sake, never do that again.'[36] But for Mary the need to survive by any means outweighed one's reputation and like her many women were forced to develop coping strategies to see their families through the depression. They had a good deal of experience to draw on since poverty was never far away in Dundee, even for those in work. Those families that were reliant on a shore labourer's wage were tied into a boom and bust cycle due to the casual or irregular nature of dock-work. Short-lived prosperity was almost always followed by periods of want during which families would have to get by on a ridiculously insufficient diet and the pawnshop. Mary describes the highs of this desperate lifestyle in her poem, 'Foondry Lane':

> There's a Juter and a Battener
> Sailing up the Tay,
> And a' the wives in Foondry Lane
> Are singing blithe the day.
> There'll be pennies for the bairnies
> A pint for Jock and Tam,
> Money for the picters,
> The auld fowk get a dram.

> We'll gie the secks the go by,
> We canna sew and eat,
> And fivepence for twenty-five
> Will no buy muckle meat.
> We'll hae steak and ingins frying,
> Lift oor claes a' oot the pawn,
> We'll gaither wulks and boil them
> In a corn beef can.[37]

But the lows were never far away. When mass unemployment devastated Dundee in the early 1930s, with 'full twenty thousand unemployed', the workers' diet deteriorated to the extent that 'the staple enjoyed [was] Breid and marge'. The only thing they could fall back on was the dole – but whatever money they received from the state it did not last the week. The coping strategies women used were varied but all involved making use of whatever resources were available. Lying in bed in the winter saved on coal, and allowed breakfast to be passed by. As Mary puts it:

> In cauld winter days tae lie lang in bed
> Saved ye fae buying mair coal;
> You could aye skip yer breakfast, hae dinner instead.
> Knock the days in tae you got the dole.[38]

In summer life could be lived more on the streets and there existed a vibrant female culture that revolved round gossip, knitting and singing. On Sundays, if the weather was warm, the whole of the street would decamp from Foundry Lane to the grassy beach. 'Women and bairns with go-carts, prams, etc, and wee boys with their . . . jeely pieces, cheese sandwiches, corned beef sandwiches, broken biscuits, sweeties, balls, [and] skipping ropes.'[39] It was an undemanding culture with little in the way of expectations and this included the men. A drink and a song on a

Saturday night was the best that could be looked forward to. As Mary put it, 'They were happy in their own humble way, those men who had so little to be happy about. The joys of their lives were their wives and bairns, their Saturday pint with their mates, and their work.'[40]

Although Mary had joined the CPGB, she recognised that in the fight against poverty and unemployment a broad alliance of the Left was necessary. She felt the need to support those members of the Labour Party who were trying to improve social conditions in Dundee in the late 1920s and early 30s. In particular, Mary confessed to having sleepless nights when ordered by the party to stand against a Labour councillor named Kidd, whom she considered to be 'a good fighter for housing' in the city. Sentiments such as these cut across the political strategy of the CPGB, which was heavily influenced by the Communist International (Comintern). Stalin in 1928 had decided that a struggle had to be waged against unemployment and the growing menace of fascism. Social democratic parties, such as the British Labour Party, were seen by the Comintern as reformist organisations working hand-in-hand with the capitalist class and as such a bulwark against revolution. Thus, Communists throughout the world had to build alternative working-class institutions to combat the reformism of the labour movement. In practice, this meant setting-up alternative trade unions and proscribing any fraternisation with the so-called enemy. The Comintern's strategy proved to be a political disaster, only succeeding in splitting the working class at a time when unity was essential. It was rescinded in 1935–6 in favour of building popular alliances.[41]

From the beginning Mary had opposed the 'class against class' strategy, not from any strong theoretical considerations, but because as someone who, through the Women's Guild, had worked with a variety of activists from the labour movement she felt that the approach was politically out of touch with the realities of organising the unemployed and defending the poor. This reflected the fact that her politics were of the heart rather than the head, based on a sense of injustice and unfairness and owing very little to the study of Marxist theory. She herself admitted that she was a Communist 'without knowin' it', and it took some persuasion by a local party leader to make her realise that she was.[42] She also admitted that although a front organisation for the CPGB, the DWWG 'was nae a party in the full meaning o' the word, we were a sort o' rallying centre'.[43] Mary's policy of collaboration and her refusal to toe the party line was becoming an embarrassment to the CPGB and, in spite of the fact that she had stood as a Communist candidate in November 1931 for Dundee's eighth ward, polling a derisory

339 votes or 7.2 per cent of votes cast, her time in the party was numbered. The final straw was her denunciation of Stalinism and the expulsion and denunciations of former Soviet heroes, such as Leon Trotsky. After a showdown meeting with Peter Kerrigan, National Industrial Organiser, in which he banged the table, accused her of indiscipline and fractionalism, and bellowed 'That's your doom', Mary was expelled in 1932.[44]

Although she only lasted ten years in the CPGB, Mary's decision to join it raises questions regarding the relationship of women and the Left in British and European politics. Mary recognised that working-class women, particularly those who worked with families, were in a much more vulnerable position, both economically and socially, than men. As she put it:

> The women in particular had much to be afraid of. Fear of losing their jobs, fear of losing their health, fear of losing their bairns, fear of offending, even unwittingly, gaffers, priests, factors, and all those whom they had been taught were placed by God in authority over them.[45]

The Left have generally appreciated this and have incorporated improvements in women's rights as a fundamental part of their political programme. However, evidence points to the fact that certainly for most of the second half of the twentieth century women in Western European countries have been the main supporters of centre-right political parties. In Britain, the Conservative Party has had a disproportionate support among women; indeed, it has been estimated that if women had not been enfranchised there would have been an almost unbroken sequence of Labour governments in Britain between 1945 and 1979.[46] In contrast, left-wing organisations, such as the CPGB, in spite of their championship of women's issues, have found it difficult, if not impossible, to win support from female voters. Even the mass based French Communist Party (PCF) in the 1960s and 70s and 80s found attracting the women's vote an elusive prospect. In 1956 the PCF electorate was 67 per cent male, in 1962 it was 65 per cent male, and in 1982 it was an incredible 86 per cent male.[47] Women seem to have been more attracted to political parties that stress family values than organisations of the Left that question the so-called bourgeois nature of marriage. Religiosity also has a part to play, particularly in countries and regions that are nominally Catholic. The atheism of the Left, and its generally anti-clerical stance, alienated many women who were, although less so today, influenced by the priesthood to a large extent on socio-political issues. An examination of the 1965 general election in France showed that 86 per cent of

Catholics voted for Charles De Gaulle, while 72 per cent of those 'without' religion voted for the Socialist candidate François Mitterrand.[48] The call to defend the faith was a more powerful appeal than that of party or class, which perhaps explains why industrial Glasgow, with its large Catholic population, has never returned a Communist MP or town councillor. Compounding the religious factor is the fact that women have been less interested in trade unionism in Britain and thus less in touch with the Labour Party than men. They also live longer and there does seem to be a proven correlation between age and voting trends, with older women being far more likely to vote for the Conservatives than younger women.[49] However, support for the centre-right has not improved the political position of women if representation is anything to go by. In British general elections in the period 1945–79 less than 5 per cent of Conservative prospective parliamentary candidates have been women.[50]

Experience in the Communist Party might also explain why women, who like Mary were socially predisposed to the Left, found sustained commitment difficult. Although there are very few studies of Communist women and their activities, those that exist would suggest that they and their concerns were as marginalized as those of women in other, more mainstream political parties. Politically ambitious Communist women did not wish to restrict the scope of their activity within the party to second rate 'women's work', and as such refused to participate in the Women's Sections that had been established by the party in 1925.[51] Even the journal aimed at women – The Working Woman – was wound up in 1929, with only a third of party branches being prepared to sell it.[52] In spite of making up 16 per cent of CPGB membership in 1938, and in places like Fife over 20 per cent, there were no women in positions of authority; men occupied all the full-time posts, monopolised administrative roles in the districts and branches, and dominated the Executive Committee.[53] What made them join? Sue Bruley, in her study of the CPGB in the inter-war period, divides women members into the politically active 'cadres' and the more passive 'supporters'. The former were a minority of politically motivated and ambitious women who were far removed from the home and domestic duties, while the overwhelming majority were housewives, recruited by their activist husbands, who prioritised their domestic roles over political engagement.[54] As a working married woman and an activist Mary was positioned somewhere between these poles, but then she was childless and untroubled by the responsibilities of raising a family, although she did care for her dead brother's son.

However, regardless of status in the CPGB, Mary like other women was drawn to the party, as one member of the Australian Communist Party put it, by 'wishing and wanting something better'.[55] Dundee had a millennial tradition that allowed the temperance advocate, Edwin Scrymgeour, to defeat Winston Churchill in the 1923 general election. Scrymgeour's appeal lay in his 'promised land beyond the formularies of pragmatic socialism, and beyond the faith of trade union officials preoccupied with the legal entitlements of paid-up members'.[56] For him this 'wretched world' was badly in need of 'a revolution [but] the revolution must be against sin'.[57] In the midst of poverty and unemployment on a mass scale, utopian visions of a new society appealed to women struggling to keep themselves and their families in some form of decency and out of destitution. Thus, the CPGB and the idea of a socialist commonwealth were not out of place in a city where millennialism flourished and where emotionalism formed the basis of political discourse. The party's documentation of the Soviet Union's achievements in the areas of women's emancipation and family life added a practical dimension and encouraged some to think that the impossible was in fact possible.[58]

The defeat of Scrymgeour in the 1931 general election marked a turning point in the politics of Dundee and millennial aspirations gradually gave way to more realistic goals as the economy began to pick up after the disastrous period of the early 1930s. Having been expelled from the CPGB, Mary's involvement in day-to-day struggles seems to have gradually tapered off as the 1930s wore on, and her class-consciousness became expressed in less overt and more personal ways, although she spoke out in favour of the Republican government during the Spanish Civil War and wrote a poem in honour of the artist and Communist, Felicia Browne, who was the first British volunteer to die in the fighting.[59]

Blacklisted by the jute employers 'through ma work in the party',[60] she found a job mopping floors in Keillor's, jam-makers, in the early 40s, but it did not last long. She insulted one of the company directors who had felt that he recognised her as a Communist and that he 'smells a rat'. In a typically confrontational manner, Mary replied that 'the country's full o' them and they're all climbing to the top'.[61] After this she turned to picking berries, while at the same time claiming out-of-work benefit. By this time her husband, Ernest, was gravely ill and he died in 1943 of coronary thrombosis. On the day of the funeral Mary was summoned to the Labour Exchange and ordered to pay back the 1s 4d she had earned at the berry picking. It was these kinds of petty indignities forced upon poor men and women that so annoyed Mary and ensured that her opposition to capitalism never mellowed or waned even in old age.

At the age of fifty Mary gave up work altogether to look after her sick mother and it was at this point she began to seriously translate her thoughts into lines of poetry. As she explained:

> My mother lay dying, she could nae sleep, and I had nae sleep, I had to keep awake. So I used to write things oot, and a used to read them to her . . . [and] she told me 'put that in a book and keep them', so I did.[62]

The weaver poet William Thom's work was very influential and it is clear that Mary saw herself as part of a working-class literary tradition dating back to the late eighteenth century.[63] A chance meeting with the folk singer, Ewan McColl, at a concert at the Caird Hall in the early 1950s, led to the presentation of her songs about Dundee and its mill culture to him. Songs and singing were, of course, central to working-class culture, especially for women, consoling them with thoughts of a better life. As Mary put it: 'Many a time I've sung to keep myself fae greetin' . . . these were hard times, but still you get through it singing and I think singing is a fine antidote to any trouble you have.'[64] In spite of her impoverished background music played a big part in her upbringing. She played the fiddle, her brother the accordion and her mother the piano, as well as being 'a beautiful singer'. 'We were with all the tunes . . . neighbours used to put up their windows to listen to us.'[65] Since then her songs, especially 'Oh Dear Me', have been recorded by artists throughout the world. In 1968, after saving up £175 over three years, her poems were published,[66] and a rather rambling autobiography – No Sae Lang Syne: A Tale of this City – followed in 1973. Mary died on 16 March 1978 at Ninewells Hospital, Dundee; all her 'means and estate' were bequeathed to her nephew and adopted son, Fred, whom she had cared for since a baby.

Mary Brooksbank's published work will never be included in the main corpus of Scottish literature; her style was derivative, her language limited and her ideas, at times, simplistic and naive. However, in spite of their gaucheness, the poems and songs provide direct insights into the inner world of a mill culture that has all but disappeared. Her world was one of hardship and poverty, of low wages and long hours, of subordination and thwarted ambitions, but it was also one that refused to accept the social limitations of urban deprivation, not only politically, but also socially. Through her work with the CPGB and the Women's Guild she tried as much as she could to improve the material well-being of Dundee's working class, particularly the women, taking on the authorities and going to gaol for her actions and principles. Outside politics, there was her love of open spaces and the landscape. With Fred in tow, Mary cycled round Pitlochry, Aberfeldy, Montrose and Arbroath to get away from the filth and stench of 'the environment where my mother lived',[67] and to climb the 'dear hills of my country, wild, rugged and free'.[68]

NOTES

1. Typescript of an interview with Mary Brooksbank, School of Scottish Studies, University of Edinburgh [SA1964-70].
2. M. Brooksbank, *No Sae Lang Syne. A Tale of This City* (Dundee, 1973), p. 3.
3. M. Brooksbank, *Sidlaw Breezes* (Dundee, 1973), p. 5.
4. W. W. Knox, *Industrial Nation: Work, Culture And Society in Scotland, 1800–Present* (Edinburgh, 1999), p. 192.
5. M. Brooksbank, '18 Dempster Street', in *Sidlaw Breezes*, p. 2.
6. Brooksbank, *No Sae Lang Syne*, p. 6.
7. Brooksbank, *No Sae Lang Syne*, p. 25.
8. Brooksbank, *No Sae Lang Syne*, p. 6.
9. Brooksbank, *Sidlaw Breezes*, p. 2.
10. E. Gordon, *Women and the Labour Movement in Scotland, 1850–1914* (Oxford, 1991), p. 165.
11. Brooksbank, *Sidlaw Breezes*, p. 40.
12. A. M. Carstairs, 'The nature and diversification of employment in Dundee in the twentieth century', in S. J. Jones (ed.) *Dundee and District* (Dundee, 1968), pp. 320–1.
13. Gordon, *Women*, p. 154.
14. Dundee Social Union, *Report on Housing and Industrial Conditions and Medical Inspection of School Children in Dundee* (Dundee, 1905), pp. 24–6.
15. Brooksbank, *No Sae Lang Syne*, p. 7.
16. Brooksbank, *No Sae Lang Syne*, p. 7.
17. Gordon, *Women*, p. 144.
18. Gordon, *Women*, p. 149.
19. Brooksbank, *Sidlaw Breezes*, p. 40.
20. Gordon, *Women*, p. 190.
21. Gordon, *Women*, p. 195; W. M. Walker, *Juteopolis: Dundee and its Textile Workers, 1885–1923* (Edinburgh, 1979), p. 199.
22. Brooksbank, *No Sae Lang Syne*, pp. 20–1.
23. Brooksbank, *No Sae Lang Syne*, p. 18.
24. Brooksbank, *No Sae Lang Syne*, p. 9. This would have been in 1918, but the CPGB was not formed until 1920, and Mary stated in her interview that she joined in 1922, which would have made her 25.
25. Brooksbank, *No Sae Lang Syne*, p. 43.
26. Brooksbank, *No Sae Lang Syne*, p. 12.
27. P. J. Dollan, *Jubilee History of the Kinning Park Co-operative Ltd* (Glasgow, 1923), p. 48.

28. Quoted in Walker, *Juteopolis*, p. 60.
29. Her claims, with the exception of the third episode, are unverifiable. There is no mention of her actions or arrest in 1919, or in 1926/7, in the Dundee press. The Dundee Sheriff Court records cannot be examined at the Scottish Record Office, Edinburgh, because of their extremely fragile condition and there are no surviving police records dealing with arrests for this period.
30. Interview [SA1970.375].
31. Interview [SA1970.375].
32. Knox, *Industrial Nation*, p. 190.
33. *Dundee Free Press*, 25 September 1931.
34. Interview [SA1965.375.A5].
35. Interview [SA1964-70].
36. Brooksbank, *No Sae Lang Syne*, p. 46.
37. Brooksbank, *Sidlaw Breezes*, p. 41.
38. Brooksbank, '18 Dempster Street', in *Sidlaw Breezes*, p. 3.
39. Brooksbank, *No Sae Lang Syne*, pp. 26–7.
40. Brooksbank, *No Sae Lang Syne*, p. 26.
41. M. Worley, *Class Against Class: the Communist Party in Britain Between the Wars* (London, 2002 edn).
42. Interview [SA1964-70].
43. Interview [SA1964-70].
44. Interview [SA1964-70].
45. Brooksbank, *No Sae Lang Syne*, p. 29.
46. J. Lovenduski, 'Sexing political behaviour in Britain', in S. Walby (ed.), *New Agendas for Women* (1999), pp. 190–209; P. Norris, 'Mobilising the women's vote: the gender-generation gap in voting behaviour', *Parliamentary Affairs*, 49 (1996), pp. 333–42. The differences, however, have narrowed since the beginning of the 1990s.
47. T. Judt, *Marxism and the French Left* (Oxford, 1986), p. 278.
48. Judt, *French Left*, p. 266.
49. Norris, 'Mobilising', p. 338.
50. J. Lovenduski, 'Sex, gender and British politics', *Parliamentary Affairs*, 49 (1996), pp. 4–5.
51. S. Bruley, 'Socialism and feminism in the Communist Party of Great Britain, 1920–1939' (unpublished Ph.D. thesis, University of London, 1980), p. 118.
52. Bruley, 'Socialism', p. 135.
53. Bruley, 'Socialism', pp. 134, 262, 295.
54. Bruley, 'Socialism', pp. 123, 295.
55. J. Damousi, *Women Come Rally: Socialism, Communism and Gender in Australia, 1890–1955* (Oxford, 1994), p. 120.
56. Walker, *Juteopolis*, p. 533.
57. Walker, *Juteopolis*, p. 350.
58. Damousi, *Women*, p. 120.

59. 'Felicia Browne' in *Sidlaw Breezes*, p. 4.
60. Interview [SA1970.375].
61. Interview [SA1964-70].
62. Interview [SA1964-70].
63. A. M. Scott, *Dundee's Literary Lives, Volume 2: Twentieth Century* (Dundee, 2003), p. 37.
64. Interview [SA1965.162.A2].
65. Interview [SA1964-70].
66. N. Watson, *Daughters of Dundee* (Dundee, 1997), p. 60.
67. Interview [SA1964-70].
68. 'Dear hills of my country', in *Sidlaw Breezes*, pp. 34–5.

Annotated Bibliography

Place of publication is London unless otherwise stated and only the most essential secondary works are listed.

GENERAL WORKS

The history of women in late modern Scotland has been badly served. There exists no general history of women covering the nineteenth and twentieth centuries. However, on the whole, the period from 1800 to c.1914 has been subjected to more historical scrutiny than the following decades and, thus, there are more works that are worth citing as providing an introduction to the subject. Among the best is E. Gordon's *Women and the Labour Movement in Scotland, 1850–1914* (Oxford, 1991), which provides an excellent introduction to the question of female subordination in the workplace and the relationship of women to the Scottish trade union movement. Gordon's article – 'Separate Spheres' – in *People and Society in Scotland vol. 11: 1832–1914* (Edinburgh, 1990) is the first sophisticated articulation of the concept of different spheres for men and women by a Scottish historian, although the underlying theoretical basis of the article has come in for heavy criticism from feminist historians over the last ten years or so. There are also a number of edited collections that cover areas of women's working lives, education and home life – E. Gordon and E. Breitenbach, *The World is Ill-Divided; Women's Work in Scotland in the Nineteenth and Twentieth Centuries* (Edinburgh, 1992) and E. Breitenbach and E. Gordon, *Out of Bounds: Women and Scottish Society, 1800–1945* (Edinburgh, 1992). Politically, women were disenfranchised until 1918 and outside of mainstream political structures, but the campaign for the vote and the distinctively Scottish contribution to the struggle has been chronicled by the late Leah Leneman in her book, *The Guid Cause; the Women's Suffrage Movement in Scotland* (Edinburgh, 1995), and by Elspeth King in her short pamphlet, *The Scottish Women's Suffrage Movement* (Glasgow, 1994). The twentieth century is served less well. Apart from the book by Esther Breitenbach

– *Women Workers in Scotland: a Study of Women's Employment and Trade Unionism* (Edinburgh, 1979) – there are no general studies of women; however, there are a number of useful articles dealing with the whole range of experience.

JANE WELSH CARLYLE

The most written about woman in the volume, but one who failed to write an autobiography. What we know about Jane and her marriage is dictated by the voluminous collection of letters, numbering around 3,000. They provide insights not only into bourgeois marriage in Victorian Britain, but also a wealth of detail and observation on such disparate things such as servant keeping, the British intelligentsia, leisure habits and household budgeting, and much more besides. An early highly selective edition of her correspondence was A. Froude's *The Letters and Memorials of Jane Welsh Carlyle,* 2 vols (1883), which created the controversy ever since regarding the Carlyle's marriage. Another small and selective collection published in 1977 was *I am Here Too: Selections from the Letters of Jane Welsh Carlyle* (Cambridge), by A. and M. McQueen Simpson. The definitive and non-partisan collection – *The Collected Letters of Thomas and Jane Welsh Carlyle* (Duke University Press) is an ongoing project, which has resulted so far in the publication of thirty-two fully annotated and indexed volumes of correspondence, with a further planned ten volumes to come.

The secondary works tend to be polarised and one-dimensional, either Thomas is depicted as an unfeeling monster that held back his wife, or is the highly strung but kind and generous individual whose wife was an attention-seeking hypochondriac. The anti-Thomas camp includes Anthony Froude whose original biography – *Thomas Carlyle: a History of his Life in London, 1834–1881* (1890) – helped polarise opinion. Carlyle himself added to this image in the publication of his own guilt-ridden memorial to Jane – *Reminiscences* (1881). Carlyle's family and physician strenuously denied the claims of Froude in a series of contemporary articles which established the case for Jane's depiction as an untalented and somewhat bored attention-seeker. This provided the basis for E. Drew's book *Jane Welsh and Jane Carlyle* (1928), which constituted a full frontal assault on Jane's character. L. and M. Hanson – *A Necessary Evil: the Life of Jane Welsh Carlyle* (1952) – drawing on previously unpublished letters, restored the evil Thomas image of Froude. However, as a result of the labours of the Duke–Edinburgh Universities' initiative a more balanced picture is possible of the relationship. This was reflected in Rosemary Ashton's award winning biography, *Thomas and Jane Carlyle: Portrait of a Marriage* (2003).

ELIZA WIGHAM

In spite of her importance, of all the women included in this volume, we know least about Eliza. She left no diary, wrote no autobiography, and of the many letters she must have written in her life only a handful survived. These can be found in Clare Taylor's book – *British and American Abolitionists. An Episode in Transatlantic Understanding* (Edinburgh, 1974) – and highlight her prominence in the anti-slavery struggle. Her religion was central to her radicalism and a number of studies, including E. Isichei's *Victorian Quakers* (1970) and J. S. Rowntree's *The Society of Friends: its Faith and Practice* (1907), provide clues as to the prominence of Quakers in social reform campaigns. The struggle against British and later American slavery and its importance for the formation of the women's movement in Britain is dealt with in C. Midgley's outstanding book – *Women and Against Slavery: the British Campaigns, 1780–1870* (1992) – and in a highly influential article by L. and R. Billington 'A Burning Zeal for Righteousness: Women in the Anti-slavery Movement, 1820–1860'.

MADELEINE SMITH

We know Madeline Smith mainly through her letters to Emile, which reveal not only much about her own sexuality, but also provide insights into class, consumerism, and manners in Victorian Scotland. The first but heavily censored collection of the trial letters was published in an anonymously produced volume – *The Story of Minnie L'Angelier or Madeleine Hamilton Smith* – in Edinburgh in 1857. The uncensored collection was published as an appendix to F. Tennyson Jesse's contribution to the *Notable British Trials* series. The originals can be consulted in the Mitchell Library, Glasgow. Of the secondary works there is not much to say. Most treat the story as a whodunit and adopt either a pro or anti position as to the guilt or otherwise of Madeline. The truth is uncoverable and the debate is sterile, but among the best of these types of publications and one that attempts to place her within some kind of historical context is H. Blyth's *Madeleine Smith* (1975). A much more fruitful way of examining the experiences of Madeline is to locate her within the continuing discourse on Victorian sexuality. The best introduction to the subject is M. Foucault's flawed but highly engaging study, *The History of Sexuality,* vol. 1 (1978).

SOPHIA JEX-BLAKE

Most of the Jex-Blake's papers were destroyed on her instruction after the publication of M. Todd's biography, *The Life of Sophia Jex-Blake* (1918); what is left is fragmentary and is mainly held in the archives of the Royal Free Hospital, London. The further secondary works draw heavily on Todd's biography and tend on the whole to underscore Sophia's iconic status. The wider story of women's entry into the medical profession is well told in E. Moberly Bell's *Storming the Citadel: the Rise of the Woman Doctor* (1953) and C. Blake's *The Charge of the Parasols: Women's Entry to the Medical Profession* (1992). The continuing difficulties women faced in establishing themselves on an equal basis with men is covered in J. Geyer-Kordesch and R. Ferguson, *Blue Stockings, Black Gowns, White Coats: a Brief History of Women Entering Higher Education and the Medical Profession in Scotland* (Glasgow, 1996), and also in W. Alexander, *First Ladies of Medicine: the Origins, Education and Destination of Early Women Medical Graduates of Glasgow University* (Glasgow, 1987).

LADY FRANCES BALFOUR

For someone who was connected by birth and marriage to some of the most important political families in Britain and an avid letter writer, there is surprisingly little primary material with which to construct her life. Apart from a diary held at the National Archives of Scotland for the year 1912, and some letters in the Women's Library, London, the main source is Frances' autobiography, which also contains a number of highly selective letters on a series of issues, from the Church of Scotland to the women's suffrage campaign. The autobiography – *Ne Obliviscaris. Dinna Forget*, 2 vols (1930) – is a rather rambling unreflective account of the political struggles of women in the period up to 1918, where the book unfortunately stops, in spite of the fact that she remained at the forefront of women's causes in the 1920s. Her daughter, Blanche Dugdale, in her autobiography – *Family Homespun* (1940) – sheds some light on family relationships that is missing from Frances' book. The history of the women's suffrage movement in Scotland is covered by Leah Leneman in, 'A truly national movement: the view from outside London', in M. Joannou and J. Purvis (eds), *The Woman's Suffrage Movement: New Feminist Perspectives* (Manchester, 1998), and in E. King, *The Scottish Women's Suffrage Movement* (Glasgow, 1994). For a British perspective books by S. A. van Wingerden – *The Woman's*

Suffrage Movement in Britain, 1866–1928 (1999) – and M. Pugh – *The March of the Women: a Revisionist Analysis of the Campaign for Women's Suffrage, 1866–1914* (Oxford, 2000) – offer an introduction to the issues and debates concerning the women's suffrage movement.

MARY MITCHELL SLESSOR

Mary Slessor has been seen by some as the greatest Scottish woman of the last two centuries and the number of publications on her is testimony to these claims. Fortunately, although most of her letters and papers were destroyed on her instruction after her death, there survives an impressive cache that she wrote to her friend, DC Charles Partridge, and these can be accessed online or in the original in the Dundee City Archives. These letters have provided the platform for the construction of a historiography that is mainly dominated by Christian writers and one that has conferred on her iconic status. From W. P. Livingstone's magisterial biography, *Mary Slessor of Calabar: Pioneering Missionary* (1915), through to J. Buchan, *The Expendable Mary Slessor* (Edinburgh, 1980), and more recently, E. Robertson, *Mary Slessor* (Edinburgh, 2001), the image is fairly consistent, but there is little attempt to contextualise Mary within imperial discourses. New ways of assessing her role in Calabar are possible through the work being carried out by feminist historians of imperialism, particularly J. Haggis, 'White women and colonisation: towards a non-recuperative history', in C. Midgley (ed.), *Gender and Imperialism* (Manchester, 1998), C. McEwan, *Gender, Geography and Empire: Victorian Women Travellers in West Africa* (2000); and F. Bowie et al. (eds), *Women and Missions: Past and Present* (Oxford, 1993).

ELSIE MAUD INGLIS

Elsie left behind very little personal correspondence, but there is a wealth of material held by the Mitchell Library, Glasgow, on the Scottish Women's Hospitals (SWH). Most of the correspondence of Elsie and other women volunteers can be found in A. F. Cahill, *Between the Lines: Letters and Diaries from Elsie Inglis's Russian Unit* (Durham, 1999). There are a number of biographies of Elsie, the best of which is Margaret Lawrence's *Shadow of Swords: a Biography of Elsie Inglis* (1971), and a more recent one by Leah Leneman, *Elsie Inglis: Founder of Battlefield Hospitals Run Entirely by Women* (Edinburgh, 1998). All the biographers fail to appreciate the link between Elsie and the SWH and the manner in which warfare has been conducted in the twentieth century which has increasingly militarised women. An introduction to this aspect of female experience can be found in the works of C. Schmitz, '"We too were soldiers": the experience of British nurses in the Anglo-Boer War, 1899–1902', in G. Degroot and C. Penniston-Bird (eds), *A Soldier and a Woman: Sexual Integration in the Military* (Harlow, 2000), C. Enloe, *Manoeuvres: the International Politics of Militarizing Women's Lives* (2000), A. Summers, *Angels and Citizens: British Women as Military Nurses* (2000 edn), C. Enloe, *Does Khaki Become You: the Militarization of Women's Lives* (1983).

KATHERINE, DUCHESS OF ATHOLL

Katherine's papers are held privately in the Charter Room, Blair Atholl Castle, and permission is needed from the Atholl family to consult them. However, as a high profile politician there is also a great deal of newspaper coverage of her career and speeches; *Hansard* is also useful in this respect. The Duchess' autobiography – *Working Partnership* (1958) – is a tepid and disappointing affair that chronicles her career, but little else. Her other publications of a factual nature throw some light on her ideological views, as regards women and Spain, particularly *Women and Politics* (1931) and *Searchlight on Spain* (1938). Published work on the Duchess is equally disappointing. Shelia Hetherington's biography – *Katherine Atholl 1874–1960: Against the Tide* (Aberdeen, 1991) – is celebratory, but rarely, if ever, critical. It also has a fundamental weakness: there are no footnotes so much of what is said or claimed has to be taken on trust. A shorter, but more balanced view is provided by A. S. Williams in *Ladies of Influence: Women of the Elite in Interwar Britain* (2001). A study of her political downfall and its impact on appeasement can be found in S. Ball, 'The politics of appeasement: the fall of the Duchess of Atholl and the Kinross and West Perthshire By-election, December 1938', *Scottish Historical Review*, LXIX (1990). The wider issue of women and politics in Scotland post-1918 is discussed in C. Burness, 'The long slow march: Scottish women MPs, 1918–1945' in E. Brietenbach and E. Gordon (eds) *Out of Bounds: Women in Scottish Society 1800–1945* (Edinburgh, 1992), and A. Brown et al., *Politics and Society in Scotland* (1996).

WILLA MUIR

Much of Willa's correspondence, notebooks, unpublished novels and articles, and other miscellany are held in Special Collections, University of St Andrews. She also left behind a marvellous autobiography – *Belonging* (1968) – detailing her life with Edwin Muir and their marriage, and other theoretical pieces on the role of women in Scottish society – *Women: an Inquiry* (1925). There are also novels and poems, the best of which is *Imagined Corners* (1931). There exists no full-scale biography of Willa, the closest we come to it is an unpublished Ph.D. thesis by K. A. Allen, 'The Life and Work of Willa Muir, 1890–1955' (University of St Andrews, 1996). There are some biographical fragments provided by her friend Catriona Soukup, 'Willa in wartime', *Chapman*, 71 (1992–3). Edwin's autobiography – *An Autobiography* (1954) – is a disappointment (Willa thought so too), but there are little titbits of information that can be used to fill out the picture. Willa's writing has been rediscovered by a new generation of literary critics and is undergoing reassessment, particularly A. Smith, 'And woman created woman: Carswell, Shepherd and Muir, and the self-made woman', in C. Whyte (ed.), *Gendering the Nation: Studies in Modern Scottish Literature* (Edinburgh, 1995) and J. Caird, 'Cakes not turned: Willa Muir's published novels', *Chapman*, 71 (1992–3).

MARY BROOKSBANK

The most important primary source for Mary is the oral interviews carried out by Hamish Henderson, of the School of Scottish Studies, University of Edinburgh, which are available on request on CD. The other source is her rambling and chronologically chaotic autobiography – *No Sae Lang Syne. A Tale of this City* (Dundee, 1973). This should be read in conjunction with her volume of poetry – *Sidlaw Breezes* (Dundee, 1973) – which also provides some autobiographical material. The essential texts for understanding the jute industry and its workers are E. Gordon, *Women and the Labour Movement in Scotland, 1850–1914* (Oxford, 1991) and W. M. Walker, *Juteopolis: Dundee and its Textile Workers, 1885–1923* (Edinburgh, 1979). The Dundee Communist Party records throw some light on Mary's political activities and are held in the Labour History Archive and Study Centre, Manchester. For the relationship of women to the Left in Britain Sue Bruley's unpublished Ph.D. thesis – 'Socialism and Feminism in the Communist Party of Great Britain, 1920–1939' (University of London, 1980) – is essential as is J. Lovenduski, 'Sex, Gender and British Politics', *Parliamentary Affairs*, 49 (1996) for women's voting behaviour in general.

Index